100
YEARS
OF
DROPPING
THE PUCK

100 YEARS OF DROPPING THE PUCK:

A HISTORY OF THE OHA

SCOTT YOUNG

M&S

McClelland & Stewart Inc.
The Canadian Publishers
481 University Avenue
Toronto, Ontario
M5G 2E9

Canadian Cataloguing in Publication Data
Young, Scott, 1918–
100 years of dropping the puck

Includes index.
ISBN 0-7710-9093-5

1. Ontario Hockey Association – History.
I. Title.

GV847.8.05Y68 1989   796.9'6'2'060713C89-094298-6

Printed and bound in Canada

CONTENTS

Chapter One

A Meeting at the Queen's Hotel

One team was called The Vice-Regal and Parliamentary Hockey Club Rebels

It is easy to become diverted, or even lost, when attempting to set a scene that took place a century ago in a hotel that no longer exists, in a form of Western civilization that we have left far behind, and among men who, with only one or two exceptions, no longer are clearly remembered. To start with the known facts: on the evening of November 27, 1890, thirteen men gathered in Toronto at the Queen's Hotel on Front Street, where the Royal York Hotel now stands. A few decades earlier the Queen's had gone by the name of Sword's, and at that time looked like a converted row of townhouses from the time of muddy York, which it was. In an upstairs parlor at the Queen's, pacing while they spoke or sitting around on overstuffed chairs and cherrywood love seats that would be a big hit in today's antique market, the ornately framed mirrors reflected mainly fit and athletic-looking men in their thirties and early forties. All were well spoken and one had a decidedly upper-class English accent. Most of them, even those in their forties, played hockey. They had gathered with the aim of bringing some order to the game that at the time was blooming in parts of eastern Canada but had no overall organization. Curling, rowing, rugby football, and lacrosse were the major Canadian team sports then. But in Montreal, Kingston, Toronto, Ottawa, and smaller centres a few teams were playing what a *Toronto Globe* writer of the time sniffily identified as "the winter game of hockey, which may be roughly described as 'shinny' on skates and reduced to rules."

Even that was an overstatement in at least one respect. The rules were so few as to be laughable. Yet over the centuries there had been some evolution.

In the original northern European game of bandy, old woodcuts show hordes of individuals wielding hacked-off saplings with curved roots, pursuing a ball or some other small object around a patch of ice, every man for himself. In Britain, almost the same game, at the same time (around 1670), was called shinny, a word said by the absolutely best authorities to have been derived from the cry of *shin ye* often heard during a game. Trouble is, nobody is sure what *shin ye* meant. In Scotland, furthermore, the game was called shinty, the derivation being a slightly different cry, *shin t'ye*. My own interpretation of what has been written on this arcane subject is that both *shin ye* and *shine t'ye* mean "shoot!" perhaps the connotation being, "Shoot, ya bum!" I also believe that the Russian cry of "shaibu!" at hockey games is related closely to *shin ye!* Anyway, the word "shinny" was used to describe not only the game but the stick and the object being hit and pursued, and had nothing to do with the wear and tear on the players' shins, no matter what you've heard. In Britain, early shinny games sometimes were played by teams, with lumps of something at each end to represent goalposts. An 1850s reference states that a favourite puck then was a rough disc sawed from the knee-joint of an ox. Another account of how the game was played in England a few decades later says that those players most prized, for a puck, the nosebone of a big sturgeon.

At any rate, after the game had sifted across the Atlantic

to Halifax, Kingston, and other places where British troops had time on their hands, the first major Canadianization of the game came in Montreal's McGill University in the mid-1870s.

Until then the game always was played on any frozen outdoor surface, where, for instance, if sixty players showed up on a sunny Sunday, simple mathematics dictated thirty to a side.

When smaller, rectangular (but still outdoor) ice surfaces were used, planks a foot or so high might outline the playing surface, that being high enough for the purpose because for years there was a rule against raising the puck. Snow cleaned from the ice was thrown behind the planks to grow into snowbanks on which spectators, if any, tended to stand.

The big change at McGill came about because hockey-playing students had available to them at least part of the time an indoor rink, not large, but roughly twice as long as it was wide, and normally used by the students for pleasure skating. Young men from other skating clubs, the Crystal and the Victoria, soon got into the game. Restricted by rink size, teams had to be reduced from the original any-sized mob of the frozen rivers and ponds; first to fifteen, as in rugby; soon dropping to eleven, nine, and then to seven.

At that time the usual skate was a single blade on a frame that could be clamped to an ordinary boot, held there by a spring which sometimes, when hit, would release with a twang that would send the blade shooting away, the skater – on one skate and one boot – hobbling in hot pursuit. Many sticks were homemade, whittled from saplings or scrub timber, but skating-club players mainly bought them (thirty-five cents each, one report stated) from the nearby Caughnawaga Indians, who were experienced in making lacrosse sticks. By the early 1880s, hockey had been played in Montreal for about ten years, in most Ontario cities except Kingston a few years less.

There was no real governing organization, but obviously the need was growing. In mid-February, 1883, Montreal's winter carnival included a hockey tournament with teams from Ottawa, Quebec, and Toronto competing against the three Montreal clubs, McGill, Victorias, and Crystals.

McGill won, spectators at the tournament were enthusiastic, and three years later the Montreal clubs, along with Quebec and Ottawa, formed what was called the Amateur Hockey Association of Canada — even though only the one team was from outside of Quebec.

Until then, except in universities and colleges, hockey teams almost invariably were formed as minor adjuncts to sports clubs that specialized in some other sport such as curling, lacrosse, or rowing. But two or three years after the AHA was formed, a new club was established in Ottawa with a more remarkable background.

On May 1, 1888, the Rt. Hon. Sir Frederick Arthur Stanley, Baron Stanley of Preston, a former senior member of Disraeli's cabinet, had been named the sixth Governor General of Canada and arrived with his wife and several of their ten children. When winter came in 1888, four of their sons, as one of their friends later recounted, "began to play hockey morning, noon and night." One of the best at the game was the Hon. Arthur, who was in his twenties. At Rideau Hall's outdoor rink, his pickup games of hockey began to impinge on the usual pleasure skating. Soon he got together a team whose very name challenges the imagination: The Vice-Regal and Parliamentary Hockey Club, a name impossible to inscribe on their bright red sweaters, especially of small players, so they tacked on the nickname, Rebels, and played exhibitions against Ottawa College and other local teams.

The lineup, besides the Hon. Arthur, included: his older brother Edward, later Lord Stanley of Preston, the best skater among the Stanley sons; two members of Parliament, Lt. Col. Henry A. Ward (Lib. East Durham), who was forty-one, and John Augustus Barron (Lib. North

Victoria), who was forty; Sydney Fisher, later to become Minister of Agriculture in Sir Wilfrid Laurier's last cabinet; and two of the Governor General's aides-de-camp, a captain named Wingfield and an officer from the Grenadier Guards, A.H. McMahon. One occasional substitute was the son of Sir Sandford Fleming. Another was Philip D. Ross, proprietor of the then newly established *Ottawa Evening Journal* – and more a coach than a player with the Rebels, while also starring with the Ottawa team in the Montreal-based AHA.

The Rebels had fun and even won now and again, but the Hon. Arthur felt that the hit-and-miss nature of exhibition matches contrasted poorly with the organized leagues, schedules, rules, and championships he'd been used to in sporting England, and which were to be found in Canada in rugby football, lacrosse, and other sports. Other hockeyists felt the same but the Hon. Arthur did something about it. He talked the ears off friends in Ottawa about the necessity for better organization. His idea was for a province-wide ruling body for Ontario, the first in Canada.

In the winter of 1889-90, the Rebels' second season, he took his team on the road. Its first game was in Lindsay, where the Rebels won. Then it was on to Toronto for two "friendly" games, beating Granites in the afternoon and losing at night to the Victorias – with both games degenerating into fist fights, boarding, high-sticking, and general snarliness. These exhibitions set off hockey's absolutely first (of subsequent tens of thousands) outraged editorial condemning hockey violence. Still, over a calming drink or two, the Hon. Arthur persuaded officials of the major Toronto clubs that forming an organization to govern the game would be a boon to everyone, spectator and player alike, and might even sell a few tickets. The decision was made to invite any club in the province that had a hockey team or would like to organize one to send delegates to Toronto on a date to be named late in November.

The Hon. Arthur was prime mover in all this, but some other high-profile help counted as well. Before he caught the Toronto train in Ottawa on Wednesday, November 26, 1890, a day raw with blowing snow, his father the Governor General had said yes, he'd agree to be patron of what would be called the Hockey Association of Ontario.

The Hon. Arthur had also arranged for two of his team-mates on the Rebels, MPs Barron of Lindsay and Ward of Port Hope, to meet him at the Queen's Hotel in Toronto in preparation for the larger meeting the following night.

The Hon. Arthur's train connected at Kingston with the Grand Trunk's Montreal-Toronto express. Barron's trip was shorter. Lindsay at that time, the railroad age being nicely under way, had twenty-one passenger trains daily, in and out. Barron's route was to Port Hope to meet Ward and connect with the Toronto train, which might have been the one also carrying the Hon. Arthur.

Together, or separately, in late afternoon or early evening that day they chugged into the predecessor of today's Toronto Union Station. The one functioning in 1890 had been built a few years earlier on the Esplanade between York and Simcoe streets not far from the Lake Ontario waterfront. After finding a porter and strolling north through the station they leaned into the cold gale and crossed Front Street through busy traffic: hurtling delivery wagons (the hot-rodders of the time), more leisurely hansom cabs and private carriages, plodding drays and public streetcars. These were all horsedrawn and all still on wheels in late November. The wheels would be changed for sleigh runners with the first heavy snow.

At the Queen's, Stanley inspected his room and met the others in the bar for a drink or two before dinner. (Whisky seven years old was $3 a gallon at the time.)

At dinner the conversation tended to politics and hockey. In hockey, other members of Stanley's Vice-Regal and Parliamentary Hockey Club Rebels were meeting in Ottawa that same night with delegates from a few other

clubs including Ottawa College and the Dey's Rink
Pirates (whose lineup included three men named Dey).
The clubs had agreed in advance to put up $3 each to
form an Ottawa city league. In politics, both Liberal MPs,
Barron and Ward, were facing a general election within
the next few months and were hoping to put a dent in
Prime Minister Sir John A. Macdonald's 123–92 Tory
majority.

Barron, an author and lawyer as well as an MP, was
somewhat of a famous person politically at that time.
Not long before, he had broken with his party over a
complicated motion that would have overthrown Quebec's 1888 Jesuit Estates Act. This was mainly a property
issue in which the Jesuits were the big winners, a situation
that was anathema to Ontario Protestants. Neither Prime
Minister Macdonald nor Liberal leader Wilfrid Laurier
wanted the act overthrown because of the trouble such
repudiation would cause in Quebec. But a Tory maverick
insisted on making the motion to overthrow. Seven other
Tories supported him, plus five Liberals, including Barron. They lost the vote by 188–13. In Quebec the thirteen
were called the Devil's Dozen. In Orange Ontario they
were the Noble Thirteen, and Barron thus became an
Ontario celebrity. A full account of this controversy may
be found in the second volume of Donald Creighton's
biography of John A. Macdonald, but as far as hockey,
and Ontario, were concerned, having John A. Barron
among the proposed association's original captains and
kings was a major status symbol.

Other prime topics of the time that no doubt were
discussed at the hockey table or others that night in the
Queen's dining room were a particularly gory murder (the
convicted man's wife was touring Ontario making the
front pages with public, and vain, appeals to save him);
the fact that the Ottawa Trades and Labour Council was
petitioning for a nine-hour day, when $10 for a sixty-hour
week was the going rate; and that John L. Sullivan had

just celebrated his thirty-second birthday and was still going strong. And so to bed.

On the following day more delegates arrived at the Queen's, both from Toronto and from out of town. Barron introduced the two other Lindsay delegates, Fred Knowlson, town clerk, and A.F.D. MacGachen. Ward introduced another prominent Liberal, a delegate from Bowmanville, lawyer D.B. Simpson, QC. The Kingston delegates were both hockey players, J.F. Smellie of what was called then Queen's College, and W.A.H. Kerr of the Royal Military College. It was evening before they met William Hendrie, Jr., of Hamilton, and the Toronto contingent: a bookkeeper named F.W. Jackson who played for the St. George's club, W. Robinson of the Athletic Lacrosse club, C.R. Hamilton of the Victorias, H. Green and player J.S. Garvin of Granites, and Army Captain Thomas Dixon Byron Evans from C Company of Toronto's Royal Infantry school, also called New Fort.

The upstairs parlor at the Queen's was redolent with smoke from pipes and cigars when this original group gathered to do business. The trio of the Hon. Arthur and MPs Barron and Ward stood out in the early going as the main movers and pushers. Barron was chosen to chair the meeting.

On calling those present to order, reported the *Toronto Mail* the next day, "Mr. Barron said the meeting had been called to organize a hockey association for Ontario, and he said this was very necessary, as he had found on his playing visit to Toronto with The Vice-Regal and Parliamentary Hockey Club Rebels the previous winter that the Toronto clubs played too roughly, probably because they had no knowledge of the rules."

This rebuke apparently did not draw any rejoinders from representatives of the Toronto clubs, the *Mail* reported, "all being evidently of the opinion that stringent rules should be formed against charging or any other form of rough play." But there must have been a few quiet smiles at the idea that because John Barron and his friends had been roughed up a little, they wished to outlaw that kind of thing in the future. At the end of this discussion, reported another Toronto newspaper, the *Globe*, it was resolved "on the motion of Mr. Stanley, seconded by Mr. Ward, that the Hockey Association of Ontario should be organized," with election of officers and other business to follow immediately.

A letter then was read from Ottawa's P.D. Ross, thirty-one at the time and one of Canada's most famous athletes. He had played football for McGill at age fifteen, starred at lacrosse, won the Quebec single shells championship in rowing, and had stroked Canadian championship fours twice, for the Toronto Rowing club in 1883 and the Lachine Boating club in 1886. He was also owner and publisher of the fledgling *Ottawa Journal* and captain of the Ottawa Capitals hockey team. P.D. Ross regretted being unable to attend the meeting, but promised that at least three first-class hockey clubs from Ottawa (he didn't specify which three were first class) would compete in the new association's championships.

Ross was the one man involved in this first organization of hockey in Ontario whose name is recognizable by some Canadians today. At his death in his ninety-second year in July, 1949, his athletic prowess was far in the past, but his newspaper – with the towering political voice of Grattan O'Leary one of its adornments – was very much part of the Canadian scene until the *Journal* ceased publication decades after Ross's death.

When the election of officers proceeded after the reading of P.D. Ross's letter, it is not clear whether other persons joined the meeting or their assent to election was obtained in advance, or was simply not obtained. In any event, several not present at the original meeting were elected to major offices. Besides the Governor General as patron, A. Morgan Cosby, manager of the London and Ontario Investment Company Limited on King Street East, a member of the Victoria club, whose address was at 214 College Street, was named president. Vice-presidents were John Barron and Henry Ward. C.K. Temple of St. George's was the first treasurer and C.R. Hamilton of Victorias first secretary.

Also, an executive committee, mostly of players, was appointed and instructed to write a set of playing rules and association bylaws – this committee being P.D. Ross, Smellie, Evans, Garvin, Hendrie, MacGachen, Kerr, and Temple. An entrance fee was set at $2 per team, which would pay for the room where they were meeting. Annual dues were set at $3 per club. When the meeting was adjourned, those who were not teetotallers toasted the association's future and then dispersed. Newspaper reports of the meeting the next day were brief and matter-of-fact. Not a single prophetic editorial was written stating that these few men, that night, had created an organization that would be a major power in Canadian sports in the century to come.

We take you now to the deliberations of the executive committee, whose first priority was to write a set of rules. Everything else could wait, as it would be no great job to separate the original thirteen clubs into three groups – three teams in the Kingston group, six from Toronto, and three from Ottawa, with Lindsay attached to the Ottawa group for playoff purposes. Play would begin as soon as the weather was cold enough to freeze natural ice, but nothing could happen without a set of rules. These rules, produced a few weeks later, constitute a period piece that now should be tacked up in every referees' room in the land. If only for comic relief.

The rules (with my comments or explanations in parentheses) were:

1. A team shall consist of seven players: goal, point and coverpoint (these two being the defencemen, who

lined up one in front of the other), rover, centre, right wing, and left wing.

2. The match should be played in two thirty-minute periods, with provision for ten minutes' overtime if needed to break a tie. (This was straight time. The earliest advertisements stated that play would start at 8 p.m. with pleasure skating to follow at nine, all for twenty-five cents.)

3. No substitution shall be allowed. If a player must retire because of illness or injury, the opposing team shall drop a player to equalize the teams. (This rule lasted a long time. Even twenty-five years later in a junior playoff game in Berlin – now Kitchener – a Berlin player broke a skate and the opposition had to drop a player, a nineteen-year-old Toronto Varsity whiz named Conn Smythe, until other skates were found.)

4. The teams shall agree on a referee and two goal judges. The referee shall have complete charge of the game, except that he cannot overrule a goal umpire. (There were no nets in those days, and no crossbar between the goalposts. The goal umpire stood on the ice behind the goalie and waved a flag when he judged that a goal had been scored, a decision that wasn't always easy – see rule 7.)

5. The match shall commence by a "face" in the centre of the rink; the referee placing the puck between the blades of the sticks of the centremen and calling, "Play!" (Many referees got whacked on the shins doing it this way. About ten years later a ref called Fred C. Waghorne called the two centres to mid-ice and said, "I'm going to toss the puck down between your sticks and from then on I don't give a damn what you do." His system quickly was adopted by the OHA, meaning that Waghorne invented the modern face-off. Later he said, "This was not by any wave of mental brilliance on my part, but was strictly in self-defence.")

6. A player shall always be on his team's side of the puck. A player is offside if he is in front of the puck. No player shall precede the player carrying the puck. "Lagging" offside will result in a face.

7. The goal shall consist of two goal posts, four feet in height, firmly fixed in the ice on a goal line, six feet apart and at least five feet from the end of the rink. A goal is scored when the puck passes between the goal posts in front of and below an *imaginary* (my italics) line drawn across the top of the posts. (Exact location of the imaginary line four feet high often had to be decided upon by a goal judge six feet or taller. There was no net to give a clue on close calls.)

8. The goalkeeper must not, during play, lie, sit or kneel on the ice. He may when in goal stop the puck with his hands but shall not throw it or hold it. Offenders may be ruled off the ice. (Another player might then play goal; goalies wore the same equipment as everyone else.)

9. No player shall raise his stick above his shoulder, except in lifting the puck. Charging from behind, tripping, collaring, kicking, cross-checking, or pushing shall not be allowed. A referee must rule off the ice, for any time in his discretion, a player who, in the opinion of the referee, has deliberately offended against the above rule. (The word "deliberately" naturally caused many arguments.)

10. Any player guilty of using profane or abusive language to any official or other players, shall be ruled off by the referee.

(As downright strange as some of those rules may appear, they provided a solid base for organized hockey to get a toehold with the public. And one must not ignore the reality that stuffy, arbitrary, wrong-headed Canadians at the time were much more common in sports other than hockey. In the line of *really* weird rules, try this: in the Ontario Rugby Union no championship could be won or lost by less than two points! So when Montreal beat Ottawa 12–11 one Thanksgiving in Ottawa, the margin being only one point, the game was declared a draw; in this corner, loser and still champion, Ottawa! The following week Queen's College challenged. Ottawa lost again, 7–6, and declined to play overtime to settle the issue. Loser twice in a row and still champion. Couldn't somebody have taken a shot at the Ottawa club for clinging to power under false pretences, rules or no rules? Nobody did.)

In hockey reports of the time there seemed a nearly complete avoidance of writing about personalities, as opposed to teams. P.D. Ross was six-feet-two, rangy, hawk-nosed, a right winger who probably would have been much sought after by professional scouts if he had been in his prime a century later. Also, one would think that a hockey star who also owned a newspaper might be ignored by opposition newspapers when possible, but surely his own paper would do him justice.

Not so. Maybe P.D. had made a rule. He was ignored by his own paper as well. His name appeared in lineups as Ottawa Capitals' captain, and he was one of the team's best scorers and had to be mentioned for goals. But never once was Ross listed at the end of a hockey story in the familiar paragraph that began, "Among the game's stars were . . . "

This attention to teams rather than players was particularly noticeable when the playoffs moved into the crucial stage. The fledgling hockey association had drawn up for its three districts what was, in effect, a knockout series to begin in January. But it was difficult to plan and be sure the plan would work. Rink proprietors, especially in Toronto, made their money from pleasure skating and looked on hockey as an unnecessary nuisance. That reluctance to oblige became a major problem in Toronto. Games for the original round-robin could be booked well ahead and went on as scheduled, but the final between Granites and St. George's brought trouble. The rink that Granites wanted was not available. When the teams could not agree on an alternate, Granites walked out, leaving St. George's as Toronto champions and Ontario finalists.

That was fairly simple, compared to what happened in eastern Ontario. Queen's beat Kingston and Royal Military College, thereby qualifying to meet the Ottawa champion in the provincial semifinal. But Ottawa hadn't declared a champion. The schedule seemed to have been rigged, just a little. P.D. Ross's Capitals were felt to be the class of the district, and Lindsay – 200 miles away by train – the weak sister. So a February 6 game was scheduled, Lindsay against the Capitals in Ottawa. This was looked upon more as a train ride for the Lindsay team than a real contest. Then the Capitals would get down to the real business. But Lindsay, perhaps having a premonition, telegraphed to cancel the game (and soon folded entirely). That set the stage for the first game of the Ottawa city playoffs.

On February 11 at the Rideau rink the Capitals went against the Dey's Rink Pirates. It was described as a glittering occasion, with Baron and Lady Stanley, plus seven sons and one daughter, in attendance. The final score was either 3–0 or 4–0, depending on which newspaper one read – or on the distinct possibility that one hotly disputed goal was allowed by one Ottawa newspaper and not by the other. This goal was scored by Ottawa just as one of the Dey's Rink players had broken his stick. Under the rules, he was supposed to retire and Ottawa was supposed to drop a player to equalize. The referee disallowed the goal on that account. Anyway, P.D. Ross scored Capitals' second official goal and passed for the third one (but still was not listed among the game's stars), putting Capitals into the district final against Ottawa College for the right to play Queen's, the winner to go to Toronto and play St. George's for the first Ontario championship – but hold!

Capitals had also been playing in a strong Quebec league, were unbeaten all season in both leagues, and were scheduled to play the Montreal Amateur Athletic Association team in Montreal for what was billed as the Canadian championship. For some reason untraceable now, that was the only game all season in which Ross was not in the lineup, and also their first loss all year. He was back in action a few days later as Capitals beat Ottawa College, 3–2, for the city championship, a game in doubt to the final whistle.

The following Saturday, February 28, the Capitals caught the afternoon CPR train to Kingston and checked into the British American Hotel – where Prime Minister Macdonald lay ill, worn out from campaigning for the national election due a few days later. Going out to inspect the rink, which they were somewhat disturbed to find was seventeen feet shorter than the Rideau rink in Ottawa, Ross and others asked around about the Prime Minister's condition.

It was a question being asked all across Canada. The previous Wednesday he had become weak and confused while speaking in nearby Napanee, and a day later cancelled all speeches before the March 5 polling day and was moved from his private railway car to a roomy suite at the hotel. This, not the hockey game, was the main topic in Kingston as Ross pulled on his skates and went out to help beat Queen's 4–0 that night and finally make it to Ontario's first hockey final, which would be played in Ottawa.

That March 5 election, incidentally, earlier had caused The Vice-Regal and Parliamentary Hockey Club Rebels to withdraw from the playoffs. The reason was that two Rebels, Ward in East Durham and Barron in North Victoria, were fighting for re-election, Barron opposed by the redoubtable Tory Sam Hughes, later, as Sir Sam, to become both famous and infamous as a wilful and self-aggrandizing Minister of Militia and Defence in World

War One. By the time the Ontario championship hockey game came up in the Rideau rink on March 7, two days after the election, Sir John A's Tories were back in power with a majority government and Barron *seemed* to have beaten Hughes by 200 votes. He attended the big game as a winner and still MP. But elections in those days were never sure until the last charge of voting irregularities had been heard; Barron later was unseated.

On that night of March 7 the Governor General, his lady, and all their family again were in the crowd. Both Toronto St. George's and Ottawa Capitals were unbeaten in Ontario play, with only the one loss in Montreal marring Capitals' twelve-game season. Nearly 1,000 fans jammed the rink.

"At 8:15," read one newspaper account, "Mr. A.Z. Palmer, the referee, whistled the teams to their places for the opening face-off. They presented a pretty contrast, the Ottawas, as usual, in white with the red and black badge of the Ottawa Amateur Athletic Club on their chests, Toronto in navy blue adorned by the red cross of St. George . . . "

The pretty contrast notwithstanding, the game was no contest. By a little before 9:30 p.m., when the two thirty-minute halves (without time out for breaks in play) had been played, Ottawa had won 5–0. One newspaper critic opined that the St. George's "inferiority to the Ottawas lay principally in the skating and lifting of the puck." After the match, the Ottawas entertained their visitors at a party—a common conclusion to games of the time—and saw them to their hotel. The next night, Sunday, the losers caught a train back to Toronto.

So ended the first hockey championship in Ontario, almost a century ago. Ottawa had A. Morell in goal; J. Kerr, point; W.C. Young, coverpoint; P.D. Ross, H. Kirby, C. Kirby, and J. Smith, forwards. St. George's had McVittie in goal; Henderson, point; Hargraft, coverpoint; and Lucas, Thompson, Pemberton, and F.W. Jackson as forwards. (Jackson had been in on the association's organization meeting three months earlier.)

But it was not quite the end of the season. When St. George's got back to Toronto, hockey interest that in previous months had been hard to find suddenly took a spurt forward. All year, matches had been played at unreasonable hours because rink managers, bowing to the pleasure skaters, consistently refused the hockeyists prime ice time. But now people on the street were asking, how could that Ottawa team massacre our unbeaten St. George's so easily?

The rink managers got the point. Ottawa was invited to come to Toronto for some exhibitions. Two weeks after the championship match – very late in the season for natural ice – Ross led his champions into Toronto. The usual rules applied. No substitutions. You put seven men out there and that was it. On that one-day visit to Toronto, the seven Ottawas beat St. George's 4–0 before a good crowd in the Mutual Street rink in the afternoon, had a good dinner, and then beat Osgoode Hall 6–2 at the Victoria rink in the evening. The skating and combination play were said to have impressed the crowds with the possibilities of the game.

That must have been so. Within a year rinks were not always big enough to accommodate everyone who wanted to lay out twenty-five cents and get in to see the action. The game was on its way to becoming Canada's national preoccupation. Yet in all the years since, one element did not change. When Lord Stanley finished his term as Governor General and returned to England, his replacement was Lord Aberdeen, whose wife kept a daily journal. Lady Aberdeen's entry for January 20, 1894, after seeing one of her first hockey games, reads:

> This game appears to be a most fascinating one and the men get wildly excited about it. But there can be no doubt as to its roughness, and if the players get over keen and lose their

tempers as they are apt to do, the possession of the stick and the close proximity to one another gives the occasion for many a nasty hit. Tonight one man was playing with his nose badly broken & the game had twice to be stopped, once because a man got hit in the mouth & the other time because one of the captains was knocked down unconscious & had to be carried out.

Chapter Two

THE WAY IT WAS

Even a rebound off the goalie could be called a forward pass.

What a game of hockey actually looked like in those days would cause your modern television commentator to change his glasses, or his brand of liquid refreshment. The puck could not be passed forward under any circumstances, so stick-handling and skating and shooting were what distinguished the stars from the foot soldiers. Even a rebound off the goalie could not be picked up by one of his teammates without being called back for a face-off. This would not be in anything like a face-off circle, which had not yet been invented, but precisely where the infraction took place. And as the goal crease had not yet been invented, either, the face-off might be right on the goalie's doorstep. Apart from that, trying to think of where a rush in those early days might have anything in common with what happens today in hockey, you can rule out anything even faintly resembling a forward pass.

Those old rinks had no bluelines or centre red lines. Even after goal nets were invented, which was by no means immediately, the net's job being to catch pucks that went between the goalposts and provide irrefutable evidence, it took an executive meeting of the OHA even to consider drawing a line on the ice between the posts. The yeas won on the grounds that a good broad line that the puck had to cross to count as a goal probably would head off many of the hot disputes. Until then, the goal line had been imaginary, invisible, existing only in the goal judge's head – and sometimes not even there, depending on who was scoring and whether the goal judge had been appointed by the home team or the visitors.

Complicating the game in other ways, some rinks had no side or end boards. Others had boards on some sides but not on others. In one particular fracas over whether a goal had been scored, a rabid crowd wishing to have some input into a goal judge's decision caused a riot by flowing through a gap behind the goal onto the ice and engaging in fisticuffs with the goal judge as well as anyone else within reach; although this version was disputed by those who claimed the fight had been started by the goal judge attacking the goalie, with the crowd merely acting as a posse in the goalie's defence.

All through this period, finding acceptable rinks was a problem. The OHA specified that its brand of hockey must be played only in covered premises. St. Catharines joined the senior series in 1893 – but had no roof on its rink so had to play all its games on the road. Also, there was no standard size for playing surfaces. It was years before rinks began to be designed specifically for hockey, or at least keeping hockey in mind. All covered rinks that weren't used for curling were designed mainly for pleasure skating, the better ones having live music – usually waltzes – for lovers young and old skating circuits arm in arm. The Caledonia rink in Toronto was almost as wide as it was long, making hockey there a different game than it was elsewhere; until demand for seats at hockey games caused the management to narrow the ice surface by building stands on either side. More than one rink had a bandstand in the middle, making it very confusing for a defenceman who not only was supposed to stop the guy with the puck, but first had to guess which side of the bandstand he was going to come around.

Curling rinks two or three sheets wide could, and were, converted to hockey once or twice a week simply by the addition of a low plank barrier around an ice surface incredibly short and narrow by today's standards. So many games were intimate, to say the least.

Think of an ice surface that was normally a three-sheet curling rink, with no seats, wildly excited spectators standing around the edges, two seven-man teams out there hacking and shooting and passing and checking, the referee, too, often having to skate within easy reach of angry fans swinging whatever they had to swing, from purses to walking sticks. Lighting was by flickering oil lamps hung from rafters wrapped in bunting, and so low that sometimes a high end-to-end shot would disappear from the view of everybody – until it dropped at the other end in front of (or even behind!) the goalie.

The substandard ice surfaces were mainly, but not exclusively, in the smaller towns. Precise measurements are difficult to find today, but a set of rules dating from the early 1890s includes this line: "The game shall be commenced and renewed by a 'face' in the centre of the rink (112 feet by 58 feet) . . ." Insert your own exclamation mark.

Compared to the 200 by 85 size now standard, that is 6,596 square feet of playing surface against today's normal 17,000. It was not until 1903, thirteen years after the Association was born, that a minimum rink size was written into the Association's constitution. This came shortly after the famous, innovative, and colourful referee, Fred C. Waghorne, announced that he would refuse from then on to referee games on rinks "not bigger than a billiard table." The resultant ruling was that "the ice size in rinks be 60 × 160" – twenty-five feet narrower and forty feet shorter than today's standard and, at 9,600 square feet, with barely half the skating room common in hockey rinks today.

Not everyone understands now, either, the make-up of
the seven-man team. What's a point, a coverpoint, a
rover? To take it position by position:

Without getting into rules for goalies more than: (1) he
could be penalized for not staying on his feet; and (2) was
forbidden to wear a garment that gave him an unfair
advantage over shooters (what kind of illegal garment the
OHA had in mind challenges the imagination), what he
did was stop pucks, as he always has and always will,
world without end.

Directly in front of him stood a player, called the point,
often chosen for size and strength in checking incoming
forwards and ruling that section of ice in front of the goal
where danger lurked, and still does.

Next in a straight line out from the goalie was the
coverpoint, good ones being strong, fast, determined
checkers who could pounce on a puck and get away
fast.

The four forwards – two wingers, centre, and rover –
normally skated in a line abreast during play, although
the rover, usually the fastest skater on the team, stood
directly behind the centre on a face-off. During actual
play, the rover was the only one whose role was more or
less fluid; he was expected to attack as well as defend, to
work hard at "checking back," as backchecking was called
in early days, and to fill any position left vacant by a
penalty.

With no forward passing allowed, of course, all players
on attack had to stay behind the puck. This meant that
the lateral pass got a workout. There was also a play that
had to be done slickly: an attacker was allowed to pass
the puck ahead for a teammate *as long as he caught up
to the puck by the time the teammate picked it up;* then
the pass qualified as a lateral.

That's the technical side, which every spectator knew
in his bones and so never had to think about. But then
there was also the beauty side.

"There is nothing more exciting and thrilling in any sport than the dash of a well-trained forward line down the ice, handling the puck with lightning speed," wrote a man in the *Toronto Star* one day, under the heading THE FASCINATION OF THE GAME. "There is a flash of skates, a clash of sticks and bodies during all of which the rubber disc is passed from man to man in a manner that keeps the spectator on edge. The spectacle is that of 14 men on a sheet of ice, all excepting the goaltender skating at their highest speed for the hour of play. It is not straightaway skating, but quick starting, sudden stopping, short turning either way, and a certain amount of body checking, just enough to give the sport that element of danger that lends to its attractiveness."

After that near-poem of praise, as true today as it was then, the writer added his rider: "The chief objection to hockey is its roughness. Whether a game is rough or clean depends very much on the referee, who is supposed to impose penalties for any unnecessary rough play. The players and spectators have almost as much to do with that. The players often try to settle old scores, and the spectators too often in the excitement cheer for any piece of rough work."

From the player's standpoint, no available firsthand account of what hockey looked like from ice level in those days seems as accurate and evocative as that of the man who eventually was known throughout the hockey world as Cyclone Taylor. Frederick Wellington Taylor was born in June of 1883 in the small community of Tara, not far from Lake Huron in western Ontario. In later years it became almost a given of any hockey biography that the star being extolled had started out by swiping his sister's skates. But a cliché has to start somewhere, and Cyclone Taylor did grab his sister Harriet's skates one day when he was five years old, and never looked back – either for his sister in hot pursuit, or later in life when making decisions others thought he might have taken differently.

When he was six or so, by then with his own skates –
the kind that that clamped on to ordinary boots, given to
him by Tara's town barber – he moved with his family to
Listowel. At the time of the OHA's first season, Fred Taylor, aged seven, was showing up with his twenty-five-cent
hockey stick and $2.50 skates on the rutted ice of a
shallow pond called The Piggery, just off the river, where
the kids of Listowel met to play hockey.

That class of hockey, the shinny class, had been played
in many communities large or small for years before the
OHA was formed. Almost every town had a patch of ice
where kids gathered after school and all day Saturday,
sometimes choosing up sides, but more often a contest
to see who could hang on to the puck the longest, skating
and stick-handling until someone took it away from him.
Fred Taylor became very good at holding on to the puck
and outskating everyone else.

When he was only thirteen, Listowel's intermediate
Mintos, the town's sole OHA representative, were suddenly in need of a centre for a game in Palmerston, a
short train-ride away. The town druggist, one of Mintos'
executives, had watched Taylor dominating the competition at The Piggery. He asked the kid to came along. On
the train the other six players, all grown men, joked about
what they'd do if the kid got body-checked into the rafters
or over the boards into some nice lady's lap. In the game,
his first ever in organized hockey, Cyclone scored three
goals. Listowel won 5–2. The older players were much
more affable on the train-ride home. They knew a future
meal ticket when it came at them out of the blue. In years
to come, they were to tell many a crowd around the
kitchen table about the games they played with Cyclone
Taylor. However, he didn't become a regular for at least
two years. Hockey players then seemed to run mainly in
the 145-pound to 165-pound range so they weren't big
men, but they were men – better able to handle the rough
stuff when it came, as it almost always did.

As a teen-ager but within a year or two playing regularly before the Listowel Arena's capacity crowds (1,200) or in other towns, what Cyclone saw with a boy's eyes lived with him for life. Fans then were "an amazingly hardy lot, they had to be," he told his biographer, Eric Whitehead, many years later. "The wind would howl and the temperature would get down way below zero, but out they'd come in the bitter cold, packing those draughty arenas, and loving every minute of it. They came on foot, by train, in sleighs and cutters, dressed in furs and mufflers, and sat huddled under blankets . . . "

During the ten-minute intermission between periods they'd pile out to the lobby's lunch counter, stomping their feet and swinging their arms to try to get warm, laying out their five-cent pieces for a cup of coffee. The spectators had it tougher than the players, Cyclone figured. "We at least had the comfort of a pot-bellied stove in our dressing room, if little else. "When the dressing-room doors opened and the teams clumped back to the ice – it was only a few feet from the dressing-room door to the ice almost anywhere in those days – the fans would be as ready as the players for the last thirty minutes. "Those crowds didn't need any organs or horns or flashing lights to whip up their fervor. They were just crazy about hockey."

So that was hockey when the OHA was still in its infancy, growing fast. At first there had been only the senior series to play in, made up early in 1892 of seven teams from Toronto, three from Kingston, a few from Ottawa and district, and others in Galt, London, Peterborough, and St. Thomas. Many players who were not quite talented enough to crack a senior lineup were left with no place to play. The OHA's answer late in 1892 was to establish another category, junior, to handle the overflow. Those junior teams had no age limit. A man of forty could play on the same team as his teen-aged sons and they'd all be juniors.

On the year the juniors came in, the OHA organized play into five districts: west of Toronto, Toronto city, Peterborough and vicinity, Kingston and vicinity, and Ottawa. Receipts, from registration fees and a small cut of playoff gates, were $145.32. Treasurer Alex Creelman reported that figure – but also that expenses had totalled only $15.81, leaving $129.51 in the bank, or in his sock, wherever he kept it. The newly structured Association seemed healthy enough. Yet that early, the OHA was coming up to what seems in retrospect the first major sign of what became a well-deserved reputation for authoritarianism. At first it was only the tiny tip of an iceberg, but it had an effect that persisted.

Ottawa had not only been an original member, but through Arthur Stanley and others had provided much of the original impetus for forming the OHA. Ottawa Capitals, the old P.D. Ross team, were obviously the class of hockey in Ontario – they won the senior championship for the OHA's first three seasons to take permanent possession of the first championship trophy, the Cosby Cup, donated by and named after the first president. In 1894, if they'd been good little boys doing what they were told, they probably would have won again.

The dispute was over where the senior final should be played. There had never been an argument on this point before. The first OHA senior final, in 1891, was played in Ottawa. A year later while Ottawa knocked off The Vice-Regal and Parliamentary Hockey Club Rebels and then Queen's University to make the final again, the Osgoode team – usually called the Legalites by headline-writers – disposed of Queen's Own Rifles (not long back from the Riel Rebellion) 18–0, Varsity 5–4, and Granites 5–0 to earn its first shot at the Ontario championship. That game was played in Toronto at the Granite rink and, quoting a report of the time, "attracted an estimated 2,500 would-be spectators, more than the building could accommodate." Ottawa, although the defending champion, did not protest against playing that title game in Toronto – and won it 10–4.

Another year later, Ottawa beat Queen's 6–4 to win its third consecutive senior championship. With that sterling record, you'd think that the Ottawa team would have some say in choosing the site for the 1894 final. Not so. Or rather, they had a say but the OHA wasn't listening. Even before it was certain that any Toronto team would be in the final (the little town of Ayr, near Kitchener, was a distinct possibility to provide Ottawa's opposition), the game was scheduled for Toronto. Ottawa complained, got nowhere, so simply refused to play.

An OHA bylaw held then and pretty well forever after that if a club disobeyed an OHA ruling "it automatically disqualified itself." Ottawa didn't wait to be disqualified. When the OHA was adamant that the final would be played in Toronto, the OHA's absolute best hockey team said, in effect, to hell with you guys, and resigned from the OHA. To make the point even firmer, OHA vice-presidential powerhouse P.D. Ross resigned from the executive. With Ottawa gone, Queen's caught the Toronto train to play Osgoode for the championship.

Why Osgoode and not the team from what every newspaper called "tiny Ayr"? That was a strange story, too. Ayr had captured a lot of fan interest by beating first London and then the strong Toronto Granites to reach the semifinal. Then, on the very doorstep to the final, Ayr defaulted to the so-called Legalites. As a result, what might possibly have been a David and Goliath final, Ayr against Ottawa, never took place. The fact that Osgoode then beat Queen's 3–2 for the 1894 title was of less importance than the side issue: the mainstream Ottawa teams were gone from the OHA, content forever after to play in their own backyard under what eventually became the Ottawa District Hockey Association.

Still, even without Ottawa, the OHA just kept on growing. In the sixth season, 1896-97 (the bank balance a princely $236.07), the OHA decided to incorporate itself and add an intermediate series, which came none too soon. Over the years community after community had been recognizing that there could be a lot more to hockey than pickup shinny games on river or pond ice. Local teams that had figured the top thrill of a season was to win their annual exhibition game against some hated rivals from down the road applied for membership in the Hockey Association of Ontario, as it was called originally, paying the $2 entry fee and the $3 annual fee (soon to go to $5) and beginning to dream of provincial championships.

Most of the new entries fitted the intermediate category – basically, players too good for junior and not quite good enough for senior. There were also some established senior teams that didn't like being also-rans to the powerful teams from Toronto and Kingston year after year and wanted a chance to win, even in something with a somewhat lower social stature. Intermediate was the answer. The category actually had started out stillborn in 1893, when Peterborough and St. Thomas dropped out of senior and played what *they* called intermediate, Peterborough winning that championship. When the intermediate series officially came into being at the 1896 annual meeting, a few weeks before 1897 play was to begin, the OHA listed eight senior clubs, twelve intermediate, and seventeen junior, all outside of the Ottawa district's own organization.

From here and there in newspapers of that time one may read, in streaked old microfilm, reports that give the sense and feel of hockey in the first decade of the OHA. Between the lines are all the optimism and enthusiasm that local hockey reporters could put into print: the cheers and catcalls of fans trying to outyell each other; the bets won and lost – there was a lot of betting, some of it leading to trouble; the smell of strong drink and the clink of glasses and the roared-out songs as crowds of geared-up fans piled onto a train in, say, Kingston and headed off to encounter their equally geared-up counterparts in, say, Peterborough, and establish who was boss.

Short trips might be made by horse and sleigh, but automobiles were virtually unknown, so trains got the hockey-fan business. The major excursions usually took place in February or March, playoff time. Because all hockey was played on natural ice, the first round of league play usually began around Christmas or early January. Playoffs had to be under way in early February at the latest so that finals could be reached by early March, before the rinks turned into wading pools.

When the list of playoff contenders was known, the OHA would set dates. Playoff matches were often home-and-home series, total goals to count, the winners to advance and the losers sentenced to return to the debating societies of the local barbershops to explain what went wrong. Railroads usually advertised their Hockey Specials in local newspapers: "HOCKEY SPECIAL! Leaving Lindsay for Port Hope at 4 p.m., leaving Port Hope for return trip one hour after game." Barring unforeseen, but frequent, incidents where games had to be rescheduled because of snowstorms, protests, or disqualifications (occasionally due to discovery that some team was trying to slip in some talented tourist under an assumed name) those dates would be kept. The boisterous crowds on Hockey Specials were mostly male but with a sprinkling of children who remembered these occasions forever, and a few women who obviously were afraid of nothing, not even Hockey Specials.

In those days when even a small city might have several passenger trains in and out every day, the trains were made up of a steam locomotive and as many passenger coaches as the ticket demand required. These coaches often had outlived their usefulness on the posher runs but were fine for the party atmosphere of a Hockey Special. Clouds of dust rose from the plush seats. Cigar smoke was everywhere. Bottles were passed, including to the uniformed conductor. The locomotives would chug into the snowbanks and, except on a few memorable occasions, through them, giving extra whistle blasts at every town and, if all went well, would get the celebrants to the rink on time. Then all hands, usually including the train crew, would march noisily through snowy streets to the rink. They'd make their bets, shout their cheers, the home folks would shout and sing back, and then there'd be the action – while the train puffed quietly at rest in the station ready for the homebound run's exuberant noise or grumpy silence, depending on the score.

Large city or small town, the competition became so fierce that soon the OHA had to deal with another natural phenomenon: the cheaters. Quickly there grew a breed of hockey executives who didn't mind altering anything alterable, from birth certificates to residence records, if it meant a better chance of winning. The residence rule, of course, was intended to head off fake amateurs or, as some called them, tourists – hockey players who shopped around for the best deal from this town or that. The earliest rule defined a man's OHA eligibility as being residence in a team's home district by November 1. This date was soon altered to October 1 and years later to August 1. But many slipped through; a little lying or cheating would do it.

Still, importing the hotshots went on, sometimes even legally. The legal way was first to induce the player to move and then (to use a word not then invented) parachute him in before the deadline. As clubs and leagues began to court good players from other towns, such recruitment usually tried to maintain the aspect of being within the OHA rule that no financial inducement was involved: that the man had moved for a bona fide better job. But under-the-table cash payments were almost impossible to prove even under oath.

Other illegal ways were much more complicated, being based simply on fraud. Let's say a man with impeccable residence credentials couldn't play the game for sour apples, but could be induced to lend his name, birth certificate, and other records temporarily (long enough for OHA inspection) to another man who could skate like the wind, had a deadly shot, and was unlikely to be spotted as a fake by a strange crowd in an away game. It seemed a simple matter to some hockey executives to make that kind of switch, even for only an important game or two. Canada, even then, was no spiritual homeland for Honest Johns.

In home games the flim-flam merchants had to be more careful – using the name of someone not well known, preferably someone who lived out of town but still in the team's OHA-approved territory. Some in the crowd might know that the smooth-skating speedster out there was not really Charlie Jones, the hired man at the old Pontypool place, but who was going to blow the whistle on the deception and become a local public enemy?

That was crooked enough, but nothing maddened the watchdogs of the OHA quite as much as the spectre of professionalism, or the slightest unsubstantiated hint thereof. No stricter amateur rules were ever applied than those of the OHA and its steely-eyed defenders of the faith. Canada, especially Ontario, was British then to an extent that today's Canadian could scarcely imagine. Speeches from public platforms were afloat with almost religious fervour for British fair play, British common law, British educational standards. It was a Canada in which an OHA president could orate to an OHA annual meeting, that "if we Britons are as great as the glory of our Empire, the flag of amateurism in your hands will be as safe from harm as the Union Jack was in the hands of your fathers and mine."

Yet despite this flaunted Britishness the OHA, in its obsessive abhorrence for the slightest taint of money in what was supposed to be amateur sport, voted to *reverse* the old British common-law practice that a person was innocent until proven guilty! The wording was:

When the status of any individual is questioned, the burden of proving his innocence shall rest with the accused, inasmuch as the real and true facts of the case must lie within his own personal knowledge, and consequently he should be in a position, if unjustly accused or suspected, to prove his innocence to the satisfaction of the Executive.

W.A. Hewitt, the *Toronto Star* sports editor who became OHA secretary in 1903 and remained in that job for more than fifty years, noted in his memoirs years later *(Down the Stretch, 1958)*, "that regulation might have violated the Magna Carta that King John signed at Runnymede at 1215 A.D., but was deemed appropriate by the OHA in 1897."

The meaning of that rule was simply that if a hockey player was suspected of taking money for competing in sport, not necessarily hockey but *any* sport, the onus was on him to prove that he had not. Meanwhile, of course, sometimes on quite unfounded accusations, he would be suspended. The numerous hassles on this score, making outraged headlines in hinterland newspapers, eventually led to the most publicized incident of the time.

Early in the 1897-98 season, just weeks after the OHA's Draconian anti-professionalism rule was adopted, the team then considered to be the class of the province, odds-on favourite to win the provincial senior championship, was Berlin. (The city's name was not changed from Berlin to Kitchener until during World War One, when the other Berlin, the one in Germany, was the enemy capital city.)

Berlin had won the intermediate championship the year before, then moved to senior. In 1898 Berlin's first league game was on Thursday, January 6, against its neighbour and natural arch-rival, Waterloo, which featured two members of the later-to-be-famous Seagram family, Joe and Ed.

Betting on big games in those days often was heavy, not in the sense of organized gambling but mostly in a person-to-person, town-against-town, my-team-can-

beat-your-team way. But this rivalry between the Berlin
Green and White and the Waterloo Black and Orange
brought out by no means only the bankrolls.

This passage describing what must have been a great
night to be alive is from the front page of the next day's
Berlin News-Record:

> The Berlin rink never before saw such a crowd of hockey
> enthusiasts. The game was called for 8:15 and as early as
> seven o'clock the entrance was blocked for hundreds of feet
> around by people scrambling and crushing to gain admit-
> tance. At 7:30 it was impossible to obtain an unobstructed
> view of the ice, the galleries being packed with spectators
> like sardines in a box, with the downstairs ditto. A low
> estimate of the spectators is placed at 2,200. And such
> enthusiasm! Berlin and Waterloo young men and ladies vied
> with each other in extravagant displays of green and white
> and black and orange, while the discordant notes of hun-
> dreds of fish horns and the cheers of lusty men went towards
> making a pandemonium . . .

In the game itself, the ebb and flow had much to do
with the rule at the time that if a man was injured or
broke some equipment and could not continue, the other
team also had to drop a player.

But this rule had an inescapable angle: the man injured
might be a star, his absence hurting the team, while the
man the other team dropped might be its worst player,
his absence *improving* the team. There were cases where
one team with a really sub-par player faked an injury.
One such incident involved a poor player having his arms
rubbed raw with a stick in the dressing room, then showing the "injury" to the referee and claiming that he could
not continue; this causing the stronger team to drop a
player and equalize the sides. However, in this Berlin-
Waterloo game the opposite occurred.

Berlin was ahead 6–0 when one of its best forwards, A.
Farrell, who had scored earlier, took a nasty slash on his

right cheek, which bled freely. But he refused to leave the ice. Then Frank Stevens, Berlin's skilful coverpoint, who had also scored earlier, came out of a scramble with blood running onto the ice from a gash in his skate-boot. He wouldn't go off, either. The most retreating he would do was to drop back to point, the closer-in defence position where he wouldn't have to skate so much. If both had retired Berlin would have been watered down considerably while Waterloo could drop two and ice its five best men.

With Berlin weakened by these injuries, Waterloo came on strong and pulled to within two goals for a garrison finish that had the Berlins reeling, the Waterloos storming the Berlin goal, the crowd limp, and the final score 6–4.

However, as it turned out, that score was not the final word.

The next day, January 7, 1898, the last sentence of the *News-Record*'s report on the drama, the bloodshed, the goals, the saves, the good guys and the bad guys, stated that "After the game Mayor Rumpel visited the boys in their dressing room and gave each of the Berlin players an X."

In those days gold coins were common enough that some in Canada and elsewhere had their own slang designation. In Louisiana, where the French tradition was still strong, a $10 gold coin (or, for that matter, a banknote) was identified by the French *dix*, eventually becoming Dix, or Dixie, to the English-speaking. This is considered by some to deserve equal billing with the Mason-Dixon line in responsibility for calling the U.S. South "Dixie." However, in parts of Canada the $10 gold piece was called simply an X, for the roman numeral on its face. What had happened was that Mayor Rumpel (who was one and the same as O. Rumpel, the team's manager) had won a substantial bet on the game and wanted to show his appreciation by handing around X's as souvenirs. Anyway, that was the story, but it simply would not wash with the OHA.

The first hint of trouble came in Toronto papers, the *Globe* publishing a rumour that the OHA was investigating three teams, Berlin, Waterloo, and Listowel, and that suspensions might follow. Within a week the most serious charge was known to be against Berlin. The club was summoned to appear before the OHA executive. The outcome, as reported in the *Berlin News-Record*:

> THE BERLIN HOCKEY CLUB EXPELLED
> The Berlin Hockey club is expelled from the Ontario Hockey Association and each member is declared a professional. This was the decision arrived at by the OHA executive at their meeting in Toronto on Thursday evening. Manager O. Rumpel and A. Farrell, one of the players, were present and subjected to an examination in connection with the presentation of a $10 gold piece as a souvenir to each of the members, but notwithstanding their explanations, the Executive ruled the team out . . .

When the OHA said "ruled out," it meant *out*. The entire team and management were disqualified indefinitely. The sentence turned out to be for the rest of the season. A strong Winnipeg team just deposed by Montreal Victorias as Stanley Cup champions (the trophy was not yet a professional one) was touring the East and was in Berlin to play an exhibition on the day the expulsion was announced. A sellout was assured. But in those days any team that even *played* against professionals would be suspended en masse. The game was cancelled. Within days, the Amateur Athletic Union of Canada followed the OHA lead by barring the Berlin team from making a projected exhibition tour through the United States.

By the time these decisions were made, the players who had spent their gold pieces sure wished they hadn't. Then they could have lined up virtuously among those who were hastily arranging to have the gold pieces mounted as watch fobs to back up the contention that they had merely been intended as souvenirs.

No matter. The watch-fob ploy cut no ice. Nobody could fool around with the OHA.

Naturally, many citizens in the Berlin-Waterloo region protested loudly over the expulsion. It had ruined their winter! They'd anticipated two months of great hockey, great Hockey Specials, betting with both hands, shoving it at all comers. Now, those expectations were all down the drain. Dozens wrote letters to newspapers denouncing "the tyrants of the OHA." Many hundreds in Berlin and area signed a petition fourteen feet long, which was carried to Toronto and presented to the OHA, pleading for a change of heart. Even some Toronto fans got into the act, one writing to the *News-Record* that "as the OHA has attained its object and in great measure has cleansed the 'Klondike' taint from its ranks, Berlin is entitled to another chance and they should get it."

From the OHA: Save your breath.

Foiled on that front, the Berlin-Waterloo hockey public then settled in to pull for the Waterloo team that had given Berlin its late scare in that fateful game and was competing in the intermediate playoffs. The Waterloos won their way along until early in March they were ready for the provincial championship series with Listowel (whose starters did not include Cyclone Taylor, then not quite fifteen).

It often seemed in those days that if you couldn't win it on the ice, try the committee room. Earlier in the playoffs Waterloo had been beaten 9–5 by the Kingston Frontenacs, but protested that a player named Harty, his first name possibly Jock, had been playing for money in New York and had played for Kingston under an assumed name. The protest was upheld and a replay ordered on neutral ice, Toronto. Waterloo took that one 7–3 in a violence-filled battle royal, but Kingston apparently couldn't think of anything to protest about so that win sent Waterloo on to the final.

In the other semifinal, Listowel had beaten northern Ontario's Waubaushene, which had protested something or other but lost, meaning Listowel would meet Waterloo, in Waterloo. When Waterloo won 10–4, local front pages rejoiced that despite the earlier Berlin suspension disaster, the intermediate championship won by Berlin a year earlier would stay in Waterloo County.

The rejoicing didn't last long. There was one more river to cross. Professionalism charges somehow overlooked by everyone else Waterloo had beaten that year were brought against three Waterloo players. The arguments, reported at length on front pages, were fun for a while. Sworn affidavits claiming innocence, eyewitness accounts of everything but virgin birth, kept hockey people reading and arguing through March, long after the ice was out.

The main focus was on charges against Joe "Grindy" Forrester, whom one assumes must have been an early version of the kind of player who is always noticed, whatever he does. An Eddie Shack, Bobby Clarke, Dave Keon. Almost every game story of the time had a comment on Grindy, the newspaper readers apparently always wanting to know. He was either "at the top of his form" or "playing below par."

There was no telling at first where the original impetus for the Listowel protest came from, but soon a possible instigator appeared, a man named Galloway, a citizen of nearby Galt. Galloway said he had come forward with information about Grindy Forrester not because he had a grudge of any kind but, although a professional himself, felt that justice must be served. His charges were that a year or two earlier Grindy had played lacrosse in Wiarton for money, had also taken some money in Fergus once, and had once competed in a speed-skating race at Lucknow that offered cash prizes for the first three finishers – who did not include Grindy, which, Galloway said, explained why Grindy's name did not appear in newspaper accounts of the race.

The OHA waved away as unimportant any tentative conclusion that if Grindy had skated in Lucknow and finished out of the money, he had not taken money for

sport. Three skaters *had* been paid. In the eyes of the OHA
that was enough to taint every man in the race and, if
Grindy had indeed been in the race, which he steadfastly
denied, enough to taint the entire Waterloo team!

Grindy not only denied the Galloway account of that
race, but claimed (front page, *News-Record*) that he had
never even *been* in Lucknow, let alone skated there. Sure,
he had played lacrosse in Wiarton, but had never been
paid for it. He thought Galloway had mixed him up with
another Forrester in Fergus.

Galloway replied in another front-page statement that
he had made no mistake, there was only one Grindy
Forrester. Galloway contended virtuously that he himself
was an honest pro and had never tried to pose as an
amateur, as he claimed the despicable Forrester had.

Grindy fired back that once Galloway had entered a
bicycle race in Fergus, swearing he was an amateur, won,
was unmasked as a pro, and curtly was refused the prize,
a nice bicycle.

As the debate raged on, Grindy and two other Waterloo
players signed sworn affidavits, which were published,
claiming that they had never been paid for playing anything. But innocence in some cases is difficult or even
impossible to prove, and where professionalism was concerned the OHA was not what you'd call a sympathetic
ear. Even to sworn statements. Waterloo's championship
was taken away and awarded to Listowel. Berlin seniors
were reinstated in March, after the provincial playoffs
were safely over. So instead of two provincial championships they might have won that year, Berlin-Waterloo got
zilch. The arbitrary nature of OHA suspensions, right or
wrong, could be documented *ad infinitum*. In some ways,
there was worse to come. Which brings us to the reign of
John Ross Robertson.

Chapter Three

THE ENFORCER

"There was a lot of deception practised half a century ago. A game was always a matching of wits as well as ability."

– W.A. HEWITT,
Down the Stretch

Years later some writers called John Ross Robertson "the father of the OHA," which is obviously an error. The OHA was going like gangbusters by the time he was invited to the annual meeting early in December, 1897, where he was nominated, elected, and welcomed aboard as a rank-and-file member of the OHA's eleven-man executive. But he *was* the richest and most powerful among them. At fifty-six, he was the member of the House of Commons for East Toronto and owned the extremely profitable *Evening Telegram*, which he had founded in 1867 after being ousted – by political interference, he claimed – as publisher of another paper, the *Daily Telegraph*. He'd followed that with a spell as London correspondent for George Brown's *Globe*, an event that stands as one of the few authenticated occasions on which John Ross Robertson changed his mind. His *Daily Telegraph* had been Tory, but he felt the Tories had betrayed him, so he went to the ultra-Liberal *Globe* briefly before founding the *Telegram*. Thirty years later when he landed in the OHA, widely known for both business frugality and public philanthropy and inevitably soon to be president, John Ross Robertson wielded more sheer clout than any president of the OHA from its founding to the present day.

A contemporary once described Robertson as being about six feet tall. W.A. Hewitt, who as OHA secretary was Robertson's right-hand man for several years, seemed to concur, writing in his memoirs that Robertson "was a big man in every way." The big man's grandson, John Gillbee Robertson, did not agree.

He is quoted in Ron Poulton's biography of Robertson, *The Paper Tyrant* (1971), as saying that Grandpa was a short and pudgy man and, perhaps speaking for a lot of people who had felt the weight of Robertson's righteous wrath, added, "I did not like the son of a bitch."

One photo of the time shows Robertson as having a strong face: probing eyes, prominent jaw, and commanding nose under a tall black hat. And he was strictly a black-hat type when anywhere, into the farthest reaches of the OHA, there was suspicion of professionalism.

It's legitimate to speculate on why he interested himself in the organization at all. He certainly didn't need the work, having a newspaper to run, a busy life as an author of several volumes of Toronto history, and operating as the chief organizer and fund-raiser in establishing Toronto's Hospital for Sick Children. But at that time, long before the national Canadian Amateur Hockey Association was born, the OHA was recognized as *the* power in hockey across Canada. Robertson liked winners. Also, judging solely by his performance as the OHA's first and greatest strongman, he might have been attracted originally by its implacable anti-professionalism.

Whatever the motives, he soon became the embodiment of the OHA's iron fist. It was in his first term as a director (under president James A. MacFadden of Stratford) that the OHA ordered the Berlin disqualification and other multiple suspensions of 1898. After a year on the executive he accelerated his rise in the organization by donating the 130-ounce solid silver John Ross Robertson Challenge Trophy for competition among senior teams. His presentation speech, about "a manly nation" being "always fond of manly sports" that would help "our boys to be strong, vigorous and self-reliant," also included the sentence, "Sport should be pursued for its own sake, for when professionalism begins, true sport ends."

There's no telling or even guessing what other hockey men thought about this unbending militancy – after all, professionals were the big deal in some other sports, including rowing and baseball – but any open opposition to the Robertson steamroller was still a few years away. Nevertheless, after only a year in the OHA he was elected one of the two vice-presidents.

His doings at that meeting, plus fulsome descriptions of the new trophy, got a much bigger news play than a really long-reaching decision made at the same time: that junior teams, instead of being open to anyone, henceforth would he limited to players under twenty years old.

A year later, on December 2, 1899, to quote an OHA summary of its tenth annual meeting, Robertson "was persuaded to accept the position of president." During his subsequent six-year presidency and for many years thereafter his stamp was on everything the OHA did, including a good deal that was arbitrary in the extreme.

Robertson prided himself as one who always listened to the other man's point of view and opposed bigots of all stripes, but there was certainly bigotry in his own contempt for professionalism in sports. The case of the souvenir gold pieces – they really might have been intended only as souvenirs, and besides, the anti-pro point might have been made by ordering the gold pieces returned to his nibs the mayor – was only a beginning. A year later Guelph Nationals, a strong senior team, were thrown out on charges of importing a couple of closet professionals. But in the 1900-01 season . . . well, let John Ross Robertson tell it in his own words.

His speech to the OHA annual meeting late in 1901 noted that the rise to fifty-seven in the number of OHA-affiliated clubs represented not only "a wish to participate in all the advantages our competitions offer," but also "from a belief that our determination is to make hockey the clean game of the honest amateur."

That noble aim, he lamented, wasn't all that easy to fulfil. "Your executive, in maintaining the honour of the genuine amateur . . . has had to meet a good deal of offside work.

"We thought that bitter experience had taught us all we could possibly learn of ways that are dark and tricks that are vain. The London Hockey Club, however, proved that the heathen Chinee [whom Robertson apparently was designating here as the ultimate trickster] was a back number. . . . We found that in the fine art of perjury there were men to the fore that could give the childlike Oriental cards and spades in this particular line of business."

To summarize drastically from his more-in-anger-than-in-sorrow account, he said that on January 16,1901, when Stratford played London in an intermediate championship series game at London, London's lineup included the name of a farmhand named Campbell Lindsay. This man worked in a nearby township and thus qualified under OHA residence rules to play for London. That no one had ever seen him actually *play* hockey was not a factor, because the plan was to have a real whiz from Montreal, Frank Winn, play under Lindsay's name.

On the night of the match almost everybody, with the exception of those who had arranged the deal, thought the stranger on the ice was, as the program stated, Campbell Lindsay. And, said Robertson, "the belief might have been held until this minute, and many minutes hereafter, had not a spectator acquainted with the township man, discovered that it was not he who was playing the phenomenally fast game on the London team."

This spectator told someone, who passed it on. London won the game. Stratford protested that the "Lindsay" on the ice was not Lindsay at all. Such cases usually were heard by the full OHA executive, accusers and defendants giving it their best shot almost as if in a courtroom.

London, defending its case, startled the OHA executive by filing a sworn affidavit from Lindsay that he indeed had played that night against Stratford.

The OHA might have been startled, but it wasn't stopped. The next day Robertson designated a member of the executive to gumshoe around the scene of the crime. When this operative tracked down Lindsay's employer, who said his hired man had not even been off the farm on the night of the game, the jig was up. Lindsay confessed that he'd been lying in the sworn statement London had showed the OHA.

It took longer to find and question the ringer, Frank Winn, but ultimately found, he confessed his part in the fake, giving details of how it had been planned and paid for. No mention was made of Lindsay making anything on the deal except a reputation as a home-team loyalist of the nth degree, but Winn admitted he was paid $45. So the OHA by that time had London cold on both impersonation and professionalism. And if that wasn't enough, Robertson declaimed, in an unrelated case the star London goalie, William Hern, was found to have "been offered financial inducements at a match in Tavistock, and confessed that later he had been paid in London."

Whether the inducements in Tavistock had been based on Hern throwing the game was not revealed. But when the OHA challenged the London club's executive on both these cases, said Robertson, "their ignorance indicated a large range of possibilities."

His immediate suspicion was that either everyone in the executive was in on the crookedness, or some knew and others had turned a blind eye. Accordingly, "your executive acted. London's career as an amateur hockey centre fell with a dull thud. The officers of the club and (all players on) the team were expelled and professionalized."

Not only that, but laying perjury charges all around was proposed. Robertson told the annual meeting that "your executive did not thirst for vengeance, but did think that perjury should not be regarded as a mere boyish folly. The legal adviser of the association – an eminent counsel – gave every consideration to the evidence. His opinion was that there was a good case for prosecution, but that the difficulties arising out of local sentiment in favour of the offenders would make success very doubtful." Robertson's regret at not being able to send the miscreants to jail was obviously deeply felt.

A few years and many suspensions later, Robertson actually engineered the suspension of an entire sport!

Lacrosse had been Canada's major sport before hockey came along, but its professionalism scandals had not been treated severely by either of the two major lacrosse organizations, the Canadian Lacrosse Association and the National Amateur Lacrosse Union. When a new incident caused all but three members of the Toronto Lacrosse Club to be grounded indefinitely by the Canadian Amateur Athletic Union, Robertson – not the OHA executive, but Robertson himself – banned *all* lacrosse players from OHA play. When the executive upheld this action, Robertson thought he might as well add an afterthought, and did: anyone who played lacrosse was barred from being a delegate at OHA meetings.

It's difficult to know whether a style other than Robertson's implacable slugging it out would have worked as well as his did in its own cops-and-robbers way, winning some and losing some. Hockey's battle for simon-pure amateurism pretty much prevailed in his day, but the seeds of defeat were in sight, if anyone was looking ahead.

It was simply that, as in rowing, baseball, lacrosse, and non-OHA hockey, money talked and young men making $10 or $12 a week in their day jobs often listened. At least one player suspended in the big London crackdown, Harry Peel – who had played point for London and was never proved to have known anything of the Lindsay, Winn, or Hern cases – went to Pittsburgh and made $20 a week playing hockey on the new artificial ice there. Of course, suspended by the OHA, he was beyond the pale in Canada, so if he wanted to play hockey he had to go somewhere. However, other players who were not making $20 a week at anything noticed this, and some found ways to do it without going to Pittsburgh.

As for Peel himself, he kept cropping up for years – an unwitting straight man for some of the most self-righteous pronouncements in the history of sport, as well as the centre of a little comedy on the difference between Robertson's presence, or absence, when anti-pro decisions had to be made. At one full meeting of the OHA executive in December, 1903, two and a half years after the London club's suspension, A.B. Cox of London made an impassioned plea for Peel's reinstatement as an amateur, the grounds being a claim that he had been an innocent victim of the original offence. With Robertson in the chair, the motion was defeated 9–1, Cox casting the only yea vote. Two months later, with Robertson away in Egypt (cat's away, mice play), an executive meeting chaired by vice-president Francis Nelson, a *Toronto Globe* sportswriter, defied Nelson's wishes, reversed that decision by a 5–4 vote, and reinstated Peel as an amateur. This caused Nelson to resign in a rage and stamp out of the meeting, waving off all pleas that he reconsider (although he did come back a few weeks later, as we'll see, to deal with another emergency where his bluestocking vote was crucial).

Anyway, when Robertson returned to Canada that spring, his wrath at the reversal of the Peel suspension put the fear of God, or of Robertson (approximately the same thing in the OHA), into everybody. In November that year, 1904, Peel's reinstatement was reversed by the

executive as being "illegal, of no effect, and contrary to
the fundamental law of the OHA."

But London wasn't finished. Four days after that executive decision, at a full meeting of the seventy-four delegates to the OHA annual meeting, London attempted to
overturn the decision once again. The debate was hot
and heavy before the professionalism of Harry Peel was
confirmed by a vote of 43–26, with five abstentions. To
hammer home the point, a succinct rule was written into
the OHA constitution that day: that no professional could
be reinstated under any circumstances. But an indication
that Robertson's influence was waning came not only in
the split vote on the Peel case, but also in the election of
officers. For the first time, he was opposed for the presidency by Bill Wyndham of Hamilton, who had been pro-
Peel. Robertson won fairly easily, 49–22, but it was not
considered a coincidence that a year later Robertson
announced that he would not stand again for the presidency. He wasn't accustomed to opposition.

The OHA's residence rule itself acknowledged tacitly
that money, or some form of compensation, was part of
the game. Otherwise residence rules would not have been
required to prevent players from shopping themselves
around to whoever could offer the best deal. Some did,
anyway. OHA protest files soon were filled to overflowing
with objections against this or that great skater and scorer
suddenly moving from his hearth and home to a strange
town where, eureka, the nice people had asked him to play
for their local team, which he was doing in all innocence.

About all Robertson could do then was okay a ruling
that raised to $25 the filing fee for any protest, hoping
this would weed out at least some of the weak cases.

A reading of what happened during the first years of the
century in the OHA's battle to the death against the taint
of money in sport turns up very few instances of even the
slightest degree of public support for the OHA. Every time
the hammer came down, almost every newspaper beyond

the confines of Robertson's own sometimes (but not always) slavish *Telegram* seethed with emotions ranging from shock to fury. A few sample newspaper comments, each on a different OHA suspension, indicate that the press (and, one might assume, the public) did not share the organization's self-righteous vision:

" . . . the OHA may find that it is one thing to attempt an injustice and another to succeed in it."

"[This decision by the OHA executive] seems to be anything but a fair one."

"To throw out the entire team seems to be far too severe."

"The OHA executive have been giving several snap verdicts lately which are not raising them in the estimation of the public."

"This iniquitous action of the OHA executive . . ."

"Not very good evidence, of course, but good enough to satisfy the OHA . . ."

"If the ears of certain members of that august body known as the OHA executive did not burn yesterday and today, there is no truth in a certain old saying, for assuredly some of the remarks that have been made about them in this city were couched in very vigorous Anglo-Saxon."

And in at least one case, the vaunted piety of the OHA was labelled a fraud.

This came about after the University of Toronto seniors travelled to Sault Ste. Marie for a couple of exhibition games during the Christmas-New Year holidays against professionals from the Canadian Sault and from Houghton, Michigan. The OHA immediately pounced with one of its prefab bans. After an initial hasty reaction in which the university banned its hockey players from all sports, cooler heads discovered that no Canadian Intercollegiate Hockey Union rule had been broken; college teams were allowed to play anybody, as long as it wasn't for money.

The university agreed that the OHA had a right to exercise its own ban, but so what? Varsity would play in its own league, as legal as ever. An editorial in the university's weekly *Varsity* took the matter a little farther, under the byline of P.H. Montague. He jabbed at the Toronto daily newspapers for "falling all over themselves for joy to think that one of our teams has got into a little mixup," while the OHA had been issuing orders about university sport that was not under OHA jurisdiction. So, he wrote, the Varsity seniors *were* amateurs. Then came the needle:

> Not OHA amateurs; not the kind of men who go to the OHA annual meeting and vote against all amateur infringements, and after the meeting make arrangements to change their residences for a money consideration; but clean amateurs. We can honestly say that we have a strictly amateur team, and that is more than fifty percent of the OHA teams can say.

The reasons behind this widespread condemnation of John Ross Robertson's lynch mob perhaps are best conveyed by a few specific cases. One such focus could legitimately be related to the late afternoon dark of Thursday, February 19, 1903, when about twenty-five citizens of Belleville, some a little boozed up, were pulling their overcoats from overhead racks while their train rumbled through the outskirts of Toronto. Among them was the anonymous hockey writer for the *Belleville Daily Intelligencer*.

He wrote well, with passion and humour, and in his blow-by-blow account published the next day he left very little out, right from, "Well, let's start at the beginning. The Flyer was nearly an hour late and it was 5:40 when she reached Toronto." There had been a train wreck that morning at Whitby and when The Flyer passed hours later "everybody rubbered at the windows to see the wreck. The great railway cars were lying in the field alongside the track where they had rolled like so many building blocks, some on their side and some bottom side up with the roof smashed. One could hardly believe that such a wreck could happen with a train going fifty miles an hour, and nobody be killed."

That was his style, telling everything he saw on the hockey trip. He described the Belleville hockey gang checking in at Toronto's Arlington Hotel at the corner of King and John streets and then, at 7:30, catching a street car to the Caledonian rink on Mutual Street. Outside, they stood on a corner to sing "In The Good Old Summer Time" and exchange jibes with passersby before crowding into the rink.

They were there for the first game of the provincial intermediate semifinal against the Toronto Marlboros – the series being in the familiar form of two games, total goals to count. In those days when radio and television did not exist, a newspaper writer was the only source, the eyes of the public. So this one from Belleville described the action in a detailed way long since forgotten on most sports pages – dutifully detailing the scene up to and including the time, 8:25, when the referee skated to centre ice and faced off the puck, and then, "There was a roar from the crowd and they were off with a rush," he wrote. "The Toronto men got the puck and down it went into Belleville territory. Wallace (Belleville's point man) cleared and play went down to the other end and there was the closest kind of call for the Marlboros. The play was now end to end and it was lightning fast . . ."

The Belleville contingent roared as Winchester (the Belleville goalie) "cheerfully bodied a Marlboro man off his feet." And so it went, check after check, shot after shot, for about 2,000 words through the Marlboros leading 3–1 at halftime, Belleville seeming buffaloed by the width of the rink (fifteen feet wider than Belleville's) and well beaten at the end, 9–4.

Disconcerting to the loyal twenty-five travellers and the folks at home? Sure. But, as the Belleville team's Boswell advised his readers in print the next day, don't abandon hope: "Give the lads the glad hand and a word of encouragement. Anybody can cheer for a team that wins; it takes a sportsman to pat a losing team on the back and say, 'Try again.' They're not all in yet, by any means." His piece ended with a bit of doggerel, including,

Red and White, Red and White,
We got licked on Thursday night,
But wait'll you see us next Monday.

As it turned out, he was precisely right. His opening lines reporting the Monday game read:

What did they do? What did they do?
They licked the Marlboros eight to two.

That second-game comeback sounded beautiful, as described in the *Daily Intelligencer*. It started, of course, with Belleville down five goals on the round – but with the home crowd cheering wildly and hope springing eternal. Belleville made one lineup change, dropping Allen, the first game's left wing, and replacing him with Jack Marks, an aggressive customer who had been playing with Belleville for some years.

The Bellevilles indeed did thrive on their narrower rink. They contained the slick Marlboro attacks, hung tough in the corners and along the boards, and with goal after goal pecked away at Marlboros' lead. Late in the second half came the great crowd roar as Belleville scored the goal that tied the series 10–10 and, scoring two more before Marlboros got one back, setting up a wild finish. Belleville hung on to win the total-goals round 12–11.

Delirious fans swarmed to the ice after the final bell and carried the Belleville goalie, Winchester, on their shoulders around the rink. No moment could have been happier for that crowd.

However, enter the OHA. Before the game began, Marlboros had protested Belleville's use of Marks on the grounds of professionalism, namely, that he had played baseball with a Toronto team called the Cadets and a Kingston team called the Ponies.

It didn't matter that Marks's baseball experience had been well known when the OHA granted him a playing certificate, as it had every year since 1900, or that he denied ever having been paid. What did matter was that a few weeks earlier at the OHA 1902 annual meeting, Robertson had put baseball on his hit list. He said that while in defence of amateurism it was hard enough to keep track of hockey players without worrying about other sports, the amateur spirit in baseball was "at such a low ebb . . . that about the only thing to do is to bar them all from the ranks of hockey." One current OHA player with the powerful Toronto Wellingtons had played baseball in the same leagues without OHA action. But the OHA executive, while admitting that in the Marks case evidence was conflicting, threw out the second game entirely (Belleville 8, Marlboros 2) and ordered it replayed on neutral ice, Peterborough.

After some agonizing, Belleville stubbornly refused to replay and ended the season bitterly, convinced that its excellent chance at winning the championship had been literally stolen away. The *Intelligencer's* parting shot exemplified this bitterness:

> It is an unsatisfactory ending to a brilliant season, but people in this city would rather see the boys cut themselves loose from the OHA than submit to injustice! Far better for a club to lose every game played than squeal like a pig under a gate, like the Marlboros did, and do the baby act.

The *Globe's* headline read: The OHA Rubbed It In to Belleville. Even Robertson's *Telegram* took a shot at the OHA over this decision. (Robertson might have been away at the time; he travelled widely.) From the *Telegram*:

If the evidence conflicted, why did the OHA act on it? Why is not one man's word as good as another's? No, no! It's another case of dear old Toronto, which always keeps in mind the old Quaker's advice to his son: "William, thee needs money. Get it. Get it fairly if thee can; but get it anyhow."

In the end, Marlboros didn't win the championship either, losing to Paris in the final. (Marks played for another seventeen years, mostly as a pro, finishing up in 1920 after three years in the NHL.) But after his disqualification by the OHA in 1903, one can imagine the situation a year later when Belleville and the Marlboros met once again in the intermediate semifinal. Belleville again won, again was ready for the final, and again was disqualified by the OHA.

This time the original charge was that a player named Aeneas (also known as Angus but mostly by the nickname Reddy) McMillan had not been a Belleville resident before the October 1 deadline. When that didn't stick, because the OHA earlier had ruled him eligible, a backup charge was produced: professionalism.

In this OHA executive hearing Belleville was represented by E. Guss Porter of Belleville, a widely respected member of Parliament and an OHA executive member. The professionalism charge was based entirely on the evidence of a Smiths Falls player who said that McMillan had told him he'd been offered $15 a week to play in Belleville.

That is the short version, but it ignores several nuances. The prosecution evidence actually submitted in detail by Ed Gilroy and F.S. Purdy of Smiths Falls went as follows. Gilroy, a player on the Smiths Falls team, had known McMillan the previous year, when McMillan played for Cornwall. Now Gilroy worked in the store of a man named Evertts, who claimed that McMillan owed him $80, which Evertts had asked the Belleville club to pay, threatening to "get even" if they didn't . Whether Gilroy was just working for the boss in the "get even" line is hard to say. But he swore that a man named Truaisch of the Belleville club had offered him money to play in Belleville and that McMillan had told him (Gilroy) that he (McMillan) had been offered $15 per week to play in Belleville. Gilroy said further that McMillan had told him that he (McMillan) had had letters and telegrams from Truaisch offering him inducements to go to Belleville. Evidence from the other Smiths Falls man, Purdy, was a good deal less complicated, declaring only that McMillan had told him that he (McMillan) had been offered $15 a week to play in Belleville.

Had the professionalism charge indeed been a malicious case of getting even in the matter of McMillan's unpaid $80 debt? Who knows? At any rate, that was the evidence against McMillan.

In defence, E. Guss Porter for Belleville submitted McMillan's sworn statement that he had never received or been offered a cent to play in Belleville and the sworn statement of Truaisch that he had never paid McMillan a cent or offered him a cent, and furthermore had nothing to do with the financial end of the Belleville club. In light of what Porter called hearsay evidence of the prosecution against straightforward affidavits by the defence, he called on the OHA executive to dismiss the charge.

The OHA did not comply. The vote was 5–4. One of the losing votes was cast by a man unnamed, but not from Belleville, who told a reporter, "I would not professionalize a yellow dog on the evidence submitted."

One of the throw-Belleville-out votes was cast by W.A. Hewitt, who at the time had been OHA secretary for a year, seemed very much the creature of John Ross Robertson, and also seemed (as we'll see later) to have some sort of connection with, or at least a leaning toward, the Marlboros. A further fillip was that all motions against Belleville, both on the residence rule and on the professionalism issue, were made by OHA treasurer A.W. McPherson of Peterborough – and Peterborough would be designated to move into the playoffs in Belleville's place, if Belleville was disqualified. Another out-with-Belleville vote was cast by OHA vice-president Francis Nelson, the Torontonian who had resigned that post a few weeks earlier over the Harry Peel vote when Robertson was away; had refused many pleas to rescind his resignation; but then *had* rescinded it to preside at this meeting where his vote was needed in another professionalism crisis, with Robertson still abroad. Little wonder Belleville felt it had been jobbed.

And then there was this paragraph in the *Intelligencer*'s account of that meeting:

> A significant fact is that, just before the meeting closed, and it sat well into Sunday morning, Mr. Nelson proposed, and Mr. Hewitt supported him, that all members pledge themselves to keep all the proceedings secret. To this Mr. Porter demurred. "If you pass a motion like that," he said, "here is my resignation as a member of the executive. I propose to show the people of this province just what an injustice has been done to Belleville."

The secrecy motion did not pass, but trying to impose it was an obvious conflict-of-interest position for newsmen Nelson and Hewitt. In their jobs they were presumably expected to report facts, not hide them. In the end, Belleville sued the OHA (for $200!) on behalf of McMillan, and lost that one with costs, but did obtain an injunction to prevent Peterborough from taking Belleville's place in the playoffs. Eventually Midland won that nod and lost the final to Stratford.

McMillan, without doubt somewhat of a hockey tourist, went on to be one of the better players as hockey continued to grow in teams, gates, and popularity, both in and out of the OHA. He later played for Cornwall in the Federal Amateur Hockey League (1907) and for Montreal Shamrocks in the Eastern Canadian Amateur Hockey Association (also 1907) – two leagues in which the use of the word "amateur" was openly suspect and certainly wasn't in accord with the OHA interpretation. But then, neither team was in the OHA.

Chapter Four

THE LONG SURVIVOR

*"All right, if you won't play for the Marlies,
you won't play anywhere."*
— W.A. HEWITT TO CYCLONE TAYLOR, 1904

Nothing in available records indicates that there was much advance planning when W.A. Hewitt was parachuted into the OHA as secretary in 1903. The job had been held for six years by A.H. Beaton, a man about whom little may be deduced at this distance. In 1901 Beaton moved up to be a vice-president. W.A. Buchanan, OHA treasurer and a man apparently eager for work, accepted the double job of secretary-treasurer. A measure of his own state of gung-hoism could be seen in a newspaper notice in which he gave his telephone number and said that if anyone had to get in touch with him on OHA business, he would take calls until 3:30 a.m. Whether total fatigue, or Mrs. Buchanan, or a little bit of both overtook him on this rash promise, he lasted only two years.

It would be a fair guess that W.A. Hewitt had been lined up in advance as his successor. Hewitt knew the game as a writer, player, and referee. His *Star* sports pages had bordered on the adulatory when dealing with John Ross Robertson. Also, it was quite customary in those days for sports editors to take jobs with the sporting organizations they wrote about, a sort of moonlighting and possible conflict of interest virtually unknown on major newspapers today. Some weeks before the 1903 annual meeting in November, the *Star* reported that "this newspaper's sports editor, W.A. Hewitt, has been nominated for the post of OHA secretary." At the meeting Buchanan resigned not only as secretary-treasurer but from the OHA executive entirely. The OHA minutes recorded that fact tersely, without the usual flowery sendoff, and Hewitt, then twenty-eight, was in by acclamation.

Another aspect is that the annual honorarium for the job, $200 at the time but to rise year by year, would be an integral part of Hewitt family finances. He'd come from a working-class family where everybody was expected to contribute. As a boy he had delivered newspapers, graduated eventually to helping in the proof room of the *Toronto News* (reading stories for typographical errors), then, at age fifteen, to being a reporter. At twenty, he'd been named sports editor of the *News*, moved to the same job with the *Montreal Herald*, then returned to Toronto and the *Star*. He was five feet six, slight of build, good-looking, and a known go-getter. When he took the OHA job he was married with one young daughter, Audrey, and an infant son, Foster. He took his income where he could find it. Besides his job at the *Star*, he wrote publicity for local theatres, baseball, lacrosse, and worked as a steward at race meetings (Toronto had several race tracks then). No one could have foreseen that as OHA presidents came and went, Billy Hewitt would be the constant— holding the OHA secretaryship and many other major jobs in hockey until he was well into his seventies.

His relationship with John Ross Robertson had some rough patches at the beginning. The competition between the established *Telegram* and the fledgling *Star* had not reached the intensity it eventually would attain, but it was there. Robertson conducted all his business from his newspaper office. Initially, he was not keen about having the sports editor from the opposition paper entering his building to do hockey business on an almost daily basis, as happened during the hockey season. But Robertson's reservations were soon laid to rest. The formal Mr. Hewitt soon became the informal Billy, the trust perhaps coming with Robertson's realization that Hewitt had his life as thoroughly compartmentalized as Robertson's own, although without the income.

The number of hats Hewitt wore and the sometimes conflicting responsibilities he took on could be handled because Hewitt had a lifelong sensitivity to the main chance. Which didn't mean that he was widely liked. He often used his power as arbitrarily as Robertson ever did. Naturally, Hewitt was a lot closer to hockey's front lines than Robertson; the general speaks, but the guy with the gun does the damage.

Just as one instance, it is rather amusing now to compare two versions of Cyclone Taylor's brush with the OHA during the Reddy McMillan springtime of 1904. This doesn't show up in any OHA documents available today, and certainly not in the passage about Cyclone Taylor in Hewitt's memoirs, *Down the Stretch* (1958). In a chapter where Hewitt is picking his own all-time all-stars, Taylor is included. One passage reads:

> The first time I had a good look at Taylor he was playing for Listowel juniors in the 1904 final against Kingston Frontenac-Beechgroves. The game was played in the old Caledonian Curling rink on Mutual Street, and it had been delayed (by a heavy storm) a whole week until the Listowel train could plough its way through to Toronto. That night Taylor played well, but the Frontenac team won the game. Soon after, the young Taylor was pursued by professional clubs . . .

According to Cyclone himself, quoted in his biography by Eric Whitehead, the first pursuit did not come from professional clubs at all, but from W.A. Hewitt.

Hewitt had no publicly known connection to the Marlboro club, but it was he who now phoned Cyclone back home in Listowel, inviting him to move to Toronto to play the following season for the Marlboro seniors, who had just won the OHA championship. Cyclone was flattered and at first wanted to accept what would be his first chance in hockey's big time. He told Hewitt that. But in a few days he had second thoughts.

> To a young fellow like me, born and raised in a small town and I guess a homebody, Toronto suddenly seemed awfully big. I liked Listowel, my home was there, and I had my job in the piano factory. I decided to stay put. I thanked Hewitt for asking me, but I said I wouldn't come. He said he couldn't believe it. I insisted I meant what I said, and he insisted that I change my mind. I said no, I wouldn't change my mind. Then he told me straight out, "All right, if you won't play for the Marlies, you won't play anywhere."

Cyclone knew that Hewitt had the power as OHA secretary to make good on his threat, but he hoped that something could be worked out if he got the right people on his side. Late in 1904 when an OHA team in Thessalon invited him to play there, he hopped the train and began working out with the Thessalon team. But just before the season opener at the end of December, a Thessalon official called Cyclone aside and relayed the bad news. Word had come from OHA headquarters (meaning secretary Hewitt) that he was barred from playing anywhere in Ontario. Thessalon had gone the official route, applying for Taylor's transfer from Listowel to Thessalon. OHA records listing a large number of transfers authorized and a few denied at an executive meeting on December 30, 1904, include this: "Fred Taylor, transfer to Thessalon, denied."

Cyclone went home again, couldn't even get his old job back at the piano factory, wound up missing the entire

1905 season of hockey – and seventy years later said, "I've never forgiven Billy Hewitt for that."

A final footnote to the season he missed comes complete with the usual charges, counter-charges, and general bitchiness that so often attended OHA playoffs of the time. The team that Cyclone had refused to join, the defending champion Marlboros, wound up in the 1905 senior final against Smiths Falls. As often happened when the OHA ordered a series to start in Toronto, favouring the big city team, Smiths Falls didn't do well on the wide Caledonian rink on Mutual Street. Marlboros won 8–3, even though Smiths Falls had one of the great goalies of the time, Percy Lesueur, then twenty-three and later to win two Stanley Cups with Ottawa Senators and to be named to the Hockey Hall of Fame.

In that Toronto game Harry Smith of Smiths Falls was injured by a heavy check and publicly threatened to get even back home. When the teams moved to Smiths Falls for the second game on a Friday night, war broke out. Play was so rough that when the second half was due to begin Marlboros declared that they had only two players fit to continue, all others being (to use the OHA's word in its official report later) "incapacitated" by injuries suffered in the first half. Smiths Falls argued that as Marlboros had finished the first half with five players on the ice, at least four should be able to stagger out there and continue the game; but if Marlboros were scared, two players each would be okay with Smiths Falls, so let's get on with it. The beleaguered referee, Hugh Rose, a lawyer from Welland, was caught in the middle as both the evening, and the argument, wore on.

One problem hindering a settlement was that Hewitt, who was the senior OHA rep for the series, had spent much of the day on a train stuck in a snowbank near Peterborough. Marlboros had made the trip on Thursday, before the storm began. Hewitt left Toronto Friday morning and by the time his train was dug out and steamed on to Smiths Falls it was 10 p.m.

Hewitt told in his memoirs that when he trotted quickly from the train station to reach the sounds of tumult in the Smiths Falls rink, at first the gate attendant wouldn't let him in, saying the rink was too full already.

Hewitt explained that he had to get in; he was the OHA secretary and was in charge of the games. This made the gate attendant laugh. "Well, if you're in charge, you're in a hell of a mess. Go on in."

Actually, Hewitt wasn't in full charge at that stage. By OHA rules the referee was all-powerful until the game ended. It had not ended, so he still had the job. Hewitt's function was to be there as a witness in case of later disputes and to collect the gate money. Referee Rose told Hewitt that the idea of letting the game resume with only two players per side was ridiculous. He was going to call it off and leave the outcome up to the OHA executive.

Which he did. The rink emptied. Hewitt, looking for the gate receipts, was told that in the ambiguous (to say the least) circumstances the county clerk had taken possession. Hewitt tracked this worthy to a nearby hotel lobby and asked that the money be handed over. The county clerk said that the game was not over and he was keeping the money until it was. The lobby was full of locals – naturally on the clerk's side and having fun giving the man from Toronto a hard time.

Hewitt finally had to leave without the money, after assuring the clerk that he was in big trouble. The lobby-dwellers loved that. Their jokes and jibes ringing in his ears, Hewitt retreated. He caught the next train back to Toronto, where he told his troubles to Robertson and a hastily called OHA executive meeting. The meeting – Robertson, Hewitt, and one other, three being a quorum – didn't take long to sort it all out.

First, a rather strange decision was made to throw out

the results of *both* games and order one sudden-death championship match to be played in Peterborough a few days later. Then Robertson got on the phone to Premier James Pliny Whitney. In an Ontario general election only a few weeks earlier, in the last week of January, Whitney's Tories had ended thirty-three consecutive years of Liberal rule. This feat had been achieved with massive support from Robertson's *Telegram*. A favour was owed. Whitney agreed to see Hewitt and hear his story first thing Monday morning.

Accordingly, Hewitt reached the Ontario legislative buildings in Queen's Park at 8 a.m. Monday and was waiting when Premier Whitney rode up on his bicycle. (This was 1905, remember, and stretch limousines for big shots were, at most, no more than a gleam in some buggy-manufacturer's eye.) Hewitt told Whitney his tale of woe, whereupon the Premier called Smiths Falls and ordered the county clerk to cough up the Friday gate receipts forthwith. The money arrived on Hewitt's desk the next day.

When the sudden-death game was played in Peterborough a few days later, Marlboros won 9–3 to repeat as senior champions. But that wasn't the whole story. In Hewitt's memoirs he wrote with his usual mildness that this game "also had its irritations, which indicated the spirit of the times." Then he provided these details:

> Marlboros had arranged for a special train to convey their supporters to the game. When the yelling, be-ribboned enthusiasts dashed to the rink, they were dismayed to find that no seats had been reserved for them. The game had been such a sellout that they were even denied entrance through the turnstiles. Then the Toronto fans found a loose door. They smashed in the door and filed through the opening like the Trojan hordes. Once in the rink, they couldn't find seats so they assembled on the ice. Finally, they left the ice, crowded every standing-room spot and howled throughout the game.

And Cyclone Taylor, still suspended, had missed all that fun.

So the fact is that W.A. Hewitt, however unintentionally, really paved the way for Cyclone Taylor's start on his celebrated wanderings through the hockey world. The suspension was effective only in Ontario, so in the summer of 1905 Cyclone did what Hewitt hadn't been able to talk him into doing – he left Listowel. Portage la Prairie in the Manitoba Hockey League invited him there for room, board, and $25 a month spending money. Cyclone took it and was on his way to his career as one of the all-time hockey greats.

In a sense related to the Cyclone Taylor incident, there was always a feeling in the boondocks of hockey that OHA residence rules favoured the big city teams against those clubs in smaller centres. Certainly the many strong Toronto clubs had a vastly greater pool of playing prospects, although – as in the case of Cyclone Taylor, W.A. Hewitt, and the Marlboros – they also were not above trying to persuade an excellent player to change his abode. No doubt Hewitt would have made sure that Cyclone moved before the October 1 residence deadline in effect at the time, but smaller towns often didn't have that kind of flexibility.

If a star player was suddenly moved by his employer, the hole left in a team in Smiths Falls, Pembroke, Belleville, "Little Ayr" – as the sportswriters of the time usually put it when Ayr was doing well against the big boys – or a host of other smallish communities could well render the team non-competitive. It was in such situations that shading the residence rule was most prevalent. Local pride was involved. If you're the team president, you have to be ready to defend yourself to everybody you meet going "down street," as Ontario village usage has it. In such a community, hockey people – not criminals, but your barber, grocer, blacksmith – sometimes felt they had to do a little cheating just to keep level with the other cheaters. If a protest led to an investigation and OHA suspension later in the season, it was lights out. Such protests rarely, if ever, were levelled against Toronto teams because they usually had so much available talent that they didn't have to try to beat the system. Don't think the out-of-town people weren't aware of this inequity. But if the OHA took any notice of this double standard, it didn't show.

The OHA's credo on residence shifts was stated plainly and often by John Ross Robertson. "When a hockey player shows signs of restlessness in his home centre and longs for scenes of greater hockey activity on the approach of cold weather, his reasons for moving will bear investigation," he informed the 1903 annual meeting.

> There are doubtless many bona-fide changes of residence after October first, but the only safe assumption is that all are induced by other than a true sportsmanlike spirit to make the move. We must be careful on claims of bona-fide changes of residence, for they are a good deal like the ruling of an eminent Irish judge. The law of Ireland was that no drink be served on the Sabbath except to a bona-fide traveller. It looked like dry times until a judge ruled that everyone with a bona-fide thirst was a bona-fide traveller. And we have to see that the OHA does not recognize a bona-fide thirst for the fleshpots of hockey as a bona-fide change of residence.

Linked to residence rules, one persistent bone of contention of OHA meetings was the Toronto Bank League. When the OHA wanted to defend itself against charges that it favoured city teams against those from smaller centres, its attitude to the Bank League often was cited as an example of how the OHA stood fast for the rights of teams from smaller towns. In the early years of the century, Bank League hockey in Toronto ran a close second in quality to OHA games. Both leagues sometimes drew crowds of thousands. Many bank head offices were located in Toronto. Strong competition among their hockey teams was natural. If the Bank of Montreal, for instance, found itself running a distant last in the standings behind Royal, Nova Scotia, Dominion, Toronto, or others, there would be a search among OHA teams in smaller centres for anyone who hit like a dray horse, skated like the wind, got goals in bunches, and (this was the important part) worked for the local Bank of Montreal branch. If one was found, the appropriate authorities at head office would be instructed to transfer this paragon to an interesting new job Toronto . . . and tell him to bring his skates. This, of course, would leave a hole in the OHA team he'd been playing for, which would cry to high heaven for the OHA to do something.

The only defence the OHA had, usually delivered in ringing tones, was that in a policy formulated and led by Robertson, the OHA refused to let any Bank League player perform for any OHA team. Indeed, the OHA would have no truck or trade with the Bank League at all. And felt good about it.

In one of his spirited defences to the effect that the OHA was on the side of the little man, not the bankers, John Ross Robertson argued:

> In the small towns it is often the bank clerks that are the life and backbone of the hockey. The OHA exists for the promotion of hockey throughout the length and breadth of our districts. The Bank League exists for the purpose of ransacking the branch offices of every chartered bank for players who are strong enough to be brought to Toronto and help to win a local championship. If there were no Bank League, good players who are now promoted to head office in Toronto because of their hockey ability would be left to play for the towns in which they live. Some of these towns are small and every high-grade player is of value to a struggling team.

A real, but usually unstressed, part of his argument was that many OHA teams in the big cities that had bank leagues wanted to get in on the talent, too, pick up players who would continue to play in the Bank League but also perform in the OHA. The ban prevented that. Still, year after year a motion came before the OHA to lift the ban, but it was still in effect on November 11, 1905, when John Ross Robertson announced that he was calling it a day as president and would not stand for re-election.

As it turned out, he wasn't exactly leaving the OHA entirely, but few could reach that conclusion from listening to his departure speech.

His six years in the presidency, he said, "will always be a green spot in my memory, yes, pleasant as the thought of summer time amid the storms of a winter night," adding that, "the OHA has so far navigated a troubled sea, and the whole coast line of that sea is strewn with the wrecks of organizations that professed amateurism and practised expediency."

He might have been thinking of the Winn-Lindsay-Hern case in London, the Harry Peel case, the way perfidious baseball had done in Belleville's Jack Marks, the $10 gold-piece "watch fobs" of the old Berlin seniors, Guelph Nationals with their two imported pros, Grindy Forrester as a speedskater, Reddy McMillan, or dozens of other real or imagined threats to snow-white amateurism, when he said staunchly, "We make no man a professional and no man an amateur. The man makes himself a professional and the OHA should never unmake him. He goes wrong with his eyes open and must abide by his own choice. He chooses his class and should be content to play in it."

For this he got a standing ovation, a fulsome resolution of thanks adopted by a standing vote, and, perhaps most typically, agreed to head a three-man subcommittee that would include himself, each current OHA president, and W.A. Hewitt. This subcommittee soon was considered so powerful in protest and suspension cases that its members were known as the Three White Czars. This nickname, wrote Hewitt cheerily fifty years later, was because of their power to "exile offenders to hockey's Siberia."

The fact that Robertson stepped straight from the presidency to become chief of the Three White Czars was an indication of things to come. He simply did not go away, which soon showed.

In the first year that Robertson was out of the presidency, the annual open-the-gates for the Bank League motion came from his successor in the presidency, D.L. Darroch of Collingwood. One newspaper report of the debate on this motion said that Robertson opened with a terse, "Keep the gates closed!" Louis Blake Duff of Welland, a future president, said that any favours shown to bankers might have to be extended to any men who were moved by their employers, such as railway workers, the men themselves perhaps "innocent of guile." Francis Nelson noted that the executive had the power to grant playing certificates to anyone, including bankers, but had not exercised that power for some years. So there was a bit of soft-shoe shilly-shallying in the opposition. (A few years later, with the Bank League's popularity waning, the OHA did lift the ban, though Robertson still led the dwindling opposition.)

Even out of the presidency, his position as head of the Three White Czars gave him considerable power and a number of other moves added to it. As immediate past president, he was entitled to stay on the executive. Another year later he was named a life member of not only the OHA but also of the executive, so that while a rule was adopted some years later that only each year's *immediate* past president got an automatic seat on the executive, that didn't affect Robertson; he was on for life.

Whether foreseen or not, this set up a powerful three-man inner cabinet of hard hats that would last for another decade or more: Robertson, Hewitt, and Francis Nelson. Nelson had been elected to the OHA executive in 1899, the year that Robertson became president. Nelson resigned as first vice-president when Robertson resigned the presidency, but a year later was appointed the OHA representative to the Canadian Amateur Athletic Union and as such was given a permanent seat on the OHA executive.

Hewitt, of course, survived them all. The smallish, outwardly mild, shrewd, foxy, pragmatic W.A. – whose baby son, Foster, had turned three that year – stayed on as secretary for another fifty years.

Chapter Five

A MURDER CHARGE, AND ENTER THE LADIES

"For years, violence in hockey was a rare occurrence. (Now) going to a hockey game is more like going to a fight. Today's players have no tolerance for being given a stiff check or ridden into the boards. (At one time) the game was played without fighting and stick swinging . . . ."

– September 1, 1988, letter on the *Toronto Star's* editorial page

"Taken all round, it was a poor exhibition of hockey, but an excellent exemplification of the rough-house sport that travels under the name of hockey in this section of the country."

– February, 1904, *Toronto Star* report on the first game of a Toronto Marlboros vs. Ottawa Stanley Cup series, in Ottawa

For nearly 100 years now, anguished wails about the rough stuff in hockey have been rising heavenward, where nobody seems to be listening. There persists a romantic idea that hockey was once a game for vastly talented gentle folk, all games consisting of Guy Lafleurs, Mike Bossys, and Wayne Gretzkys zooming around like barn swallows and never ever doing anything nasty, mean, or just plain vicious. Be assured by one who has read al-

most 100 years of hockey journalism: 'twas never like
that.

The mention of rough play between Ottawa and Marlboros is from an unsigned account, probably written by
W.A. Hewitt, who was the OHA representative at the game
and in the normal course of events would combine that
official capacity with his reportorial one.

"The Marlboros encountered a far different proposition
to any they had met in their OHA experience," the report
continued. "They were unaccustomed to the style of game
that permits downright brutality, cross-checking in the
face and neck, tripping, hacking, slashing over the head,
and boarding an opponent with intent to do bodily
injury."

The reader then was told that game delays occurred
when: Toronto's Charlton was knocked unconscious by
Ottawa's Alf Smith cross-checking him into the boards
(two-minute-penalty); Toronto's McLaren was rendered
wonky in the same way by Harvey Pulford (no penalty);
Toronto's Wright caught a flying skate in the thigh and a
stick across the nose (no penalty); Tom Phillips took a
painful blow in the mouth (no penalty). Also, "Moore
nearly broke McLaren's back with a cross-check over the
fence, " and Frank McGee cracked Toronto goalie Geroux
with his stick several times on the top of the head during
goalmouth action.

With all that, there were only four penalties: two
minutes each to Moore and Smith of Ottawa and Phillips
of Toronto (who, the report said, gave back as good as he
was getting). There was also a three-minute sitdown for
Frank McGee of Ottawa. The light and tricky Marlboros
led 3–1 at the half, but the physical toll seemed to show
in the second thirty-minute period when Ottawa scored
five times, three by McGee, to win it 6–3. Physical toll?
Many years later in Hewitt's memoirs he dwelt on Ottawa's second-half reversal of form.

Of course, the victory could have been quite fairly achieved; but the rumor was widely circulated that during the halftime the Ottawa management had salted the ice and softened it so that the faster-skating Marlboros would lose their effectiveness. Whether or not that trickery occurred was for long a subject for debate; and even though I was the OHA representative at the game I was never able to prove it.

That opinion, of course, could have been Toronto bias, Marlboros bias, or sour grapes. In the second game two days later Marlboros, except for Phillips, were never in it. Ottawa won 11–2, with McGee scoring five. But at a time when it was commonly believed that time clocks went faster when the home team was ahead and slower when the home team was behind (this chicanery eventually being countered by having two timekeepers, one from each team, which more than once led to fist fights between the timekeepers), salting the ice was certainly a possibility.

That series provided evidence, as well, that intimidation in hockey wasn't born yesterday. To complaints from some Marlboros about the rough play in that Stanley Cup series, one Ottawa player remarked, "You fellows got off very easily. When the Winnipeg Rowing Club team played here last week most of their players were carried off the ice on stretchers."

One lesson might be taken from that beating and others that came almost like clockwork each time an OHA senior champion challenged for the Stanley Cup. The lesson was that with the stricter refereeing in the OHA, stricter residence rules, and much stricter rules against professionalism, which tended to drive many of the best OHA players to where they might make a few dollars from the game, OHA seniors were usually well outclassed when they met the real big boys. Even with the first-rate play of a goalie named Hiscock, a long-time hockey hero around Kingston, the bids of Queen's University for the Stanley Cup led to bad beatings in 1895 and 1899. Toronto Wellingtons made it closer (losing two 5–3 games) against Winnipeg Victorias in 1902. Marlboros' humiliation came two years later. The fact was that outside of the OHA, the accelerating move elsewhere toward paying players – still secretly – was the forerunner of open professionalism.

In 1893, when Lord Stanley presented the Cup that bears his name, the conditions were that it would be held by "the champion hockey club of the Dominion," which was bound to defend it against any reasonable challenger. Because all teams in Canada in Lord Stanley's time were amateur, there was apparently no thought that the Stanley Cup *should* be specified as being for amateurs only. It was not until 1908 that the amateurs got their own trophy, the Allan Cup, donated by Sir Montagu Allan. By 1910 the Stanley Cup had become the purely professional trophy it remains today.

But really it should have been an all-pro trophy years earlier. By 1905, outside of the OHA, the game was dominated by closet professionals who played a much rougher type of game. Mixing pros and amateurs was so common that in November, 1906, the Eastern Canada Amateur Hockey Association (teams from Ottawa, Quebec, and Montreal) decided to legalize the mixture; the only provision being that each player's status would be declared in advance and published in the newspapers. To what end, it's hard to say. Anyway, a couple of years after manhandling the Marlboros so roughly, the supposedly amateur Ottawa team was squabbling in public over money. Harvey Pulford and Frank McGee were said to be on the way to record paydays. These events were outside the control of the OHA, of course, but are mentioned because the relentless move into professionalism had an impact, a constant talent drain, on all other teams.

In the OHA itself, amateurism certainly was no guarantee of clean, gentlemanly play – and newspaper writers tended to poke away at the bad guys. Here are some accounts from the early 1900s.

A dispatch from Iroquois, Ontario, remarked that the Cornwall team had run a special train there filled with confident supporters who had the game won before leaving home, but eventually lost because they had "reckoned without the referee, Chaucer Elliott, who insisted on good clean hockey, a style of game foreign to anyone who has learned the game in Cornwall."

In Perth, Malcolm Isbister of the Ottawa Aberdeens – the first Ottawa club in the OHA for many years – was hit by a stick across the eyes and wound up in a dark hospital room, his sight in danger and never totally regained.

In Morrisburg, a goal umpire stationed behind the Cornwall net at an end where the ice surface was not enclosed jumped to the ice and attacked the Cornwall goalkeeper, whereupon the umpire was hammered by a Cornwall player. But referee George Stiles of Cornwall, in his official report to the OHA, thought there were extenuating circumstances. "The goal umpire was followed to the ice by such a crowd that I couldn't tell who the principal offender was," he stated in his game report. "This is not the first time this mob trouble has occurred in Morrisburg and I would strongly recommend the executive compel the rink (management) to board up the west end, which is entirely open, and to close, during matches, the gate at the east end, where the trouble occurred tonight, and which, unfortunately, resulted in a nasty injury to Mr. Meikle, the umpire."

A rink with both ends open during a game? Those were the days. When that could happen in what was relatively a mere whistlestop in the hockey world, as one may imagine, the higher in the game one looked – the pros then being mainly found in places like Pittsburgh, New York (with a four-team league), and Michigan's Sault Ste. Marie and Houghton – the rougher the going. The *Brooklyn*

Eagle (Brooklyn had a team!) put it this way: "Hockey in this vicinity makes football seem as mild as croquet, and prize-fighting like caresses in comparison. The unversed onlooker would judge that cracked ribs count one point and broken heads two points for the side inflicting the injuries."

But the rough stuff really knew no geographical boundaries. In 1904 Toronto Varsity beat McGill 9–4 at the Mutual Street Arena in a contest that had a bearing on the intercollegiate senior championship. "Deliberate cross-checking, tripping and slashing predominated all through the game," one newspaper trumpeted. "Referee McDowell allowed the players the greatest latitude and they took full advantage of it." Singled out for special mention was a McGill player named Young, who "got away with the most remarkable species of cross-checking, giving his opponents the stick right across the face and neck. If the rules had been enforced as they should have been, everybody but the goalkeepers would have been off the ice a score of times during the match."

Yet, then as now, dirty play often was allowed to dominate reports and public perception of the game. On the same night as the blood-and-thunder intercollegiate game, which took up a column or more in Toronto newspapers, an OHA senior match was played in Perth (Perth 6, Brockville 2). On the same page as the McGill-Varsity bloodletting a tiny story datelined Perth read: "The game was one of the fastest ever seen here, and was remarkably free from roughness, not one player being ruled off during the game."

And yet, rough play or clean play, winning or losing, what the OHA had that the pros didn't have was an idea so inflexible that one might call it a creed, a yardstick of behaviour that kept the most dangerous events from causing tragedy. The OHA was one of the wonders of the sports world, a stature certainly not due to the association pandering to the weak and easily tempted. But what it did, worked. It persisted. New leagues, avowedly amateur but really flirting openly with professionalism, came and went while occasionally luring, or trying to lure, OHA clubs into what was promised to be a more salubrious hockey climate. One of these new leagues was the Federal Amateur Hockey League, born at least partly because of strife within the powerful old Canadian Amateur Hockey League.

The Federal started play with fanfare in 1904 with four teams, Cornwall defecting from the OHA and Montreal Wanderers and Ottawa Capitals from the CAHL. The Wellingtons of Toronto, OHA senior champions for three consecutive years, unaccountably dropped out of the OHA the same day as Cornwall and were expected to show up in the Federal but didn't, so another Ottawa team, the Nationals, made the league's fourth team. Over the next few years teams moved in and out of the Federal until, by 1907, only Cornwall was left of the originals. Weeks before that season began the Federal's two leading teams, Wanderers and Ottawa Capitals, broke away to join the Eastern Canada Amateur Hockey Association. That left the Federal with Ottawa Victorias, Ottawa Montagnards, Cornwall, and Morrisburg.

On February 15 Victorias were beaten 4–2 by Cornwall in a league game but protested on the grounds that two Cornwall players, Owen (Bud) McCourt and Laurence DeGray, had played a couple of games a few weeks earlier with Shamrocks in the ECAHA. (Both, incidentally, were under an earlier OHA suspension along with the entire Woodstock club, because Woodstock had imported them illegally from Cornwall.)

Perhaps because of the Federal's weakened state the decision on the protest seemed to go both ways. A replacement game was ordered to take place in Cornwall, but both McCourt and DeGray were okayed to play. At the time, McCourt was the league's leading scorer with sixteen goals in eight games. Cornwall won 11–3. The game was followed a day later by the only murder charge ever recorded as a result of hockey violence.

Early in the second half McCourt and Art Throop of Ottawa crashed together and began to fight. Other players joined in with the usual name-calling, punching, and stick-swinging. When the fight was broken up, McCourt left the ice bleeding from a head cut. In the dressing room he became unconscious, was taken to hospital, and died the following morning.

A few hours later that same day, a coroner's inquest called witnesses and found, on their evidence, that McCourt "came to his death by a blow from a hockey stick in the hands of (Ottawa's) Charles Masson," that there had been no evidence of animosity between the two previous to the assault, and that there had seemed no personal provocation for Masson's blow. The jury recommended what many an investigation of hockey violence has recommended since: "that legislation be enacted whereby players encouraging or engaging in rough or foul play may be severely punished." Masson was brought before a magistrate. The crown attorney read the charge, murder, and objected strenuously when, after some preliminary evidence had been heard, the magistrate reduced the charge to manslaughter.

Five weeks later the case was heard in Cornwall by a judge and jury. The many witnesses called at the three-day trial included referee Emmett Quinn, Cornwall player Zian Runnians, Ottawa goalie William Bannerman, and Ottawa players Jack Ryan, Alfred Young, and Jack Williams.

Several witnesses swore that McCourt had been hit by another Ottawa player, unnamed, before being hit by Masson. With this uncertainty over who had struck the fatal blow, Masson was acquitted. As far as can be judged by available records, he never played hockey again.

Pro pressure caused many other defections (like Cornwall's) from the OHA, teams as well as individuals. The

Ontario Professional Hockey League, the first avowedly all-pro league in Canada, was formed late in 1907 to begin play early in 1908 with teams from Brantford, Guelph, Berlin, and Toronto. In a separate instance, officials of the Sault Ste. Marie, Ontario, OHA intermediate team abruptly decided to go pro in a league with Sault Ste. Marie, Michigan, and Houghton, Michigan. But just as abruptly three of the Sault players left town, not wishing to be professionalized. The remaining players couldn't beat anybody. The team folded.

Many other amateur leagues operated outside of the OHA or on the non-championship fringes. A prime example was the Western Ontario Hockey Association, which – with former OHA men among the organizers – came about as an aftermath of the Berlin and Waterloo suspensions back in 1898. People in that area felt maybe they should try hockey without Toronto's OHA headquarters calling the shots. The well-run WOHA had only five teams to start with and professed no animosity to Mother OHA (indeed, at least one WOHA president was OHA executive member H.E. Wettlaufer), but arranged season-long schedules that were a welcome relief from the OHA system under which, in effect, every team that didn't win its group between January 1 and January 31, and go on to the playoffs, was out of business for the season. Within a few years the WOHA had grown to more than twenty clubs, senior, intermediate, and junior, involving a lot of players who otherwise would have been with OHA affiliates.

Also, a lot of hockey was being played in the north, with occasional moves toward OHA membership – one of which, a dozen years later, brought the Northern Ontario Hockey Association into the OHA as an affiliate that played its own schedule to championship levels, but then could send its winners south to test the OHA champions for all-Ontario titles (and sometimes win).

Along with the ebb and flow, teams coming and going,

players going pro and finding it was forever as far as the OHA was concerned, playing rules were constantly under scrutiny. Almost every year as OHA membership rose steadily (to a total of ninety-seven clubs by 1904), new ideas were considered, tried out, and – if they worked – adopted. Taken over a period of its first thirty years, the OHA led, or helped to lead, or welcomed good ideas from other hockey jurisdictions that brought about a veritable revolution in the way the game was played. As in many profound changes, the extent of hockey's change over even its first decade or two could only be seen by taking the long view and remembering what the original rules had been.

So consider a time, 1893, when a goalie for the Toronto Granites was banished from the ice for dropping to his knees to block a shot. It was right there in the rules that he had to stay upright, a rule written because most shots were along the ice and a goalie lying prone between the posts would be taking an unfair advantage. In that case, as the goalie was dressed exactly like all other players, with no goal mitts, no goal stick, no pads, his point man dropped back to play goal and Granites still won the game.

Two years later, with more shots coming in at thigh height or better, one goalie in Ottawa and another in Winnipeg showed up for work in cricket pads – and another, evidently fearing for the safety of his family jewels, during games used to wear his fur hat where it would do the most good, stuffed down the front of his hockey pants.

As the 1890s wore on, players at the point or coverpoint positions sometimes wore cane shin pads on top of their hockey stockings, while forwards tended to wear lighter pads under their stockings. Helmets and face guards? Forget it. There were not even rudimentary hockey gloves until the early 1900s. One player with a bad elbow drew ribald comments by showing up with a knee-pad from some other sport tied to his arm as protection.

As for sticks, each of which at the time was made from a single piece of wood, those used by goalies and defencemen were a little heavier than the ones carried by forwards, but a few years went by before forwards started shaving the upper edge of their stick blades. Skates were mostly of a single-unit sort that resembled modern figure skates, but without the sawtooth points. Early in the 1900s some players in western Canada began to use the first tube skates.

But none of these changes or refinements had the importance of an idea that came originally from Frank Stocking, who played goal for Quebec from 1893 to 1901 and who had experienced all too often the violent arguments, shoving, and physical attacks involved in a goal umpire's decision on whether a puck had passed above or below hockey's famous imaginary line between the tips of the goal posts, four feet above the ice. When the annual meeting of the Canadian Amateur Hockey League was held in Montreal late in 1899, Stocking and Arthur E. Scott of Quebec submitted a small model of a goal net that could be strung between the posts by a crossbar.

Their reasoning was that if a shot was really a goal, the puck would wind up in the net. If it was high, it wouldn't. If it hit the crossbar and bounced out, what always had been the closest of all a goal umpire's calls would be history. As a supplementary advantage, Stocking figured the net would help in another way – by providing a catch basin for the tangles that ensued when an onrushing forward, unable to stop, would crash into the goalmouth and carry puck, goalie, and all sliding between the goalposts to hit the end of the rink, which by the rules had to be no less than five feet behind the goal.

The goal nets were accepted in Montreal, and within weeks the OHA ran a test and announced with enthusiasm that as soon as nets could be manufactured they'd be in use. Which they were, although in Ontario at first the iron crossbar, for some reason lost in antiquity, was not directly between the posts but six inches back of the imaginary line. This flaw was discovered in dramatic circumstances during a senior game between the University of Toronto and Toronto St. George's when a shot struck the crossbar, bounced into the air, and landed on the top of the net. Varsity claimed a goal but the goal judge disallowed it – whereupon he was removed at the request of the Varsity team, which had this right under the rules, even though in this case the referee supported the goal judge. Varsity's claim was based on the fact that the shot, from close in, had been *rising* when it struck the crossbar and therefore at the instant of crossing the goal line the puck was *below* our old friend the imaginary line. They still didn't get the goal. However, that little hitch was corrected some time later by having the crossbar go straight from one post to another, and never again did a goal umpire have to judge the exact whereabouts of the imaginary line. A few weeks later the OHA also introduced a broad line painted on the ice between the posts, eliminating a few more hot goalmouth arguments.

Oddly enough, more than sixty years later when hockey historian Charles L. Coleman was compiling the first volume of his monumental work, *The Trail of the Stanley Cup*, he wondered what effect the goal nets had had on scoring. His finding: "In the period 1893–1900 when unpadded goalkeepers defended goalposts with no crossbar (or net) for support and used a narrow bladed stick, the average number of goals per game was seven, compared to six per game scored throughout the entire National Hockey League schedule in 1963."

Almost every OHA annual meeting dealt with dozens of suggested rule changes. Most were concerned with procedural matters, duties of game officials, and obligations of member clubs, rather than with playing rules. The OHA's method of handling the several rule changes of whatever category proposed every year was, weeks before the annual meeting, to publish such proposals on easy-to-read sheets with the old rule in a left-hand column and the proposed new rule and the name of its proposer alongside on the right. That way delegates could consider and discuss possible rule changes long before they hit the floor of the annual meeting.

One such motion in 1902 was that teams be restricted to six players where ice surfaces were no larger than 60 by 160 feet. The idea was defeated after heated debate, opponents saying that a game of that sort wouldn't be hockey, just as, they argued, taking the shortstop out of baseball would leave a game that was not baseball. The proponents didn't have many answers and the six-man hockey idea was dead in the OHA for another thirteen years. But in 1904, for instance, accepting a personal tryout by referee Fred C. Waghorne, the OHA ruled that in future the referee could start play by dropping or tossing the puck between the centres from whatever distance he considered safe, rather than placing it between their sticks and either being agile enough to get out of the way or getting whacked by their sticks.

One rule passed in 1905 specified that sticks had to be "composed entirely of wood." Research has not turned up exactly what alternatives had been proposed to cause that ruling. That same year the minimum rink-size rule came in: 60 × 160, and roofed, unless the OHA had ruled otherwise for some temporary reason (such as fire).

Also in 1905, goalies for the first time were allowed to pass a puck forward three feet without the pass being called offside. To facilitate precise calls on that new rule, a line was to be painted on the ice three feet out from the goal line. As small as this particular change was, it was the first break in the game's sacrosanct no-forward-pass rule. This line defining how far such a forward pass could be made was the granddaddy of the blueline, many years away, and later the centre red line, even farther into the future.

One area of the game definitely not taken seriously

then or for a long time thereafter, at least by men, was women's hockey. Although establishment of what came to be called the Ladies Ontario Hockey Association was still more than twenty years into the future, even at the turn of the century there were women's (or "girls'" as the usage tended to be) teams in Toronto listed for Havergal Hall, the girls school then on Jarvis Street, St. Hilda's, Victoria College, and Varsity, as well as a team called the Marlboro Ladies.

Not taken seriously, but not ignored. One day in 1901 several OHA league games of some importance had been played throughout the province, but the lead story on the *Toronto Star*'s sports page the next afternoon looked like this:

LADY HOCKEYISTS
PLAY ON LOCAL ICE
Tam-o-Shanters defeated the
Picture Hats of Victoria College

Upon the Victoria College Rink yesterday afternoon the Picture Hats played a practice match with the Tam-o-Shanters, which was exciting – to the spectators – while it lasted.

The teams were selected from the young women of the college. They have been practising hockey for some time and have enough knowledge of the game to make trouble for the referee. The game started without a referee, but the players refused to abide by the OHA rules and regulations, so a husky young college hockey player was pressed into service. The players took kindly to male discipline and thereafter the game progressed without dispute.

"Oh, say! I wasn't ready," said the Picture Hats centre forward when her Tam-o-Shanter opponent took the puck from her on the face-off. The puck was brought back.

The Tam-o-Shanters had two very fast forwards, a tall young woman in a brown skirt and a young woman who wore a red blouse. This pair kept the puck in their opponents' territory the greater portion of the time.

"Oh, excuse me, Clara!" exclaimed the Picture Hat's point player, an athletic looking young woman in a grey tailor-made suit, as she took the puck from an opponent who was about to shoot a goal. Clara accepted the apology with dainty grace. Then the Tams secured the puck again and rained in shots upon the goal. Miss Russell, the goalkeeper, stopped a half dozen hot ones and then let an easy one slip by her.

During the next attack on goal, in a fierce rush by the Tams' two speedy forwards, the Picture Hat's point player was knocked down in front of the goal posts.

This jar disarranged her hat and she calmly sat upon the ice, removed the hat pins, rearranged her tresses, and replaced the hat. Down the ice came a Tam with the puck.

"Is my hat on straight?" asked the young lady on the ice when the player with the puck tried to lift the disc through the goal. Being assured on this point, she scrambled to her feet and rushed it down to the other end.

"Oh, my goodness, excuse me, Clarence!" exclaimed the Tams' cover point as she saw this happening and hastily broke up a tête-à-tête with a young man on the fence and rushed across the ice to defend the threatened goal.

"Half time, Mr. Referee," gasped a young woman, very much out of breath, as she threw her arms around a convenient fence post. The game had only progressed five minutes. Mr. Referee tried to explain this, but the young lady said she was out of breath and that settled it.

The score at halftime was Tams 3, Picture Hats 0.

When the game started again, the Picture Hats made a determined attempt to even up the score, but their big hats persisted in sliding to one side at critical moments and the rude Tams absconded with the puck while their opponents were rearranging the refractory headgear. Finally, Miss Alice, a Picture Hat forward, solved the problem by sitting on the puck while she manipulated hatpins. Tired players sat around in picturesque attitudes on the ice, and the referee called the game when the only players on their feet were the goalkeepers and the young woman who was whispering sweet nothings to dear Clarence at the end of the rink.

The Victoria ladies team will play the Havergal team next week, and "may we be there to see," remarked everybody who saw yesterday's game.

Chapter Six

THE YEAR OF THE CROOKS ... AND SAINTS

*"With the competition keen everywhere . . .
there were ringers and black sheep and
crookedness. Some were found out and
doubtless not a few escaped."*

— PRESIDENT D.L. DARROCH,
summarizing the OHA's 1907 season

With a lot of exciting hockey being played, games won
by last-second goals, first-game leads of eight or nine goals
occasionally being overcome in the second contest of the
standard two-games, total-goals series of the time, this
account might seem unbalanced in dwelling so much on
the crookedness uncovered season after season. But the
long, annual state-of-the-union speeches delivered by
OHA presidents tend to set that tone. Great hockey seemed
more or less taken for granted, or at least took a back seat
in public notice to those who would do anything, legal or
illegal, to put together a team with a chance to win.

At that time, each season's usual registration of eighty
to ninety Ontario teams involved close to a thousand
players as well as coaches, managers, and those local
poohbahs usually associated with any team. Given the
rigidly authoritarian cast of the OHA and the rampantly
free-enterprise inclination of many players and club executives, there was bound to be larceny.

To take one season, 1907, as a case in point: that year

the OHA had eighty-five teams: senior (ten), intermediate (forty-one), and junior (thirty-four), ranging geographically from northern Ontario to the United States border and from Lake Huron to Quebec. They played 275 league and playoff games in all during that ten-week hockey season, blessed by what Darroch called "good steady ice" – or, in other words, the frigid weather that was normal for Canada.

However, good ice was the only break the OHA got that winter. W.A. Hewitt by then was recognized as the OHA's most indefatigable official, part obedient servant and part private eye. He knew all the procedures, precedents, and home phone numbers – and if he chose to do this or that club a favour, or to shoot another down in flames, that was one of the benefits of being born before the phrase "conflict of interest" had been invented. There wasn't anything in OHA hockey that he couldn't handle, and did, for his annual honorarium (by then $400). The OHA's first blow of the 1907 season came early. Just as play was about to start, W.A. was stricken by pneumonia. It was a killer disease then, antibiotics being far in the future. For much of the winter his life was to hang in the balance. How to replace the irreplaceable?

His most experienced possible pinch-hitters were the other two members of the trouble-shooting subcommittee dubbed the Three White Czars, John Ross Robertson and first vice-president Dwight Turner. But that winter both Robertson and Turner were out of the country for much of the season. Normally, D.L. Darroch, the president, would have been on the subcommittee instead of Turner, but he was preparing to move to Calgary and often was unavailable. Also, he lived in Collingwood, several hours from Toronto by train. For all these reasons he had been excused from the kind of quick decision-making the subcommittee was always being called upon to make. If Hewitt had been healthy, it could all have been handled. With him confined to bed and business

visits forbidden, chaos threatened. So in the end Darroch
had to go on active service anyway – travelling back and
forth between his home and Toronto so often that, he
told the next OHA convention, "it almost convinced me
that our president should live in Toronto, or very close to
it, at least during the hockey season."

To help in day-by-day matters, the OHA called in as
acting secretary Hewitt's principal journalistic adversary,
J.P. Fitzgerald, sports editor of Robertson's *Telegram*. The
courtly Fitzgerald, who was the *Telegram* sports editor
for many decades thereafter, survived that tumultuous
season somehow. What made it worse was that with
Hewitt too ill even to be consulted, there seemed more
than the usual thorny problems emanating from hockey's
underworld.

A selection from that winter:

1. In a junior semifinal between Lindsay and Belleville,
   Lindsay won the first game in Belleville. The second,
   in Lindsay, turned out to be your standard hockey
   bloodbath. When the teams were down to three players a side through penalties and injuries, referee Fred
   C. Waghorne, one of the most experienced in the
   business, stopped the game and called it no contest.
   For this decision, he got a fiery ticking-off by the
   harried Darroch a few days later. Under the OHA constitution, a home club was responsible for maintaining law and order in its own rink or would forfeit the
   game. On those grounds Darroch maintained that
   Belleville should have been awarded that second game
   and the series prolonged into a third game. While
   Darroch didn't say so, the prospect of another sellout
   crowd in a third game to determine a winner wouldn't
   have hurt anyone's feelings, either. The discussion
   must have got hot. Waghorne didn't take criticism
   willingly, on or off the ice. The meeting ended with

Waghorne suspended from the refereeing staff. On the basis of winning the only game officially completed in the series, Lindsay advanced and went all the way to the final before losing to Stratford.

2. Peterborough protested arch-rival Kingston being declared winner of their five-team senior group, which Peterborough had been leading. This happened because for some unrecorded reason, probably to make up a postponed game, a late-season meeting between Kingston's 14th Regiment team and Midland had been designated as having a value of four points instead of two. Kingston won and thereby, without having had to deal with Peterborough on the ice, vaulted over Peterborough into the playoffs. Peterborough thought, rationally, that this situation stunk. When the OHA did not agree, the Peterborough club angrily quit the OHA.

3. Guelph was making a runaway of the other senior group when the OHA stepped in and demanded details on how Guelph had convinced one player from Port Hope, two from Fenelon Falls, and a fourth from Ottawa to move to Guelph. The players involved and the Guelph manager, Norman Irving, were ordered to appear before the Three White Czars and explain. Their explanations, said Darroch, "were nothing if not damaging. (Their) carefully rehearsed story failed to hang together when closely questioned, and the men would not take affidavits." Also, it was discovered that the Guelph recruit from Ottawa, Ouelette, "had been rung in under an assumed name by Lindsay the year before." Manager Irving then issued a long list of professionalism charges against players and officials of eight other teams. The OHA paid its own lawyer to investigate all these charges because, as Darroch said, "we felt in duty bound to pay expenses of men charged with an offence and not proven guilty.

One or two men in the dim and distant past had received from 50 cents to a couple of dollars over and above expenses."

In face of such meagre pickings, Darroch concluded that Irving's scattershot charges had been intended to embarrass the OHA to the extent that during the fall-out he could form a semi-pro league in competition with the OHA. Irving, said Darroch, "had some support in a certain section of the press which was not prompted by a love of clean sport, but for various reasons best known to those irresponsible howlers after the fleshpots."

End result: all Guelph players, and the club, were suspended, as well as manager Irving.

4. But the problems in that senior division were not over yet. Berlin, back in the OHA only a couple of years after the gold-coin suspension of nine years earlier, was running neck and neck with Stratford and Toronto St. George's (with a fifth team, Galt, trailing) when OHA investigators targeted Berlin once again on various charges. All players, except one named McGinnis, cleared themselves with sworn statements. Because of a reported, and perhaps even real, illness in the McGinnis family the OHA allowed McGinnis extra time to put forward his defence. He still had not done so when he showed up in Toronto with Berlin for a game with St. George's. The OHA sped instantly to action stations. Calling from Collingwood, Darroch instructed acting OHA secretary Fitzgerald that McGinnis was not to be allowed on the ice unless he signed an affidavit swearing he was an innocent amateur and always had been.

The OHA lawyer, former secretary A.H. Beaton, bore this ultimatum to the rink—where both teams, and the crowd, were impatient for action. Challenged outside the dressing room, McGinnis would not sign the affidavit. Also, he admitted having been paid for playing hockey a couple of years earlier (proving, incidentally, that he was somewhat more honest than many others who had signed affidavits that later were proved to be lies). That admission, of course, normally would get him and the whole team suspended. But in the circumstances, including the impatient crowd, a deal was offered.

The OHA representatives, with Berlin's agreement, proposed that with McGinnis ruled out, St. George's could drop a man as well and the game go on with six a side. St. George's ("certainly ill-advised by their management," opined Darroch) at first refused. Then when they changed their minds, the Berliners huffily changed their minds, too, and refused to drop McGinnis. Amidst some rather wild scenes, Berlin forfeited the game and was suspended.

That meant, if anyone is still counting, that of ten senior teams that started that season, in the eastern section one, Peterborough, had quit in a rage and in the western section two, Berlin and Guelph, had been suspended for professionalism. However, as always, nothing really ever *stopped* the OHA. With both Berlin and Guelph out of the five-team west group, leading survivors St. George's and Stratford played off. Stratford won, and went on to beat Kingston's 14th Regiment team for the senior championship and the John Ross Robertson Trophy.

5. Gore Bay, being refused a change-of-residence certificate for one player, defaulted to Little Current and told acting secretary Fitzgerald they had never been treated right by the OHA anyway and would blankety-blank well form a league of their own, an option that had quite a few precedents, one way or another.

6. Ingersoll, Paris, and Woodstock were tied in the lead of their junior district. However, when some opposition sleuth discovered that Ingersoll had played a man on his brother's birth certificate, it was good-bye Inger-

soll. Then it was found that Woodstock unwittingly had used an over-age player. Woodstock "was manly enough to admit it when they found it out," said the OHA minutes on the subject, those minutes also recording that Woodstock was tossed out of the play-offs exactly the same as if it hadn't been manly at all. So of the three original contenders for that group's championship, only Paris was left in the intergroup playoffs – where it promptly was eliminated.

7. Markdale was suspended because, possibly due to its inexperienced and youthful (under legal age) secretary, its playing certificates were all found to be unsworn-to, unattested, and totally against the rules.

8. After outlining these and other misdemeanours in his speech to the OHA annual meeting later that year, Darroch also reported that in the finals of one junior group (teams not named) "there is more than a suspicion that the games were not played to win, but were fixed."

The main point is that none of this was really unusual, except in terms of numbers. The litany of such offences was part of every season's summing-up. Each succeeding president – Dwight Turner of Toronto followed Darroch into the presidency for two years before giving way to Louis Blake Duff of Welland – almost could have used a blank form and just filled in the names of the offenders. One year John Wiggins of the Goderich team was expelled for life for assaulting a referee at Clinton, and the Goderich team was suspended for its part in the riot that followed. Another year Markdale was suspended for playing an ineligible player, Wiarton got the ax for playing two ineligibles, and Simcoe was suspended for taking its team off the ice in protest of a referee's decision. Bracebridge and Baden were bumped out of one season for minor infractions and all Chatham players and club executives were expelled for what the OHA called "crooked work," that is, playing a couple of men under assumed names.

And so it went year after year, sometimes good hockey and sometimes a jungle of impropriety out there. Louis Blake Duff, the eloquent Welland newspaperman, set both the good and the bad scenes nicely in his presidential roundup in 1910:

> Today, after these score of years, we find the domain of the OHA reaching to the uttermost West of Old Ontario, east to within hailing distance of Montreal, north to the edge of civilization, and south to the edge of winter – a domain that would make a dozen European principalities.
>
> The game has taken a tremendous hold upon the interest of the Canadian people, and it is not strange, for it typifies wonderfully the sturdy pluck, the courage, the stamina, the resolution, the dash and go, that is lifting this country up to the heights of splendid achievement . . . The hockey stick struck a responsive chord in the breast of young Canada, and in the breast of Canada that is not so young . . .

Then he came to the nitty-gritty.

> As you know, the referee is required in every game to report upon the penalties for offences, and to comment touching the character of the play. I have made an analysis of these reports . . . Let me quote to you some of the phrases: "Nice clean game." "Wholly free from roughness." "Two teams of little gentlemen." "Nothing dirty and no back talk." And so I might go on reading from 230-odd reports.
>
> Now I am going to quote you from every report in which the game of hockey was not honored.
>
> One referee says, "Slashing, tripping, fighting." Another one comments. "Everyone off but the goalkeepers, some two or three times." "Two spectators were put out of the rink for taking a punch at players over the fence."
>
> "The team laid on the hickory with a vengeance." "I put two players off for mixing." Mixing is not an offence covered by our code, but doubtless it is something very bad. I have

but one other offence to report, that of a player using very bad language at a match in the presence of ladies.

All this while, despite the strenuous efforts of the OHA, the erosion of amateurism went on. For example, the Eastern Canada Amateur Hockey Association, although with the avowed intention to set itself up on OHA lines, didn't even take the word "amateur" out of its name when play-for-pay was permitted. In addition, the Ontario Professional Hockey League, usually called the Trolley League because electric trains connected all its towns, was out-and-out pro and thriving. Seventeen-year-old Newsy Lalonde, eventually to become an all-time professional great, was among its stars. But that league actually paid its players less than some teams that were avowedly amateur. (Berlin joined this league after the disqualification over McGinnis.)

The job of staying amateur and still keeping the best players was soon to be beyond the OHA. Professionalism continued to be punished for decades thereafter, but every year many of the best players moved to the pros. The triumph of the OHA idea was that for every player who turned pro there were a hundred boys who got their first pairs of skates and twenty-five-cent hockey sticks and staggered out on frozen ponds or corner-lot rinks to have a shot at becoming hockey heroes. For every burgeoning professional organization there were hundreds of men in communities of all sizes who would put up a few bucks to support the local junior, intermediate, or senior team from whence, originally, every great star came.

The word "awesome" had not then become a sports cliché, but this endless annual flood of incipient hockey talent can only be described by that term. The ones who didn't go on to play as adults remained behind, as they do today, to cheer from the stands for the ones who did scale the heights.

But every once in a while the pattern of the old amateur

ideal did manifest itself. The 1898 rule change that limited junior play to players under age twenty had brought
some major boys' schools into OHA competition. None
reached a late playoff round until, in the winter of 1902,
Upper Canada College made it to the junior final against
Stratford. This produced not only the parades, the college
cheers, the extension of schoolboy sports enthusiasm into
what had been largely adult crowds, but also one of the
most remarkable playoff series of the time.

It began with a 4–4 tie in the first game at Stratford
and continued into a 5–5 tie in regulation time of the
second game, in Toronto. The OHA had ruled that this
game must be played to a conclusion. After all, it was
March 6 and this was natural ice – a thaw could happen
anytime. Overtime then was not sudden death. There
was no score in the first ten-minute overtime period.
Then, with the crowd in a near-delirium, there were
three goals in the second overtime, two by the hometown
Upper Canada College, which won 7–6 to take the series 11–10.

A year later St. Andrew's College of Aurora made it to
the junior playoffs over Upper Canada College but didn't
reach the final. The next year Upper Canada College was
the best school team but lost in the playoffs. In 1905 St.
Andrew's College reached the junior final against Stratford for two one-sided games, Stratford 10–3 and St.
Andrew's 7–2, for a total favouring Stratford 12–10.

This set the stage for the first tentative step in the
emergence of St. Michael's College of Toronto as a hockey
power. By mid-century St. Michael's graduates were to
be found almost everywhere hockey was played on this
continent. It all began in 1907 with a St. Michael's junior
team playing in what the OHA called its college group,
including St. Andrew's, Upper Canada, and Parkdale
Canoe Club.

Against those more experienced teams, St. Michael's
went through its season unbeaten. That was only in the

college group, but the unbeaten record still wasn't all that easy to come by. It was on the line in the group final when St. Michael's played two ties with Parkdale Canoe Club and won the third game in overtime before being knocked out in an early playoff round by Stratford, the eventual junior champions. The following year St. Michael's once again won the college group and once again faced Stratford, but this time in the provincial final. It was a weird series: a win for St. Michael's on Toronto ice by a single goal and a loss in Stratford by 21–4!

A year after that hammering, amazingly enough, St. Michael's – with three of its seven players veterans of the previous year's junior slaughter – moved to senior and won the OHA championship. The college's establishment nationally as a hockey power was close at hand.

We can take it for granted that, even with no forward passes as fans today would know them, no bluelines, red lines, or indeed any line at all except the goal line, hockey in those days had the same – or perhaps even greater – appeal than it has today. When the hockey nuts gathered for the OHA senior playoffs of 1909, jamming into the rinks to watch St. Michael's beat Kingston's 14th Regiment team 12–9 in Toronto and 11–8 in Kingston, there was no television, or radio, and an automobile was something to stop and look at as it passed.

There was no Maple Leaf Gardens and therefore no necessity to pay 1989's $30.50 for the best seat at a hockey game. Most seats were under $1 (however, a good weekly wage at the time was $15). But when playoff time came around, hockey fans of any era would recognize the spirit abroad. Eighty-odd years ago, the excitement was much like that of today.

There is no ready explanation – except possibly the sudden burgeoning of professional and semi-professional leagues – for the fact that when St. Michael's won its first senior championship in the spring of 1909, there were fewer senior teams in Ontario, only five, than there ever had been. The senior group was always much smaller than the less-pressured intermediates and juniors, but there had been twelve senior clubs in 1904, ten in 1905, nine in 1906, a starting ten in 1907 (before Peterborough quit and Guelph and Berlin were disqualified), seven in 1908, then five in 1909. Of course, there were several new pro leagues, with OHA seniors a prime recruiting area.

Yet in 1910 when play began in the National Hockey Association, forerunner of the NHL, even though it gobbled up a lot of good and not-so-good seniors for its teams in Cobalt, Haileybury, Renfrew, Montreal Wanderers, and a new club called Les Canadiens (within a few weeks Ottawa and Montreal Shamrocks also were admitted), at exactly the same time the number of OHA senior clubs jumped back to eleven, among them St. Michael's. This more-than-doubling of OHA senior teams in one year could have been just a freak. More likely it was a reflection of the growing popularity of the pros. To many players, senior hockey looked like the stepping stone to the huge salaries they'd heard about: $3,000 a year or more for the likes of Cyclone Taylor, Bad Joe Hall, Lester and Frank Patrick, Hod Stuart, and others.

Another undoubted element was that many men, rural, big city, or wherever, the ones who always could be found beating the drums for how fame and fortune lay waiting for any community that could beat its neighbours at hockey, had a new focus – the Allan Cup representing the Canadian senior championship.

With the Stanley Cup by then impossible to wrest from the pros, Sir Montagu Allan's Cup represented an essential filling of the big-time playoff gap. Play for the Allan Cup was national in scope. At season's end winners of provincial or other organized-league (such as Intercollegiate) championships would meet in sudden-death games until only one was left as undisputed national amateur champion. So the Allan Cup promised amateurs and their fans that any community, large or small, now had a chance at national prominence – which indeed did come years later to the likes of Kitchener-Waterloo Dutchmen, Whitby Dunlops, Belleville McFarlands, Montreal Royals, Port Arthur Bearcats, Winnipeg Falcons, Sydney Millionaires, Trail Smoke Eaters, Penticton Vees, and the rest, right across the country.

St. Michael's College was in that parade. When St. Mike's, as it became known across the land, won the OHA in 1909, it challenged Queen's University for the Allan Cup but was refused because the trustees of the Cup ruled that the challenge came too late. St. Michael's then requested that the challenge be held over until the following season but was refused on the grounds that, by that time, perhaps neither club would have repeated as champion of its respective league. So by 1910 the St. Michael's players had the Allan Cup very much on their minds. Senior hockey was thriving in many parts of the country, and St. Michael's in many books was the class of the competition.

The team that year was still unbeaten when it reached the OHA senior semifinal against the old nemesis from junior days, Stratford, and the battle was on. The teams played to an 8–8 tie in Stratford, but St. Michael's won 4–3 in Toronto to reach the final. Meanwhile, Parkdale Canoe Club and Toronto Argonauts were going at it in the other semifinal. The weather was mild enough that, reported the *Toronto Star* from one game, "the ice was like molasses in January, and the puck as obstreperous as a girl's hair after she has washed it." Playing the puck, the *Star* said, was like batting fungoes in baseball.

Parkdale apparently was better at this than the Argonauts, winning by a single goal scored ten seconds from the end of the second game. This brought on resumption of that earlier rivalry, St. Michael's vs. Parkdale, and the hockey world was more than somewhat agog. The crush for tickets was so great that the doors of the rink were barred early, the rink full to overflowing. The 4–4 tie in the first game did nothing to lessen the fan interest. The second match was played on a Saturday night. Again the doors were locked even earlier than before. The OHA had ruled that this game would be played to a finish, in overtime if necessary, which turned out to be the case.

After twenty-five minutes of the first thirty-minute period, Peter Spratt, the St. Michael's point player, rushed end to end, shot hard, and the rebound came out to right-winger Herb Matthews, who blasted it back in for a 1–0 lead. That held until near the end of the final period when Andy Kyle made a brilliant rush that ended with a waist high shot that tied the game, whereupon, said a news report, "that Parkdale crowd simply went mad; they shouted and cheered and threw their hats away and acted like Queen Street asylum patients on a jamboree."

The overtime, in ten-minute periods, was not sudden death. The first overtime period was scoreless. Only a few seconds into the second overtime, Matthews made a hard shot that was stopped but the puck rebounded eight feet and straight to the St. Michael's captain, Jerry LaFlamme, who put it back in for the goal that stood up to win the game 2–1. The last few minutes were bedlam and the whole game so close that rink manager Alex Milne, among many spectators quoted later, coined a felicitous phrase: "The series was a draw in favour of St. Michael's."

Meanwhile, that same night in Kingston, Queen's defended its Allan Cup for the first time – beating the Interprovincial League champion Ottawa Cliffsides 6–3 on ice described as sloppy, and setting up another Cup defence four nights later against St. Michael's.

That, on Wednesday, March 16, 1910, turned out to be the last great, close game of the season. More than 1,700 fans crammed into the Kingston rink, which normally held several hundred less. The doors were locked at eight o'clock when it was found that not only was the building full, but that although two policemen had been detailed to guard seventy-five seats bought and paid for by St. Michael's for their supporters who had just arrived by train, Queen's students had overwhelmed the policemen and filled those seats.

With the doors locked, the rink manager scoured the rink for space, any space, and finally got the Toronto fans either seated or standing in time to watch Queen's take a 4–2 lead in the first half. St. Michael's came back in the second half with three unanswered goals, the winner scored by Herb Matthews with about five minutes left to play to give the visitors the Allan Cup.

The *Daily British Whig* the following day covered the game in the main headline on its front page:

QUEEN'S LOST

The Allan Cup captured by St. Michael's

EXCITING GAME

RESULTED IN FIVE TO FOUR IN ST. MIQUES FAVOR

A social note on the financial side of hockey at that time was found in a *Daily British Whig* sidebar. Seats for that game cost fifty cents each. There was a discrepancy between the announced attendance of 1,607 and the announced total gate receipts of $861 – which would indicate that 1,722 had paid to get in. Of those receipts, $344 covered rink expenses and $517 went to Queen's athletic committee, the visiting team's expenses (unrecorded) being paid from that amount.

Three days later in Toronto the hockey season ended when St. Michael's (or St. Mike's, or St. Miques, as many papers had it) easily defended the Cup, winning 8–3 against Sherbrooke, Quebec, the St. Lawrence League champions, to become undisputed champions of Canada.

Through the next few years both the OHA and the Allan Cup underwent growing pains, starting right away. Louis Blake Duff, who had succeeded Dwight Turner as OHA president, had to bear the brunt in 1911 of what turned out to be a year of pitched battles between the OHA and the Allan Cup trustees. The crux of it was disagreement on when, and by whom, the Cup should be defended.

The OHA position, as outlined in this year-end review, could be summarized as contending that the Allan Cup trustees didn't know what the hell they were doing. This reaction stemmed from the trustees having ordered St. Michael's to defend the Cup on February 20 and 22, 1911, against Winnipeg Victorias. Victorias' championship season had ended February 2, but the OHA playoffs were still far from being over, no champion decided.

The OHA contended that this order from the Allan Cup trustees "was manifestly unfair and in direct contravention of the Allan Cup deed of gift to make such an order." The deed of gift provided that the Cup was to be "competed for only at the end of a season, between clubs having won the championship of some recognized league or association in Canada."

Anyway, St. Michael's, following OHA advice, declined to play the Victorias in mid-season. The trustees, after much correspondence, awarded the Cup to Winnipeg. The OHA was furious, said the trustees had no right to make any such ruling, and refused to give up the Cup, telling the trustees that if they wanted it handed over they could go to court. At the same time, they made sure the press was well armed with arguments supporting the OHA cause. Ontario newspapers, especially the ones in Toronto, worked over quite thoroughly what was obviously (a) the party line and (b) indisputable.

The OHA arguments went something like this. What was the hurry? In 1909, when Queen's won the Allan Cup, the game had been played on March 16. In 1910, when St. Michael's took the Cup from Queen's and defended it against Sherbrooke, the games had been played March 16 and 19. So why order an Allan Cup series in February involving one champion, Victorias, and another team, St. Michael's, which might not wind up as Ontario winner at all?

As it happened, St. Michael's did not win the Ontario championship that year so any Allan Cup defence could have been disputed. They were beaten in both semifinal games by Parkdale, which in turn fell to the winnah and new champion, the Eaton Hockey Club of Toronto. (This club already was a subject of OHA debate as to whether a team named for a commercial establishment, in this case a department store, should be allowed in the OHA at all.) The championship was decided March 4, which would have left lots of time for Eatons and the Winnipeg Victorias to play for the Allan Cup — except that the OHA still had the Cup locked up somewhere while engaging its trustees in a battle to the death.

In the end, the OHA kept physical possession of the Cup, defying the trustees' order that it should be sent to Winnipeg. So there was no Allan Cup championship game that season at all. The argument ran on until December 5, 1911, by which time a process had been worked out by lawyers representing the OHA and the Allan Cup trustees, with stiff upper lips on both sides. The Allan Cup trustees unconditionally withdrew the Cup from competition, whereupon the OHA returned it, also unconditionally, *not* to the trustees but to the original donor, Sir Montagu Allan, who must have wondered what the hell he had gotten himself into. W.A. Hewitt's letter accompanying the return of the Cup repeated the OHA's conviction that the disputed ruling by the Allan Cup trustees was "most unsportsmanlike and unfair to the OHA Cup-holders."

However, the "unconditionally" really meant that either side could do what it wanted from then on. The trustees sent the Cup to Winnipeg Victorias, a year late. Final word on the matter came about three months later, in March of 1912, when both Eatons of Toronto and

Winnipeg Victorias had repeated as regional champions. Eatons challenged for the Allan Cup, travelled to Winnipeg for the series, and got walloped 8–4 and 16–1. The OHA graciously conceded that Winnipeg had an exceptionally clever team and "won absolutely on their merits." But one must suspect that there was a sigh of relief in the OHA when Eatons lost. It might have tested the most implacable spirits in the OHA executive if they'd had to expel an Allan Cup champion from the OHA because it bore the name of and was bankrolled by the T. Eaton Company Ltd. department store.

When the OHA annual meeting was held on November 16 that year, Louis Blake Duff's successor to the presidency, H.E. Wettlaufer of Berlin, was in the chair. Part of the news was good: the total number of teams competing that year had jumped to 113 from the previous year's eighty-eight. But the self-satisfaction evaporated during a spirited debate on a motion to bar from membership not only Eaton's but any club playing under the name of a commercial organization. Eaton's had its supporters, but the motion passed. So it was good-bye Eaton's, and when at least one other commercially sponsored team applied for membership that same year, the application was rejected.

Worth notice in this period, when players were turning pro either because they had good offers or were caught and convicted by the OHA and had to start taking their money openly or quit hockey, was the time a year earlier when one George (Goldie) Prodgers, a big eighteen-year-old redhead playing intermediate hockey for his hometown London team, made the fastest known go-pro decision on record.

At the time, Waterloo in the Ontario Professional Hockey League had just lost three star players – one of them the later great Newsy Lalonde – to Quebec in the National Hockey Association and was having trouble finding good replacements. Someone had seen Prodgers play and implored him to come to Waterloo and play just one game. According to an account by *Toronto Globe* sportswriter C.W. (Baldy) McQueen published in Bill Roche's *The Hockey Book* (1953), Prodgers was reluctant to endanger his amateur status for one game but finally was convinced that he could easily make a few dollars by playing under an assumed name. "Just one game, Goldie! No one will ever know the difference."

The game was played on January 23, 1911, Waterloo against Berlin, in Berlin. McQueen's account:

> Prodgers slipped quietly into Waterloo on the evening of the game, went to the rink all by himself, and eased out toward the ice after all the regular Waterloo pros had begun their warmup. He was just starting to skate away from the gate when somebody spoke to him.
>
> "Well! What are you doing here, Goldie?"
>
> The husky boy turned and saw Eddie Wettlaufer of Waterloo, one of the top OHA referees and a longtime member of the OHA executive committee.
>
> Prodgers knew the jig was up right then and there, and while he fumbled mentally for a reply, Wettlaufer cornered him, asking, "When in blazes did you turn pro?"
>
> Goldie made the quickest decision of his life, answering, "Right now!"
>
> So started one of the most brilliant professional careers of that decade.

It doesn't really matter much that McQueen had a few of his facts wrong. The "Eddie Wettlaufer from Waterloo" was actually H.E. (Eddie) Wettlaufer of Berlin, not only a member of the OHA executive but first vice-president, only a few months away from becoming OHA president. Prodgers went on to play sixteen games for Waterloo that year, scored nine goals, then moved to Quebec in the NHA and Victoria of the Pacific Coast Hockey Association before returning to the NHA with Quebec, Wanderers, Canadiens, and in 1917 to the NHA's 228th Battalion Canadian Army team (for whom he once scored six goals in one game). He then starred for Toronto for a season and later Hamilton in the National Hockey League until he finally retired after playing one game at the beginning of the 1925-26 season.

Chapter Seven

WAR YEARS

"Any player who is under suspension from the OHA for any cause whatever (except professionalism) and who enlists for overseas service shall automatically be reinstated . . . (and may play) with their home team, their regimental team, or with any team in the town in which their company or battalion is located."

— Decision of the OHA annual meeting,
December 4, 1915

Although World War One began in the late summer of 1914, it had very little effect on the hockey played that winter. The total number of OHA teams registered dropped from 107 to ninety-eight, but in only a few scattered instances could that be attributed to enlistments. At the time Canada lacked training facilities for the huge numbers trying to get into uniform. One of those turned away was Conn Smythe, a nineteen-year-old bantamweight who had been captain of good hockey teams at Upper Canada College and Jarvis Collegiate before enrolling in the University of Toronto's School of Practical Science (later to become the engineering faculty). Again he was a hockey captain, this time with Varsity juniors in the OHA, a team known officially as Varsity 3 because the university also had teams playing senior (Varsity 1) and intermediate (Varsity 2). Smythe was Varsity's star scorer. He got six in one 9–3 win over Brampton and, against a strong Orillia team in the first game of the OHA final in March of 1914, scored all four Varsity goals in a 4–3 win. That was in Toronto. The second game, in Orillia, was different. "We never saw the puck, " Smythe said. They lost the game 10–3, and the series.

When war began later that year, Smythe tried to enlist. Short and fair-haired, he looked about fifteen as he faced a grizzled old recruiting sergeant wearing ribbons from the South African campaign. The sergeant apparently was no hockey fan. He told Smythe, "No children allowed in this battalion. Go home and see if you can grow some hair on your face."

Still, wrote Smythe in his memoirs, "I had a feeling that my time would come." Which it did, a year later.

Just before the war the OHA had flourished as never before, with well over a hundred teams entered most years. Among the seniors, the TR&AA (Toronto Rugby and Athletic Association) was the class of the field, winning in 1913 and 1914, while Toronto Victorias won in 1915. In all three of those finals St. Michael's College had made it close as runner-up. Collingwood, London, Berlin, and Orillia were the best of the intermediates, with Orillia, Berlin, and Varsity the junior powers. Charles Farquharson of Stratford, who had replaced H.E. Wettlaufer of Berlin as president in December of 1913, had a fairly easy break-in period – the usual suspensions, for the usual reasons: residence eligibility (Hamilton Alerts), fraudulent birth certificates (Waterloo juniors), and a few others.

That year also, the game was changed from two thirty-minute halves to three twenty-minute periods; and the old point and coverpoint positions became known as right defence and left defence. Other housekeeping procedures included a ruling that a player allowed exemption from normal residence rules to play hockey where he was attending school must show up at lectures and not just at the hockey rink. If not, suspension came swiftly. Also, team captains had to wear four-inch armbands bearing the letter C on the right arm above the elbow, so referees would know who was yelling at them. And so on.

But to fans the most interesting rule change in many years, dealing with rebounds off goalies, came just before the season of 1913-14. In a game that at the time still barred *all* forward passes, it had been nothing short of revolutionary in 1905 for the OHA to allow a rebound off a goalie to be fielded by his own side, *as long as the puck had rebounded no more than three feet*. If the rebound was more than that, a face-off would be called on the spot where the infraction occurred, which could be a few inches over three feet from the goalie (and present-day goalkeepers think they have it tough).

Now, for 1914, the OHA had gone even farther. It would allow a whole ten feet per legal rebound! Noise levels soared in taverns as hockey fans debated this crime against hockey or miracle of sound thinking (depending on the point of view). This while the fans imbibed some of the dozens of locally brewed ales and lagers available at the time, among them O'Keefe's Pilsener Lager, described in the ads as being "a bottle of liquid food and strength for all workers. It restores the flagging energy and refreshes the whole system."

Apart from such changes and occasional losing motions urging a cutback to six-man teams, the big amateur hockey news of the period was creation of the Canadian Amateur Hockey Association. A national association – at last! This came to pass in Ottawa on December 4, 1914, one day before the OHA annual meeting in Toronto, a factor that emphasized the OHA's position as a prime mover in creating the CAHA. Representatives were there from provincial hockey associations of all four western provinces, the Intercollegiate League, the Quebec Amateur Athletic Union, the Amateur Athletic Union of

Canada, and the Canadian Olympic Association, as well as representatives of several major teams.

The CAHA, all present fervently intended, would bring order out of the chaos of differing residence qualifications across the country, set up a system to police inter-branch transfers, and generally govern hockey – including the national senior championship for the Allan Cup – pretty well as the OHA had done in its own bailiwick. The first president was Dr. W.F. Taylor of Winnipeg, with long-service man Francis Nelson of the OHA executive elected first vice-president and John Ross Robertson named honorary president.

The necessity for the CAHA had been obvious for years, especially to hockey associations that had found that to some players, the footloose and fancy-free, a suspension didn't necessarily mean much. The wrath of the OHA, for instance, sometimes – as in Cyclone Taylor's case in 1905 – seemed little more than a suggestion to begone, try some other province or one of the pro leagues.

One might think that the most popular option to a suspended player then would have been to go professional. Yet, the prospect of being barred from all amateur athletics was still a powerful deterrent. To be branded a professional was considered a permanent stain and many good players simply did not want that. One eloquent testimony to this state of mind came, remarkably enough, from a professional, Art Ross, well known then as a player and later famous as coach and manager of the Boston Bruins.

In November of 1910, when pro players of the NHA were talking of striking for basic salaries of $10,000 and club owners were holding out for a ceiling of $5,000 and claimed they could fill their sweaters with senior players for much less, Ross wrote a letter to the *Montreal Herald*. In it he argued that with such a short season, the constant threat of serious injury, and little opportunity to establish satisfactory careers elsewhere as long as they played hockey, pros *should* get more. Furthermore, fill-in amateurs "from the bush," he argued, would be crazy to give up their amateur standing for a paltry few dollars. They might not make it permanently as professionals, "but their amateur standing would be gone." Which meant forever.

His letter continued:

> During a period of four years my own salary as a professional hockey player has varied from $1,000 to $2,700, the amount I got from Haileybury (of the NHA) last season. But I would gladly give back all I have made as a professional player to regain my amateur standing, and there are a good many other professionals who feel the same way I do.

That rather wistful statement about the personal value of amateur standing, from one of the giants of the pro game, was often cited in pro-amateur debates of the time.

Apart from the nuts and bolts of organizational changes, rule changes, and the settling of hockey into clearly defined pro and amateur ranks, OHA hockey was still a steamy game at ice level for both players and referees – and sometimes even on the timer's bench. The old system of using one home-team timekeeper who might let the clock run fast or slow, depending on who was ahead, had led to establishment of two timekeepers, one from each competing club, plus a third timekeeper for penalties. That didn't always work, either. In 1914, one J.C. Dore of Sarnia was fined $10 and costs in court and barred for life by the OHA for punching his timers'-bench colleague, Thomas L. Swift of Watford, during a game between those two towns.

Referees? Some, such as Fred C. Waghorne (called Wag), were as well known as the players; others were sportswriters, small-town lawyers, old players who wanted to stay in the game somehow. The job was not all that enviable. The base pay was $5 plus mileage of ten

cents a mile *one-way*, split between the competing clubs.
Jeering fans almost invariably followed the referee to his
hotel or train after a loss. It was fairly common in such
situations that the beleaguered referee would exit the rink
with a skate in each hand, blades out menacingly, to
protect himself if need be. One player was suspended for
attacking a referee physically after a game. Another was
barred for life "because he led a crowd in an assault on
the referee." In addition to all this, the referee was a busy
fellow even before a game. In 1915 the OHA ruled that,
henceforth, before a game each referee had to watch as
each player signed his name on the form provided to
referees for that purpose, possibly on the grounds that
one playing illegally might not remember his *nom de
stick*, or might not know how to spell it.

Noting this rule, an unsigned column in the *Toronto
Star* (perhaps written by Lou Marsh, a referee and sportswriter with a good eye for colour) commented:

> The OHA stuck another job on the poor old referee. In
> addition to hustling around and getting the teams out on
> time, looking after two goal umpires and three timekeepers,
> inspecting and measuring the nets, looking after the black
> line in front of the nets, scrutinizing certificates, calling the
> roll of players before the game starts, tossing for choice of
> goals, protecting players from rowdy spectators, making note
> of all the goals, calling all offsides and fouls – the big Associa-
> tion now compels him to cart around a fountain pen and
> watch every player sign his own full name on the official
> report.
>
> After he gets all that done, he collects $11.85, changes his
> skates and wet underclothes, dodges a few snowballs from
> disgruntled friends of the losers, chases back to the hotel for
> three hours sleep and grabs the 3:30 a.m. train back home.
> Then he has nothing to do until tomorrow!

In February and March of 1915 two men who were to
become major builders of pro hockey met in conflict.
Varsity juniors, with Conn Smythe as captain, worked

their way through three rounds of playoffs with wins over Welland, St. Andrew's College, and Lindsay. At the same time, Berlin Union Jacks with Frank Selke as manager (the "Union Jacks" name having been adopted as a hoped-for antidote to anti-German wartime sentiment in many crowds) kept pace by beating Woodstock College, University of Western Ontario, and Collingwood.

That made it Varsity against Berlin in an OHA junior final that Conn Smythe described in his memoirs. Referring to the anti-German barracking by crowds in many rinks, Smythe wrote:

> The home crowds in Berlin weren't any too respectful of us, either. In the first game of the home and home, I came out of it with my hair stained brown from tobacco juice that people would spit at me every time I came near the boards.
>
> It was quite a game in other ways. The goal umpire stood right behind the net in those days. Selke always said that any goal umpire who wasn't worth two goals to his home team (one for the home team and one disallowed for the opposition) should be fired. People he had hired were robbing us so openly that twice in the first period goal umps were ordered out of the game by the referee.

There was another little matter. Smythe was an inveterate gambler. All his life he had a good won-lost record in bets. His closest friend from their Jarvis Collegiate days was one Harvey (Wreck) Aggett, who was at the game as a fan. The two pooled their finances ("every cent we had") to bet on Varsity. The man holding the money was to meet them at Berlin's Walper House hotel after the game. With only minutes left, Varsity was down 7–5. Smythe scored two goals to tie the game 7–7 and, he thought, at least protect their investment. When they went to the Walper House, however, the money-man said their bet had been to win and that with a tie they were plumb out of luck.

Wreck Aggett's father, John, a Toronto plumber, was

among those present in the hot argument that ensued. A small man, Mr. Aggett stood on a chair so he'd be noticed and shouted that if those boys didn't get their money back, the crown attorney would be there in ten minutes to see about it. Wreck and Conn got their money back.

With that tie, it all came down to the second game of the series two nights later in Toronto. On that night of Thursday, March 11, 1915, nearly 5,000 poured in by car and trolley and on foot to the Arena Gardens on Mutual Street, which was in its third season then and was much bigger than the old Mutual Street rink. (A few weeks earlier Victorias and St. Michael's had drawn 7,366 in their first game, 6,982 in the second, of the OHA senior final.)

The Arena's artificial ice, in contrast to soft ice conditions that had slowed the Berlin game, figured to be an asset to the faster Varsity team. Then another element intervened. Although the OHA often debated (and defeated) motions to allow substitutions, the only player who could be replaced in case of injury was the goalie. For everyone else, the old rules prevailed: if a player got hurt or had to retire for any reason, the other team had to drop a man, too. Smythe described what happened.

> The score was 3–3 late in the second period when one of their men, Irving Erb, broke a skate and had to go off.
>
> Our coach came to me as captain and said, "Who do we take off?"
>
> "Me," I said.
>
> He protested. "The captain can't come off!"
>
> I'd taken a big body check about then. I was groggy. I insisted, so I came off.
>
> We didn't do so well against them, each playing six men. We each got another goal before the end of the period, making it 4–4. It was still tied in the third when something happened that Selke later called the biggest boner of his life. His brother-in-law, a Canadian featherweight boxing champion named Bert Ayerst, came to him and said to be

sure not to put Erb back on the ice. "Without Smythe out there, Varsity isn't the same team," he said. I'm quoting Selke, not me. Anyway, Selke always was a suspicious fellow and that was his downfall.

We weren't ahead, but Selke was standing right behind the timer instead of being at his own bench [when] someone at the bench produced another pair of skates for Erb. Without Selke there to tell Erb to stay where he was, Erb put on the borrowed skates and jumped over the boards.

That meant I could jump on, as well. Back at seven-man hockey, we scored five goals. I got two of them, to go with one I'd scored in the second period. The 9–4 score gave us the Ontario junior championship and although it had never been done before for a junior team, we were given Varsity letters as a reward. I still have mine, someplace.

By that mid-March of 1915, many parts of the city looked like Army camps: tents on the university campus, recruits marching here and there, military bands, posters and speeches of exhortation for men to join up. Four days after Varsity's win, the entire team walked downtown to enlist. Most were accepted, and by the end of the day Smythe was Gunner C. Smythe. (With almost the entire team in uniform, as it turned out, the Varsity juniors were no more. The following year the university did not enter the junior series, although two players from the 1915 champions, G.R. Gouinlock and Mac Sheldon, turned up with the next spring's junior winner, Aura Lee.)

In that springtime of 1915, as well, only three months after the CAHA was formed, the OHA and the CAHA had a clash (not the last) over their occasionally differing inter-pretations of rules. One was the residence rule. Toronto Victorias, senior winners that year, had played a game in Melville, Saskatchewan, early in March. At the formation of the CAHA, one regulation adopted was a three-month residence rule.

The OHA—whose residence deadline, August 1, was more stringent—contended that for everyone else the three-month rule had become hockey law immediately. The CAHA argued that the rule had not been intended to take effect until the beginning of the following season, to avoid disrupting teams already formed under looser residence requirements. Several Melville players did not qualify under the OHA's interpretation of the three-month residence rule. But the Victorias had played against them nevertheless.

The OHA summarily suspended the Victorias, whose officers fought back fiercely and, one must conclude at this distance, with good reason. But the OHA saw this as showing "a singular lack of loyalty to their own association" and invoked the time-honoured rule that if a club defied the OHA it automatically disqualified itself. Victorias angrily disbanded, donating the disputed game's receipts to the Patriotic Fund for needy families of soldiers.

A footnote for aficionados of the tiniest rule changes: the next winter, when hockey fans were still criticizing the expulsion of the Victorias, the OHA also ruled without substantial debate that in face-offs, all players in future "will have to stand with their lefthand side toward the opponent's goal."

By the time hockey began in the season of 1915-16, many players and club officers all across Canada were in Army khaki. Troop movements were supposed to be secret, although the public learned to read between the lines when several soldiers were missing from a lineup, or a notice appeared in the sports pages stating that a particular Army team was unable to fulfil the balance of its schedule. Some service teams playing in the OHA never knew if they'd still be around for their next league game. Kingston Frontenacs had an unbeaten season until several of their soldier players had to leave for the front, whereupon Frontenacs were knocked out of the playoffs.

In February of 1916 Toronto's 40th Battery team — managed by Lieutenant Conn Smythe — was running neck and neck with Riversides and Argonauts in the OHA's Toronto senior group and was considered to have a good chance to win the province. As so often was to happen in the next half-century or so in various circumstances that included Conn Smythe, this had at least one remarkable outcome.

Smythe had been commissioned in July, 1915. His officers' course at Kingston included a man he greatly admired, Gordon Southam of the publishing family, a famous athlete in court tennis (North American champion), football (a Grey Cup), hockey, and cricket. Southam was planning to do what several other well-off men did at the time: organize his own unit to take overseas. His own specific idea was to put together a Sportsmen's Battery, which would have a hockey team.

First he managed to enlist some of the Orillia players who had beaten Varsity in the junior final of 1914, including two genuine greats, Quinn Butterfield and Lovering Jupp. He'd also picked up Jack Pethick, a famous Regina player, goalie Skid James from Peterborough, and others equally well known, including F.J. (Jack) Gooch from the disbanded and suspended Toronto Victorias. Gooch's eligibility had been restored under the OHA's ruling that cancelled suspensions for servicemen.

When Southam outlined his plans and asked Smythe if he was interested, Smythe replied, "I'd give my life's blood to be with you."

The Battery trained that autumn at Niagara-on-the-Lake. When cold and mud came and the horses, guns, and marching men moved to barracks in Toronto (and the OHA elected a soldier president, Captain James T. Sutherland of Kingston), Smythe was put in charge of organizing the team. He played one game himself, a 6–1 shellacking by Riversides, was criticized for his lack of back-checking, and decided to be strictly the manager from then on. Reg Noble, eventually to be an NHL star, played for Riversides, but the next time the teams met, the 40th Battery won 5–4.

Patriotic Toronto loved this Army team. Crowds grew from four thousand to five and six. The Batterymen, as they were called in the newspapers, were a feisty lot. In one game Sergeant Mawk McKenzie and a TR&AA player named Sullivan dropped their sticks and fought. They were ejected from the game, but the fight continued in the corridors. Toronto police, called to restore order, did so in a mêlée in which, the *Star* reported, "batons were freely used" before they arrested both players involved in the original fight as well as some civilians and a few soldiers who actually had come back into the rink when they heard their war had started early.

Another memorable contest in the league that winter was covered in the main sports-page story of the *Toronto Star* on January 10, 1916. Below the main headline we read this:

SENIOR O.H.A
ARGONAUTS.....9 RIVERSIDES.....7

WHY RIVERSIDES LOST

**Because Goalkeeper Collett went to his knees
and Riversides lost three goals while
he was on the penalty bench.**

A goalkeeper in the penalty box? Because he went to his knees? And the opposition scored three while he was off? Answer to all three questions: yes.

The rule that a goalkeeper had to stay on his feet had been among the originals back when the OHA's first simple code was written. Goalie Ernie Collett rarely broke it or Riversides would not have been the powerhouse of the OHA senior series that it was.

The *Star*'s report on that game, although unsigned, was most likely – a guess based on a racy style that soon was to become familiar – the work of Lou Marsh, who soon began to get the first bylines ever given on the *Star*'s sports pages.

Eventually, either under or despite W.A. Hewitt's guidance as sports editor, Marsh was as famous in sports, especially hockey, as his younger *Star* colleague Gordon Sinclair became as a globe-trotting adventurer. Whoever wrote it, this story mentioned that Riversides were unbeaten until that night and that in the ever-present pre-game betting ring were 2–1 favourites, with some supporters offering to take small odds that the team would double the score on Argonauts – never dreaming (or should that be nightmaring?) that Argos would have so many chances at an empty net. Or that Riversides' goalie would be penalized not once, but twice, during a game that was wild enough even without the goalie-penalties.

Collett's first penalty did most of the damage. In the game's opening minutes, just after he had let one in by fanning on a long shot, one of his defencemen by name of Percy (Pete) Reesor illegally flattened an incoming Argo forward and got the gate. "Right on the heels of this came a two-minute penalty to the Riversides goalkeeper for going to his knees," the *Star* reported. The writer considered this was a severe penalty for a first offence, but its real importance was in the way Argonauts reacted to Riversides being short not only their goalie but one of their two defencemen. As the *Star* put it, "while Collett was nursing his knees in the penalty box, Argos, led by the quick-witted LaFlamme threw everybody up on the attack and playing seven men to five, landed two goals."

The quick-witted LaFlamme? Who's he? The name is virtually unknown now except to perusers of eighty-year-old sports pages, but any hockey fan of the time could have answered. In any careful reading of hockey reports through almost ten years before this game with Riversides, many lineups are dotted with the names of men who went on to professional renown.

But none could be ranked above a stocky, dark-haired

defenceman named W.J. (Jerry) LaFlamme who by 1916, captaining the Argos, had an illustrious career behind him, with more to come. No one in Ontario hockey, and few anywhere, could match the way championships or near-championships followed Jerry LaFlamme around. The bare bones of his hockey career go like this. He was a star with the first-ever St. Michael's OHA team, the juniors of 1908 who surprised all hands by getting to the final against Stratford before winning one game and then getting slaughtered 21–4 in the second. The following year, 1909, he moved up to St. Michael's seniors. They won the OHA championship and repeated in 1910, when they also added the Allan Cup.

Parkdale beat them in a group final in 1911. In 1912 he was with the short-lived Eaton Hockey club that won the OHA but lost in Allan Cup play. Then it was back to St. Michael's in 1913 for three successive years of being OHA senior runner-up. In 1916 when St. Michael's dropped out of hockey due to the war, LaFlamme, by then a dentist stationed in Toronto with the Dental Corps, went to Argos – where we pick him up leading Argos' seven-man horde against Riversides' five, none of those being a goalie.

The *Star* writer's verdict on that game was that "Local hockey fans have to go back to the famous battles between St. Michael's College and Parkdale Canoe Club juniors in 1908 to obtain comparison for the titanic struggle which raged from 8:45 p.m. to midnight at the Arena Saturday night . . ."

Those fans nearly seventy years later who lament for the old days as being more law-abiding are lamenting for something that never was. Dr. Jerry LaFlamme and Dr. Frank Knight on the Argos' defence were cases in point. Many times during this game report one or both were mentioned:

" . . . time and again Argos, led by Knight and LaFlamme, broke loose and only had Merrick and Collett to beat, but if

Merrick didn't get the puck with a diving poke check, Noble, steaming back with desperate speed, batted the puck aside, or Collett, who had recovered his form, came out and gallantly met the invader. Knight and LaFlamme knocked him down but they couldn't beat him . . ."

"Once Farr hooked Applegath under the chin when he was through and ready to shoot, and LaFlamme and Knight knocked them down and tripped them time after time . . ."

"Pete Reesor, the Riverside defenceman, was laid out with a broken collar bone by a heavy body check by Dr. Frank Knight . . ."

"LaFlamme stood Merrick on his head and foxily laid down beside the knocked-out Merrick and got away with it. A second later Dopp plowed into LaFlamme and almost gave the dentist a job for himself. He cross-checked LaFlamme in the mouth and split his lips."

Good old days? One is reminded of a toast occasionally found on birthday cards exchanged by long-ago friends, or even lovers:.

> Here's to the good old days,
> When we weren't old,
> And we weren't good.

After the opening bad breaks Riversides were down 4–1 at the end of the first period and 7–2 finishing the second. In the third they came to life to score five and send the game into overtime at 7–7. Then, after twenty more minutes (overtime then was played in five-minute periods) they were finally beaten, Argos' ninth and final goal coming when Collett once again had been penalized for falling to his knees. That was one of only two defeats Riversides had that season.

Meanwhile, the 40th Battery was waging some titanic battles of its own against LaFlamme, Knight, and the rest of the Argos. Twice the Argos beat the Batterymen in overtime. For their next one against Argos a record crowd was expected. But right then Major Southam got orders with train departure times and other details involved in the basic message. The 40th Battery was headed for action overseas.

This was secret, but Southam entrusted Smythe with the information so that, for one thing, he could wind up the team's bank account and pick up the team's accumulated gate-receipt money. Not many minutes before the Argo game Smythe and Southam were standing together when a big bettor named Brenner came up and asked Southam if he wanted to put a bet on his team. Southam said yes. Smythe chirped up that he had $100 he'd like to throw in as well. Brenner said rather contemptuously to Smythe that he had something bigger in mind than betting for peanuts.

This rudeness annoyed Southam. He shot a long look at Brenner and then took Smythe aside to ask how much the hockey team had in its kitty. Smythe told him $2,800. That was the team's share of the whole season's gate receipts. He had it all with him because of the unit's imminent departure. The idea had been to use the hockey money overseas to provide extras for the Battery, when required.

Smythe's account:

> Southam turned back to Brenner.
> "How much can you handle?" he asked.
> "Anything you've got, major."
> Southam turned to me and said, "Give me the $2,800, Connie." That kind of blanched Brenner but he put it up. We handed the $5,600 to somebody to hold.
> In the dressing room I stood up in front of the team: Lieut. Jack Gooch, Driver Lovering Jupp, Gunner Jack Pethick, Driver Skid James, Driver Quinn Butterfield, Sergeant Squaw MacNab, and Sergeant Mawk McKenzie, and told them that every nickel this hockey team had in the world was riding on this game. That was all they needed.

One can imagine Smythe doing that. He won a lot of

hockey games, including Allan Cups and Stanley Cups, because he had that instinct. His guys poured over the boards, led 4–0 after nine minutes, 5–1 at the end of the first period, 7–2 after the second, 8–3 at the end. Smythe and the major picked up the $5,600. The crowd that night was a season's record 6,378, with part of the gate receipts going to each club and some to the OHA. The Battery's share was $1,106, building the team kitty to a total of $6,706.

As mentioned earlier, if a hockey team with the label of potential champion suddenly disappeared in mid-season, the public understood. Southam's 40th Battery team was one of those that disappeared. It was close enough to being of senior championship calibre that, like Argos, it had once beaten Riversides –who did win the Ontario senior crown that year over the last team that carried the name Berlin.

In England a few weeks later every 40th Battery man going on leave was given some of the winnings to spend. And for the rest of the Battery's war, the money provided sumptuous Christmas dinners.

Leaving only the questions: Did such largesse make professionals out of those players who were among the happy recipients of this benefaction? And, what would John Ross Robertson have thought of them apples?

Chapter Eight

SURVIVING – AND CHANGING THE RULES

"Very sorry we cannot play this year. Our boys are fighting Fritz."

– Telegram to OHA late in the war
from the Wiarton Hockey Club's secretary, Al Corrigan

On December 7, 1916, the registration deadline for OHA teams, one newspaper's sports-page banner headline read: HOCKEY PLAYERS SCARCE IN ONTARIO. The following story led off by quoting the terse telegram from Wiarton and continued:

> This is the most expressive way of putting it that has come to hand, but all clubs are affected in the same way . . . . Most of the towns have been depleted of hockey players by enlistment, but many of the clubs will remain in the game and use juniors to fill the gaps. Military and junior teams are very much in evidence.

An interesting element of World War One hockey was the absence of any substantial public criticism of the game for doing business as usual while men were dying in battle overseas. One reason was that the OHA *didn't* do business as usual. It improvised, season after season, as if it were quite normal to have teams here one week and gone the next either to a new training area or to board a troopship headed across the Atlantic.

Many famous names were gone. St. Michael's had

dropped out of hockey before play began in 1916. Orillia, winner of several championships, reported that every man from its old championship teams was now at the front. But the OHA kept on working through the blizzards and thaws and the shocks of casualty lists to the playoffs and then the finals with the equanimity born of experience.

Indeed, a reading of the normally dry OHA proceedings during those years late in the war projects a remarkable image. Enthusiastic and unquestioning patriotism could be found in other parts of Canada as well, but it seemed deepest, most felt by the most people, in the most British province, Ontario. Berlin, Ontario, was no more. The city was renamed Kitchener after the famous British general, and of course remains Kitchener to this day. The young women who handed out white feathers to healthy-looking young men not in uniform were a manifestation, however jingoistic, of a population that was faced with staggering casualty lists almost daily. Enlisting for overseas service was seen throughout much of the land, but nowhere more so than in Ontario, as being the unquestioned first priority for any man who loved his country.

Whether or not he played hockey, or how well, had no bearing, but it was common to see in newspaper accounts, printed with sports-page pride in men they saw as their own, that this or that player had been decorated, was mentioned in dispatches, had performed heroically in the trenches, or was in the casualty lists.

The OHA president, Captain Sutherland, was overseas as quartermaster of the Canadian Army's Casualty Training Battalion when he was re-elected unanimously late in 1916, the OHA minutes recording "our hope for his early and safe return to our councils." But there was also the fact that enlisting and playing hockey were not by any means mutually exclusive. In the season of 1916-17 virtually every OHA team included men in khaki. Seventeen teams organized by and named for military units were manned entirely by soldiers. Most of these teams were intermediate, but some were juniors – soldier teams in which by OHA rule every player had to be under the age of twenty as of January 1, 1917. And the two Army teams in the senior series were, at first, among the most successful.

One was the 227th regiment of Hamilton, which had recruited an entire hockey team from Sudbury. The other was the 228th of Toronto, a unit that must have been richer than any in hockey talent, not to mention the front office. The 228th that season iced not only OHA junior and senior teams but a pro team in the National Hockey Association: the one Goldie Prodgers played for.

The NHA hadn't been all that eager to take on the 228th or any other Army team, due to the possibility that a sudden overseas draft would entirely disrupt the league schedule. But a never-named someone among the organizers of the 228th's hockey program must have been quite an operator, possibly trained in the old amateur school of fake residence papers, somebody's younger brother's birth certificate, and everything considered legal unless you were found out. He placated the NHA doubters by taking out, or saying he would do so, an insurance policy for $3,000 to compensate other teams if a war-related withdrawal occurred. He also picked up for the NHA team experienced players, some by means that only were revealed later.

And in their first four games in the NHA, talk about a scare – the 228th beat Ottawa 10–7, Montreal Wanderers 10–4, Toronto 4–0, and Quebec 16–9. Four consecutive wins! Forty goals! Give 'em the Stanley Cup!

It didn't last. Many losses followed. When the 228th was ordered overseas in February and a new schedule had to be drawn up, the NHA clubs left behind tried to collect compensation. This got them a very bad press, with the newspapers averring loftily that the soldiers had merely withdrawn for a more important game. But an at least partly funny scandal was rolling east toward an Atlantic port.

On this troop train a former OHA star, Gordon Meeking, who'd worn an officer's uniform ever since the 228th entered the NHA, suddenly was seen to have switched to the breeches, tunic, and puttees of the private soldier. On investigation, it turned out that he had been *promised* an officer's commission to play for the 228th, had been assured that authorization was a mere formality, and in the meantime had been told that he might as well dress as a lieutenant. Only when the overseas orders came was he told, well, um, Meeking, old chap, you're actually just a private; better put on the right uniform.

In the fuss that followed, one other player turned out to have been another victim of the 228th's somewhat ingenious recruiting methods. Eddie Oatman, a player of some note (a Stanley Cup with Quebec in 1912, and eventually a pro until 1926) said that he had been promised $1,200 to play for the 228th, the understanding being that he *would* enlist, for sure. Both he and Meeking claimed adamantly to have enlisted and passed their medicals, but there were many doubters on that score when the troopship carrying the 228th sailed from Saint John with Meeking and Oatman left behind on the dock, discharged, civilians once more: a case of a couple of gullible, or grasping, men being aced by some Army officer who wished to win a few hockey games.

Of course, the 228th's senior and junior OHA teams sailed at the same time as the pros, leaving the OHA to go about its business. That season a new senior team from the Dental College in Toronto, usually called the Dentals for short, cut a swath. With some familiar names from earlier champions, including Mac Sheldon of Smythe's 1915 Varsity juniors and the 1916 Aura Lee juniors, and with the ubiquitous Dr. Jerry LaFlamme as team captain, Dentals won the senior championship over Riversides, then travelled to Winnipeg to take the Allan Cup in a round-robin of senior league champions. That year also, Hamilton won its first-ever OHA championship, the intermediate, beating Kitchener; and Aura Lee won the junior, with Kitchener the runner-up there as well.

Eight months later at the annual meeting in December, 1917, the temper of hockey was much the same, the players even scarcer, and some important rule changes in the offing. But in his remarks as incoming president Sheriff J.F. Paxton of Whitby reflected something else – probably part of what kept hockey going and largely uncriticized throughout the war. His speech was about hockey players who had become soldiers, not glorifying them above other Canadians who were losing their lives in Europe's bloody trench warfare, but simply putting some of them in the context of the times.

Of the OHA's hundreds of members who "had answered their country's call," many had already died in action and "let us revere their memory," Sheriff Paxton said, mentioning that Francis Nelson of the OHA executive had lost a son in the war, W.A. Hewitt a brother, and others had close family members at the front. His eulogy was both for the living and the dead. Among the dead he dwelled on two who had played on championship teams, Frederick John Gooch and Maurice Edward Malone.

Jack Gooch had been with two senior champions, TR&AA in 1914 and Victorias in 1915, before joining the Southam-Smythe 40th Battery team for its truncated 1916 season. Maurice Malone had played first-rate goal for Smythe's 1915 Varsity junior champions.

Paxton said that during the 1917 summer's terrible battle at Vimy Ridge, Jack Gooch

. . . for weeks was so busy with the guns that he never took off his clothes.

On the morning of August 15 he was in front of the trenches acting as infantry observation officer for his battery's guns when a shell hit him. So well was he liked by his men that five different attempts had to be made before they could recover his body from No Man's Land. Each attempt added to the casualty list but there never was a lack of volunteers for the work of giving decent burial to an officer who was worshipped . . .

Maurice Malone celebrated his 21st birthday in the trenches . . . always a sunny-tempered boy with a merry twinkle in his eye. Through every big fight since St. Julien he came unscathed until that terrible battle on the Ypres salient. His company, suddenly recalled from rest billets, walked back at night through 15 miles of mud to the trenches to take part on June 3, 1916, in a counter-attack to regain trenches taken by the enemy. He bade goodbye to his major and said he was going to his finish, but would show what a 48th Highlander could do. Lieut. Malone went first over the trenches to lead his men, when he was caught in a hail of machine gun fire and fell . . .

Many other OHA members have fallen in the great struggle, and still further sacrifices will be made. Let us in great humbleness of spirit and in all humility, honor and revere their memory.

Finishing, he paused briefly and then changed gears with the words of many an OHA president before him and after him. "Another season is upon us," he said. "What of the future?"

The meeting that followed made unquestionably some of the most important decisions in the OHA's long years of dropping the puck. It was a meeting with an aura of change about it. The situation was pressing. For the season about to begin the number of teams was down to sixty-seven with the meeting being told that many towns could not make firm plans until it was known how the new Military Service Act, a wartime conscription measure authorized by a bitter general election a few weeks earlier, would affect players they were counting on.

Subsequent decisions were not reached without long and heated argument, but at the end as a bow to the way all clubs had been depleted of players, the number on a team was reduced from seven to six, with one substitute allowed. Six-man hockey had been played in the NHA and by several leagues playing on small or outdoor ice, but the OHA had rejected it until then. A lot of the suspense was removed when John Ross Robertson, approaching eighty by then and not well, pushed himself to his feet, was recognized by the chair, and spoke in favour.

Next came the rule that had allowed forward rebounds off goalies to a maximum of ten feet. It had still not solved the problem of lengthy scrimmaging in front of the net; indeed, it had made the situation worse. Even during the old total ban on any such forward passes, the game had been faster. So the ten-foot limit on rebounds off goalies was doubled to twenty feet, and progress toward the still-distant establishment of today's bluelines took another major step.

Using all these new rules in that spring of 1918, Kitchener, with the future NHL great George Hainsworth in goal, won the senior championship over the 1917 Allan Cup champion Dentals and went on to beat Port Arthur and the Winnipeg Ypres team for the 1918 Cup.

Nobody knew it at the time, but by the following season the soldiers would be flocking back home and the world, including hockey, would be able once again to resume what passed for normalcy in its sometimes fractious affairs.

Before that happy day arrived, John Ross Robertson died. At the annual meeting early in December of 1918, a few weeks after the war-ending armistice of November 11, a resolution moved by Francis Nelson and passed by a standing vote recorded the OHA's gratitude to the organization's unquestioned early-days strongman for "the aid, counsel, and guidance so unsparingly bestowed by him on our affairs for more than a score of years . . . invaluable services which went so far to bring the Association to its present high position."

If John Ross Robertson was the great executive of that era, Jerry LaFlamme seems to have been the prime candidate for his era's Most Valuable Player award (if there had

been one). Besides all his earlier triumphs, including his
second Allan Cup while captaining the Dentals of 1917,
in 1918 LaFlamme was player-manager of that team as
senior runner-up to Kitchener, didn't show up in the
playoffs of 1919, but in 1920 was on defence for the
OHA senior champion Toronto Granites – and thus was
around for the next wave of rule changes.

Some of these seemed to come from a whole new attitude. There was relief from the strains of war. Hockey
players no longer were in short supply, returning servicemen causing a jump from the seventy-one teams of the
previous winter to ninety-three for the first months of
1919.

Simultaneously, the OHA began to lean toward changes
that would make the game better for both spectators and
players. The intense fatigue of the same six or seven men
playing an entire game had often been seen. Many a
contest started at a furious pace, with everyone fresh, but
became more like a slow waltz by tired men at the end.
The 1916 Argonauts-Riversides overtime classic was one
of dozens of examples of tough hockey games that turned
as much on endurance as skill. By then also, as OHA
playing rules were those used by the Canadian Amateur
Hockey Association, there were outside influences that
no doubt were a force for change.

Whatever the reasons, changes came thick and fast
during the annual meeting in December of 1918, effective
for the 1919 season about to begin. Goalies still were
obliged to stay on their feet at all times, but for the first
time teams were allowed to carry two goalkeepers – so
that if one was injured he could be replaced by another
goalie rather than some other player hastily drummed
into service without pads, goalstick, or the skill required
to play that position. (Such substitution still did not
extend to a goalie who had been penalized.) No offsides
would be called on the defending team for forward passes

in the twenty-foot zone in front of the goal, a privilege allowed only to the goalkeeper until then. Also, instead of only one substitution being allowed during a game, the substitutes were increased to two who could enter the game at any time there was a stoppage in play. (Changing on the fly was still decades ahead.)

One of the most lasting decisions of that annual meeting, however, was not concerned with playing rules. This was agreement that the OHA should establish a memorial "of some enduring character, to OHA members who have fallen on the fields of war." This, done immediately, was called the OHA Memorial Cup, for Canada-wide competition among junior teams. The Memorial Cup for juniors had much the same terms of reference, and function, as the Allan Cup for the Canadian senior championship. A few months later the first Memorial Cup was won by University of Toronto Schools – a result that pleased everyone except the team UTS had beaten in the OHA's junior final, Woodstock. For decades thereafter many in Woodstock and elsewhere contended that their team had been cheated out of the chance to play for that first Memorial Cup – not by UTS, but by gamblers. In his unpublished memoir, "Days of Real Sport," Leonard W. Taylor, who retired as one of Canada's most respected journalists, marshalled impressive evidence to support that belief.

Gambling on all sports in those days was endemic, as it is now. The money involved would not match what would be at stake today (or even then, in the World Series fix by the Chicago White Sox later that same year), but it could be substantial. The Woodstock-UTS series had all the ingredients for a gambling coup. According to Taylor, there was even an unconscious (one must believe) role played by W.A. Hewitt.

Woodstock's credentials going into that series were impressive. The Woodstock team had won both games of its group final against Stratford, despite brilliant play by

Stratford's all-time great Howie Morenz. Then there'd been an easier victory against the powerful Sudbury Wolves. UTS was next.

The first game was in Woodstock. At the end of the second period Woodstock had a 5–0 lead. At that point Woodstock's Frank Hyde, an OHA vice-president, was approached by W.A. Hewitt, who said (Hyde told Leonard Taylor years later), "For God's sake, Frank, tell your boys to lay off. If they score any more goals we won't draw a corporal's guard in Toronto."

From Taylor's memoirs: "Hyde conveyed this remark to members of the Woodstock executive and he suspected that it got around to the coach. In any event, Woodstock eased off in the final period and UTS scored a single goal." Even that goal was flukey – a long shot that went in off a defenceman's glove. The final score was 5–1.

The next game was in Toronto on a Saturday night. Two special trains, one CPR and the other Grand Trunk, carried about 800 Woodstock and district fans to the game. One was a Thames River quarry manager named Charles Downing. Years later, Taylor wrote, Downing told former NHL linesman George Hayes, "When we got off the train a number of gamblers were there offering to bet even money that UTS would win not only the game but the round and the championship."

From Taylor's memoirs: "Outside the rink, gamblers offered to give 5–2 on the game and even money on the round. Downing . . . quickly came to the conclusion that something was up, that 'something rotten in Denmark was going on.' If that was true, the difference in the game odds and series odds makes sense, from this distance. Even if a remarkable reversal of form gave UTS the game, they still had to win by more than four goals to take the round.

Taylor continues: "Something was wrong, and it had begun to happen some time before the teams took the ice. As they were dressing, the Woodstock players found that their jock straps and undershirts had been coated with an itching powder mixed with cayenne pepper.

"Coach [Bill] Breen also thought that someone had tampered with the skates, which had been left on Friday to be sharpened [by a professional skate sharpener] and were not in the place to which they had been returned [to Breen] on Saturday. The edges had been dulled and had to be hastily sharpened in the rink as well as it could be done.

"After ten minutes of play in the first period starry Bill Carson had been forced to leave the game with a broken skate. Examination showed it had been filed part way through the blade near the heel. He had to use an old pair of skates he hadn't used since the previous season . . . Further examination [later] showed that the skates of two other star players, King and Shea, had been similarly treated, but they held up for the remainder of the game."

Two goals were scored while Carson was off in the first period, but, from personal interviews plus published reports and interviews at the time, Taylor felt that the main effect was nervous upset: the Woodstock players were young, inexperienced, felt under attack, and simply did not play their game.

Whatever the cause, UTS won 7–2. Its last goal, in the third period, was the margin in an 8–7 series victory, which certainly could not have been foreseen by W.A. Hewitt when he made his really unforgivable (no matter what the circumstances, or even the eventual outcome) first-game plea to Woodstock to stop running up the score. The fact remains that if they had run it up a goal or two more, Woodstock, and not UTS, would have had the chance to win the first OHA Memorial Cup.

Woodstock protested, wanting the game to be replayed, demanding a meeting of the OHA executive to investigate the tampering with clothing and skates. Newspapers raged equally at the OHA and Hogtown, where such a dastardly thing could happen. But in its report on the matter the OHA waxed somewhere between dismissive and philosophical. It found (without mentioning Carson's broken skate) "no evidence that the skates had been tampered with," admitted that the jock straps had been dosed with itching powder "by someone unknown," pointed out that this had been discovered before any Woodstock player felt any discomfort, and concluded:

> Every latitude was offered the Woodstock team by the officials before the game to procure new clothing before going on the ice, and the referees were instructed to hold the game until the Woodstock team was perfectly ready to proceed with the play. Investigation by city and private detectives failed to discover the culprits, though both reported that, in their opinion, every reasonable precaution had been taken by Arena Gardens management . . . In view of this evidence, it was decided that no action should be taken by the Executive and the game should stand as played.

Quite understandably, this official account made no mention of W.A. Hewitt's remark to Woodstock's Frank Hyde during the first game that Woodstock should ease up. When the verdict refusing the protest was announced, Hyde made his own protest by resigning as OHA vice-president.

Meanwhile, with Joe Sullivan (later a famous physician and Canadian senator) in goal, UTS went into the OHA history books forever. They beat Montreal Melvilles and later the Regina Patricias – all games being played in Toronto – and won by lopsided scores: 8–2 in sudden death against Montreal for the eastern championship, 14–3 and 15–5 in the final against Regina.

The UTS win that year gave the OHA a rare sweep of Canada's two major amateur hockey championships. Hamilton Tigers, as OHA senior champions, beat the western champion Selkirks of Manitoba 6–1 in the first game of their Allan Cup final. The second ended with Selkirks ahead 5–0 and the series tied. Ninety seconds into overtime Hamilton scored and then hung on to win the series 7–6, in, as the OHA records put it, "a sensational ending to a splendid series."

Over the next seventy years the Memorial Cup has become the most sought-after trophy in Canadian amateur hockey, and nowhere in the list of winners is the name of Woodstock.

From then on, practically every time the OHA met rules were changed. Some might seem small from this distance, but each was a step into the future. Soon a substitute goalie could enter a game at the beginning of any period instead of only when the regular goalkeeper had been injured. And then there was one new rule that still challenges the imagination. In future "each rink must have a penalty box *large enough for 18 persons*, the referee to see that only timers, managers, coaches and spare players occupy the enclosure."

That was also the year the Northern Ontario Hockey Association, which had successfully organized hockey on all levels in the north, became a full-fledged affiliate of the OHA – with the right to meet the OHA champions for "the championship of greater Ontario and the opportunity, if successful, of competing for the Allan Cup and the OHA Memorial Cup." There was, however, just the slightest tinge of patronizing in one provision: when the NOHA senior champs came to the big city, they would play *not* the OHA titlists, holders of the John Ross Robertson Trophy, but the intermediate champions. If they won that, *then* they could have a shot at the seniors.

As soon became evident, few hockey people in southern Ontario knew much about the class of hockey being played in the north. Toronto newspapers carried scores, but little more, as Sudbury won the NOHA senior championship handily over New Liskeard, 16–7, on the home-and-home round. No mention was made of a rather sensational play early in the second New Liskeard game when goalie George Duncan of Sudbury was sent to the penalty box for going to his knees on a save – and from the subsequent face-off in front of the vacant Sudbury net, centre Shorty Green of Sudbury (to quote the *Sudbury Star*) "grabbed the puck in front of his net and tore right through the entire New Liskeard team at terrific speed, not stopping until he had drawn Montgomery out of his net and slipped the puck in behind him." Which must rank among all-time shorthanded goals, anywhere.

Then came the usual OHA-versus-the-world situation. Sudbury fans had hoped for a home-and-home series. There was always ice in Sudbury until late in March, sometimes into April. But because that was not true in either Kingston or Collingwood, the two OHA intermediate finalists, the OHA ruled against home and home, ordering a single sudden-death game to be played on the artificial ice at the Arena Gardens. W.A. Hewitt's telegram to this effect was debated, but not protested. The *Sudbury Star* mentioned that thus "the great majority of the hockey public will be prevented from seeing games they had waited for all season, but Sudbury is only a small cog in the big hockey wheel and it is a forced case of 'take it or leave it.'" So they took it. The *Sudbury Star* headlined: HUNDREDS OF HOCKEY FANS TO MAKE TRIP, and passed on the assurance of the CPR that extra sleeping coaches would be hitched to the Toronto train and a second section of the train would be run if required to accommodate all who wished to make the trip. "Mr. J.M. Rothschild, president of the Sudbury club, has the matter in hand and sleeping reservations can be made with him at his office, the New Ontario Raw Fur Company, Rothschild Block, Elgin street, phone 96. A block of seats has been reserved for Sudburians at the Toronto Arena."

The subsequent arrival on the morning of March 11 of a cheerful band of about 500 free-wheelers from Sudbury stirred up the Toronto hockey pot more than somewhat. By then Collingwood had beaten Kingston to survive the OHA's seventy-team intermediate series. It was a team of veterans who had disposed of Newmarket, Bracebridge, Welland, and Seaforth before meeting Kingston in the final, winning 2–1 in Kingston and 14–2 in Collingwood. As a result, Collingwood was thought to have a pretty good chance against Sudbury on Toronto's artificial ice.

Surprise: the final score was Sudbury 11, Collingwood 2.

Well, wrote the wise men of the Toronto sporting press, that's all very well for these people from the north to beat an intermediate team. Now they have to go against something else entirely.

The OHA senior champions that year were the mighty Toronto Granites, with such notables as Alex Romeril and the ever-popular Dr. Jerry LaFlamme. In the OHA final Granites had beaten a good Hamilton team that included future NHLers Leo Reise (the elder) and Carson Cooper. Again, the Toronto press wrote as if Granites versus Sudbury was an issue never in doubt. The rough and rowdy first period decided nothing, but Granites came out of it leading 1–0. That was the last lead they had in the series. Sudbury came back with three unanswered goals in the second period and two more in the third before Granites scored, then Sudbury, for a final score of 6–2. The second game, three days later, was even more decisive, 5–1 for Sudbury. With only two more bridges to cross, the Intercollegiate champion and the great Icelandic team from Winnipeg, the Falcons, Allan Cup fever was rife in Sudbury. So what happened?

The big city had one more chance. Although there had been agitation among some University of Toronto faculty and students to enter the university's senior team in the OHA, it hadn't happened yet. But the university won the Intercollegiate championship that year, which meant eligibility for the Allan Cup playoffs.

The first game between Varsity and Sudbury was a 2–2 tie, with one goal by Sudbury unjustly disallowed. Late in the game while a dangerous Sudbury attack was in progress, a seventh Varsity player jumped off the bench, making too many men on the ice. Both referees reacted, sounding their bells just as the puck went into the Varsity net. Obviously, play should not have been stopped until Sudbury lost the puck. To add insult to injury, Varsity was not even penalized. The second game was tied 3–3 at the end of regulation time, which would have given Sudbury the series if they'd won the first game. Varsity won it with a rather flukey overtime goal, a rolling and spinning puck.

But overall, the *Sudbury Star*'s verdict was this: "The boys of the North were the victims of their friends. Seven days lounging around a Toronto hotel . . . with meals interrupted, rest broken, and adulatory fans everywhere it was not the same team that had trotted out to meet the Granites . . . " The writer scorned rumours that the team had been living it up, calling that rumour "vicious libel."

Varsity then met Winnipeg Falcons for the Allan Cup and lost both games, 8–3 and 3–2, Falcons going on to win the first Olympic hockey championship at Antwerp. But nobody ever took the NOHA champions for granted after that great run they made the first time they competed outside of their own territory. They didn't do badly in the next few years, either. Sault Ste. Marie Greyhounds made it into the all-Ontario final the next year before losing to the Varsity seniors, who then beat Brandon for the Allan Cup.

The NOHA juniors were strong, as well, year after year. In 1922, Iroquois Falls might have made it all the way to the Memorial Cup except for a remarkable turn of events. They were in Toronto to face Aura Lee, the OHA champions, in a sudden-death game. The day before, when that game had been advertised and tickets sold, the NOHA allowed an age-eligibility protest by North Bay against Iroquois Falls. North Bay and Iroquois Falls were ordered to replay the NOHA championship game, in Toronto, on the same day as the all-Ontario final! Iroquois Falls did win that morning against North Bay, using their best six men all the way. A few hours later the same players skated out against the strong Aura Lees, who starred future NHL great Harold Cotton, and lost 4–0. Considering that two tough playoff games on the same day might stretch the endurance of any team, there was a certain quality of understatement in the OHA's official record to the effect that "consequently the Iroquois Falls players were not at their best." In future years northern teams were always a factor, usually living up to Sudbury's initial success of 1920 – and in 1924 surpassing it, when Soo Greyhounds took the Allan Cup.

A couple of other matters seem worth noting from that period. One is that the hockey seasons were getting marginally longer, starting late in December and running to mid-March before championships were decided – often with junior, intermediate, and even some senior games outside of the major cities being played on soft or even water-covered ice. The only artificial ice under OHA jurisdiction was in Toronto and Hamilton, meaning that when teams from smaller cities or towns (Kitchener, for one) made it to championship playoffs they had to leave their familiar rinks and play away from home. As such games sometimes were ordered by the OHA to be played in Toronto, favouring Toronto teams, there were occasional complaints to the OHA that it was Hogtown-dominated.

But the OHA, just as obviously, was not really a Toronto outfit. In a normal year, for instance 1921-22, when teams registered had burgeoned to 164 (up from 132 the previous year and more than double the seventy-one of four years earlier), the OHA executive was led by president A.E. Copeland from Midland. Immediate past president was R.M. Glover from Peterborough. Vice-presidents were from Dunnville and Stratford, the treasurer from Whitby, and executive committee members from Cobalt, Lindsay, Woodstock, Galt, Kingston, and Kitchener. That left on the executive only two Torontonians – the OHA's representative on the Amateur Athletic Union of Canada, W.W. Davidson, plus the perennial and powerful secretary, W.A. Hewitt. The days of Toronto domination through the power of Hewitt, John Ross Robertson, and Robertson's close ally, Francis Nelson (who resigned in 1921 and was made a life member) were over and pretty well stayed that way through the years.

With the OHA by far the most powerful of all CAHA affiliates, nothing much was done without Ontario consent, or even instigation, as the CAHA worked to homogenize playing rules and off-ice regulations right across the country. Often OHA consent was by unanimous vote, as happened with a CAHA-devised rule in 1921 providing that all of the OHA's 4,000 registered players (five times as large a number as the closest other hockey association, the 810 from Quebec) had to fill out and sign new playing certificates. These were coloured blue for senior, pink for intermediate, and white for juniors. The OHA wording of the regulation specified that "the executive may in its absolute discretion issue, revoke, or refuse to issue such certificates" and that no team could play a game unless its captain "furnished the referee with a full list of the players and their playing certificates."

There were other specifically Ontario rulings. Every senior team was required to maintain a junior team "to encourage the development of young players without which the Association cannot hope to live forever." A goalkeeper would be allowed to wear a mask "to protect his face and head if he so desired." (Few did; general use of goalie masks was still nearly half a century away.) No overtime would be more than thirty minutes. An official goal net was prescribed, called the Lesueur net after the fine goalie, Percy Lesueur, who had devised it. The net's top covering extended seventeen inches from the goalposts to the back bar on a line, and at the base stretched along the ice for twenty-two inches back of the goalposts. And, this was not a rule but a strong urging: the minimum size for the ice surface of new rinks be not less than 70 to 75 feet wide and 170 to 175 feet long. A wistful postscript added that the ideal hockey rink would be 85 by 185. This in a city where a new rink had just been built with an ice surface 70 by 100.

Application of these forms, rules, and intentions over the years gave the CAHA a uniform, Canada-wide way of playing the game. Sometimes the process had a faint aroma of bureaucracy gone mad, but there was already the sense that hockey was part of the national consciousness that had to be regulated, for reasons of the sport's future health. As it turned out, even then hockey was on the threshold of two decades of tumultuous changes that would turn upside down many of the precepts on which the OHA had been founded.

CHAPTER NINE

INTERLUDE

*"Canada has never had a major civil war.
After hockey Canadians would probably have
found it dull."*
                                        — JIM BROSNAN,
                              Chicago White Sox baseball star,
                                      author, and hockey fan

*"The disorders peaked in the third period
when St. Thomas defenceman Moose Watts
took a two-fisted swing of his stick and
poleaxed Woodstock left-winger Cecil
Mooney, who fell to the ice gushing blood."*
                                      — LEONARD W. TAYLOR,
                                              in his memoir,
                                        "Days of Real Sport"

One hazard in trying to depict a century of hockey by means of its committee-room decisions is that movers and seconders, the devious as well as the well intentioned, come across as infinitely more respectable and less lively than the game itself. Back in radio's infancy and before television, the game of hockey was best depicted in news-paper accounts written at white heat within an hour or two after a game, the reporters hammering out their stories on old portables in a makeshift pressbox or a handy hotel room and handing them a page at a time to boys whose job was to run it to the telegraph office, where a man with arm garters and a green eyeshade was "sending" at a Morse key, rattling out the game stories to the *London*

Free Press, Toronto Globe, Toronto Mail and Empire, and other papers. By early morning they would be on sale in cities and towns all over Ontario, as storekeepers ripped open the newspaper bundles thrown off the morning train. Just about every little settlement, however small, had a morning train. The stories were usually long on colour, passion, lively observation, and some actual facts, with objectivity not highly prized.

Scores in both goals and fights were important on the sports pages. BRANTFORD RINK COLLAPSES might make a front-page headline. An irate crowd chasing a referee out of town would get only passing mention – it happened all the time.

Leonard W. Taylor, when the blood-letting he describes happened early in 1928, was eighteen years old and sports editor of the daily *Woodstock Sentinel-Review*. The incident came in an ordinary mid-season league game in St. Thomas, with Woodstock the hated visitors. The two communities were arch-rivals in a senior hockey group in western Ontario.

Moose Watts was given a match penalty for felling poor Cecil Mooney. Without big Moose as the backbone of the hometown St. Thomas defence, the team lost 3–2. As usual, the fans more or less dismissed from their minds the stick-swinging that had got their star banished. Those Woodstockers, the dirty bastards, had got away with murder themselves, between them and the blind referee, and shouldn't be let out of town in one piece. So at game's end, wrote Taylor, "the St. Thomas fans swarmed around the Woodstock dressing room and threatened to break down the door." Only the sub-zero temperatures "finally discouraged the hundreds who had hung around outside to get a poke at the winners, who stayed behind the locked dressing room door for two hours before they were able to get into their bus and drive home."

This entire evening was acknowledged tersely in OHA records in a single sentence suspending player Moose

Watts for three years. His loss helped eliminate St. Thomas in subsequent playoffs, leaving Woodstock and London in the final.

London won the first game 4–1. That made the second game, in Woodstock, all or nothing. London won again – but in the process Woodstock star Doc Douglas, a clean player and key to the Woodstock attack, was high-sticked and badly cut.

So at game's end, Taylor wrote, "London was clear of the round but not out of town. Hundreds of people waited for them at the Perry Street front doors of the rink. Defying them, the London boys dashed to their bus but the mob was ready," armed with what Taylor called "Irish confetti"; that is, stones, bricks, anything heavy and throwable. "There was a sound of crashing glass as the bus strove to move through the many who stood in front, daring it to run over them. By the time the police arrived and opened a passage there wasn't a pane of glass in the vehicle but its occupants were glad to get away for a cold 30-mile return trip to London, a journey warmed only by the fact that they'd won the group championship."

So it was a high old life for Ontario sportswriters in those days, especially an eighteen-year-old like Taylor who was brash and opinionated and knew the game. Try as he and at least some of his contemporaries did to remain fair-minded, home-town sentiment was bound to show through, reflecting fury, joy, whatever. They saw their own players, club officials, and the team's most rabid supporters every day, and prudence was the better part of valour, with criticism most commonly reserved for the opposition. Playoff time, as forever and ever, amen, was just one constant round of excitement: the riotous special train or bus to some opposition rink, the pre-game crowds making their bets, friendly and not-so-friendly exchanges with opposing fans or reporters, a hot dog or two, then the game itself.

In the late 1920s press-box conditions were primitive.

No one suggested they should be otherwise. Foster Hewitt broadcast football from a freezing tin roof at Queen's University and called hockey from a perilous perch in the rafters of Toronto's Arena Gardens. In many small-town rinks, the few game reporters on hand sat on the timer's bench, squeezing over or standing up alongside when the space was required for penalized players, as could happen.

Actually, this timer's-bench system had its advantage, tending to give one a rare slant on the game. (But that is only the idle reflection of this book's author, who covered many games long ago from timers' benches.) Anyway, young Len Taylor's coverage of a game in Brantford on Thursday, February 19, 1929, is presented here not exactly as something that could happen anywhere – but what did happen that one night. You could look it up.

The Brantford rink, a ramshackle affair, had only one great advantage: artificial ice, assuring a good fast surface for every game, which natural ice rinks couldn't provide in mild weather. So, fast teams loved the Brantford rink. Referees did, too. A lot of odd things happened on natural ice that were not specifically covered by the rule book. For instance, one of the little strategic offshoots of slushy or water-covered ice was that goalmouth skirmishes would feature one attacking player using his stick to scoop water into the goalie's face while another got his shot away. (That kind of thing was hard for a ref to call, although it was not the worst that could happen; the worst was the unspeakable but effective ploy of the occasional tobacco-chewing defenceman who might squirt a stream of the stinging juice into the eyes of an incoming forward.) Anyway, the consensus was that Brantford had an okay rink from an ice standpoint, if nothing else.

The building's makeshift nature actually was due to the fact that the rink itself was only a business offshoot of its owner, the Arctic Ice Company, whose main income was from manufacturing and supplying blocks of ice to households in the area. These ice blocks, gripped by heavy sharp-pointed tongs and carried over the ice man's leather-shielded shoulder, would be carried through kitchen doors and dropped into the ice compartments of the large wooden refrigerators, or ice boxes, commonly used at the time to keep perishables cool.

It seems Arctic's owners had felt that as their machines were making ice anyway, they could do the job for an ice surface as well and make money from hockey and pleasure skating. That didn't require a palatial home, and in Brantford they didn't get it. The building would make a rink-builder of today faint dead away. According to Taylor, four-by-fours were the main beams, two-by-fours the uprights. There were no seats, but rows of bleacher-like benches that would hold about 800 spectators along each side and about 400 at each end. So normal capacity was 2,400. But for the big Brantford-Woodstock playoff game of February 19, 1929, 3,500 fans from Brantford, Woodstock, Ingersoll, Paris, and villages and hamlets between had jammed, pushed, and fought their way into every square inch of space. The first game of the two-games total-goals series had been played in Woodstock a few days earlier, ending in a 3–3 draw. So this was the decisive second game, ordered by the OHA to be played to a finish.

Naturally Alan Rose, sports editor of the *Brantford Expositor*, had picked Brantford to win this game on its home ice before a supportive home crowd and thereby take the series. Just as naturally, Len Taylor, representing the *Woodstock Sentinel-Review*, had called it the other way.

The referee was Lou Marsh, a busy man during playoffs because he was also the *Toronto Star* sports columnist. He was generally considered to be one of the best and fairest of referees – although a few winters earlier in Paris, Ontario, fans had chased him down the main street without even giving him time to take off his skates. He'd made his escape only by leaping aboard the night's last outward-bound trolley. This extracurricular athletic event had caused the OHA, always vigilant in support of referees, to ban the Paris rink from OHA play for three years.

Near game-time Taylor climbed into the press box, which had been built about twelve feet above the centre-ice benches at one side of the rink. His climb was "up a frail vertical ladder obviously fashioned from leftover scantlings," and, he wrote, the press box itself, with room for four occupants, had been built from planks laid on two-by-fours that were nailed to the four-by-four beams. There was a twelve-inch plank on which to make notes, another on which to sit, and a third on which to rest one's feet. Taylor was the third to arrive, after the local paper's Alan Rose and a telegraph boy who sat "nervously clutching a post and looking down at the swelling mob below." The boy's job was to run copy to the local telegraph office, Rose being a stringer for Toronto and London papers.

Soon the fourth press-box resident arrived, somewhat in the manner of a royal visit. He was a big-town sports-writer, Howard Broughton of the *London Free Press*, and had brought a typewriter. This, he said tersely, was because he would be writing play-by-play copy for the London radio station, CFPL – a custom of the time for important games. A few sentences at a time, mainly on goals, penalties, and fights, would be telegraphed to the CFPL studio. There, an announcer would broadcast a running account of a game he couldn't see, using his imagination and canned crowd noises to keep the illusion alive.

When Lou Marsh dropped the puck to start the game, the crowd began to cheer, bellow, and scream imprecations, the deafening noise undiminished except briefly when Woodstock scored once in the first period and again early in the second. That put Woodstock ahead 5–3 on the round. Ten minutes later, still in the second period, Brantford scored to make the round score 5–4.

"In the uproar that followed," wrote Taylor, "we felt the press box swaying and beginning to pull loose from the upright near the ladder." This caused Broughton's typewriter to slide forward dangerously, seeming about to fall into the mob below. "Broughton shouted for help. We helped him get his machine back on an even keel. We now agreed that the press box was unstable, a conclusion hastened by the sounds of splintering wood. It was hardly safe to stay where we were, and impossible to leave."

Meanwhile, another factor: the heat generated by the excited, heavily clad crowd rose to the sheet-metal roof, causing moisture to congeal and fall like rain, "big, fat, nasty-looking drops that splotched the hats of those below us," Taylor wrote. "It must have been the first-ever indoors hockey game to be played in a steady shower. The least affected seemed to be the hockey players, who thumped away madly on what was becoming very sticky ice. Then, with six minutes of the period remaining there was a particularly dangerous and sustained drive on the Woodstock net. The chance to tie the series sent fans at that end into a frenzy of excitement, jumping up and down, which might have precipitated what followed."

At the same time the press box began to sway even more dangerously, forcing its four occupants to cling to the uprights. Then, "there was a sound of breaking wood and the entire south bleachers collapsed, about half of it quickly, the rest dissolving majestically and so slowly that a couple of hundred fans were able to scramble away from their seats. Screams and groans sounded from the wreckage. In seconds the rink became absolutely silent, punctuated only by the sound of bits of wood falling somewhere below.

"This was the moment that Lou Marsh earned his fee. With barely a halt in his motion he skated to centre ice and announced that the game was abandoned and cautioned all fans to proceed in careful and orderly fashion to the exit. His confidence helped calm what might have quickly become a panicky crowd. There was no danger if they stayed calm, he assured them. Some sat still, a few moved to leave, others went to the broken bleachers to help victims in and under the debris. Some were carried out, others limped away. Soon that end area was cleared and it was found that, miraculously, no one had been seriously injured."

Then came what one has to treat, in retrospect, as the funny part.

In the undamaged areas of the rink many of the most diehard fans, at least a couple of thousand, had simply stayed on. Marsh, looking for some authoritative local support, found in the crowd the chief of police and a deputy magistrate. They inspected the building, after which Marsh made another announcement: the game had been abandoned; he was notifying the OHA to that effect.

In short: go home! The fans still did not leave.

Still later Marsh reappeared at centre ice. This time he was no longer on skates, but in his galoshes, overcoat, and hat. The game would be replayed in Paris the following night, he called, ordering the remaining fans to depart. This time they did. Broughton from London caged his typewriter, climbed down, and left the rink.

Taylor was about to leave as well when suddenly a thought struck him. When Marsh had made his final announcement, his galoshes had not been buckled up!

This would hardly have been the case if he was planning to go out into the snow!

These are the hunches from which great journalists are made.

Taylor walked across the empty ice and found Marsh in the referee's cubicle, putting on his skates. "Stick around," he said with a wink. "We're going to finish the game as soon as the rink is cleared."

With this news, Taylor, generously eschewing the scoop, rushed outside after Broughton – and found him moodily clearing snow from his windshield before starting for London. The two of them went back to the press box. Meanwhile, fans who already had gone home turned on their radios to find the indefatigable announcer from London, who by then had gone ninety minutes without a word from Brantford, was still running on pure, if puzzled, imagination, broadcasting the game as if it were still on, and suddenly sounding as if the game still *was* on.

Which by then it was.

So, wrote Taylor, "the 'greatest game of the season' was finished before about a hundred ticket sellers, ice cleaners, concession booth workers and a few others who would never again believe anything said by a man who was not only a newspaperman, but also a referee.

"It was strenuous hockey but without the crowd noises it seemed tame as Brantford strove valiantly and desperately to equalize the score. It was almost impossible to carry and pass the puck over ice scarred and soiled by the thousands of feet of those who had walked across it earlier to get out of the building. Because some parts of the ice were worse than others, Marsh stopped the game half through the final period and had the teams change ends.

"Eventually, at around 2 a.m., the game ended, Woodstock the winner. After all that excitement no one was left around to throw insults, or rocks.

"The building was closed, later rebuilt, but even then was never more than a poor excuse for a hockey rink."

There were other rinks not much better being used for hockey in those days. For a rink to shatter and fall under the weight of abnormally heavy snow was uncommon, but not unknown. But by coincidence almost exactly thirty years later, Len Taylor, by then sports editor of the *Kitchener-Waterloo Record*, was at his desk one Saturday noon when a frantic stringer phoned from Listowel to say that the fine modern arena there, built only in 1954, had collapsed during a morning of minor hockey. Taylor dropped everything and drove with a six-man reporting and photography team to Listowel.

"There had been some humor and no tragedy at Brantford back in 1929. As I stood in the mess of twisted girders, splintered beams and torn sheet metal of the Listowel rink, I wished I could have found something less tragic here. Seven minor hockey players, and the civic recreation director died in that wreckage."

Chapter Ten

THE MAN FROM
MIDLAND

*"Let us remain true to the ideals of our late
lamented life member, John Ross Robertson."*
— CAPTAIN JAMES SUTHERLAND,
fighting a losing battle

During the middle decades of this century the name
of barrister George S. Dudley, along with his telephone
number in Midland, Ontario, his lifelong home, appeared
in the source files of many sports journalists in Canada,
the United States, and eventually in Europe – the unruf-
fled Canadian who, when the hockey world was being
rocked in ways large or small, always had the answers or
knew where to find them.

The road to his eventually powerful role in the game
was deceptively low-profile. He never said in records now
available that his intention all along was to make Canadian hockey face the fact that the best "amateur" hockey
players were being paid for their skills, deserved to be, and
should be allowed to accept their due in a more socially
acceptable manner than having a few twenties slipped to
them surreptitiously now and again by a coach or manager. Indeed, he probably did not have that target originally; if not, over the years it grew of its own accord.
Nevertheless, within ten years after the first time the
name George S. Dudley showed up thirteenth and last in
a list of those attending an OHA executive meeting in

1925, he was the OHA president and a major factor in bringing pay-for-play "amateur" hockey out of the closet. A few years after this had been achieved, he was to say (by then as CAHA president) that if Canada's way of dealing with the game's realities was not acceptable in the big world of Olympics and world championships, "then we just won't be going."

And he stuck around to make sure. For twenty-four years after his OHA presidency ended, he was the association's treasurer. In the CAHA he went straight from being president to being, more powerfully, secretary-manager. Both jobs ended only when he died.

His long and at first low-key record is best seen in the perspective of OHA executive meeting minutes typewritten (usually with a worn-out ribbon) by W.A. Hewitt and kept in a series of small ring binders.

One of the earliest OHA executive meetings Dudley attended began at 8 p.m. on November 6, 1925. During discussion of the forty items on the agenda, Dudley's name appears only twice: seconding a motion to admit a Walkerville team to the intermediate series, and an hour or so later moving to admit a Wingham intermediate team as well. When one adds those two innocuous motions to one he'd made a year earlier from the floor of the annual meeting – suggesting a change in residence rules for students, for which he failed to get the necessary support – it is plain that he did not burst upon the OHA as the man who was to help lead Canadian hockey into the future at a clip that would make him one of the best-known figures in the game. It could be that his quality of endless patience was born of, or honed in, decades of hockey meetings both in the OHA, where he began, and in the much larger amateur hockey world in Canada and abroad, where he eventually was recognized among the greats – without ever losing his Midland cool.

The OHA executive and annual meetings of Dudley's neophyte years sometimes come across through W.A.

Hewitt's minutes as torture through repetition. In hockey as elsewhere, ability to deal with major events often depends on understanding the most picayune, and your average OHA meeting at any level positively reeked of the picayune. There was not only the routine of dealing with protests or complaints over everything from playing schedules to unruly crowds, blizzards that blocked roads and caused cancellations, and the occasional referee who was reportedly well foxed by the grape before he wobbled out trying to decide whether to blow his bell or ring his whistle.

There were maps showing town boundaries that affected the issuance of player registrations, disputed birth certificates, a vote to refund a $6 entry fee to a club whose grand intentions and dreams of glory never quite made it to the ice, requests for reinstatement after suspension, transfer of this player or that from one branch to another or one club to another. Each piece of paper had its own life.

There was also the fact that when change of any kind was suggested in the OHA, there was an almost automatic opposition from men who still quoted John Ross Robertson in the way that, in other circumstances, they quoted Holy Writ. Still, there were people – among them Frank Selke, then representing Kitchener, and, surprisingly enough, W.A. Hewitt – who tended to look forward instead of back, and with whom Dudley seemed more in tune.

For instance, for much of the 1920s there was one ancient, and ongoing, rule that banned from any OHA club's executive or coaching staff anyone who was or had been a professional in *any* sport. Hire a former pro to coach your local heroes and boom, you're expelled from the OHA. To some, by the 1920s, this seemed ridiculous – but they might as well have been debating with trees in a petrified forest.

One favourite argument of the old-guard delegates was

that if pros were allowed to coach, the rich teams, the big cities, would be the ones who could afford them, and (cue the violins) "on the night of the match the small town that couldn't afford to pay a professional coach would be at a disadvantage." Never mind that a former pro might have gone back to his own small-town roots and might want to pay his "debt" to society by coaching for nothing. Or that he'd been out of pro hockey for years while making his pile from some honest business like stockbroking, real estate, or politics and wanted to polish his image as a guy who cared enough about the sport to give up evenings when he could have been down at the Legion living it up. No dice.

But people who wanted the game to progress by giving young players expert coaching hammered away. One year W.A. Hewitt spotted what seemed to him, as well as to George Dudley, Frank Selke, and a few like-minded citizens, a likely opening. Queen's University had hired a year-round athletic director who, Hewitt did admit, took his salary in the form of money rather than honorary degrees. In the natural course of events he would be required, to use Hewitt's genteel phrase, "to render assistance" to the hockey club. Did the OHA rule against paying a coach mean that this exemplary person would be barred from having anything to do with hockey at Queen's? "The object of the rule as I understand it was to eliminate the *undesirable*," he argued. Should not the man Queen's had hired, a paragon of his kind, be acceptable to the OHA?

Knowing the nature of the opposition, he craftily moved a constitutional amendment in which the Queen's situation was not even mentioned. What he suggested was that the executive should be free to scrutinize the experience and character of *any* coach, pro or amateur, and accept or reject as the case may be.

But that still didn't fly with those delegates who lived only on the high ground. It wasn't the *undesirable* that they wanted to keep out but "simply the *professional*," one stated. And not only because he was, or had been, a professional: "Hiring a pro would cast a slur on the proficiency of the amateur coach."

That rather spectacular example of sensitivity toward the feelings of amateur coaches didn't seem to get anywhere at first. Speakers in favour of Hewitt's position laughingly cited cases of men with pro backgrounds who had become pillars of their communities, elected officials, much loved everywhere – but still couldn't be appointed by the local hockey club as chief cook and bottlewasher, let alone coach. Which seemed unnecessary overkill.

Frank Selke, as delegate from Kitchener, piped up for the new wave. His style, then as later (both in the OHA and when, with Montreal Canadiens, he became one of the most powerful voices in the pro game), was a mixture of firmness and folksiness. The question of paying a coach didn't really affect his Kitchener club, he said with a disarming smile.

> We never have anything left over to pay a coach – usually our officers have a deficit to wipe out – but we would like to see a little more broadminded attitude. . . . Think about this: We are proud of our hockey team that went over to France. [He had managed the 1924 Canadian Winter Olympics team at Chamonix, where Toronto Granites were a walkaway for the hockey gold.] One of the best of those players has since been signed as a pro coach. I refer to Mr. Beattie Ramsay. I don't think the less of him. He is one of our finest players. But does the fact of his being a pro coach now prevent him from taking your boys and making hockey players of them?
>
> Let's get the best OHA we possibly can! If our old players are willing to help again, surely they should be encouraged, and if the clubs are willing to give them something for it, then that is their business. The OHA executive has the authority to turn down *any* man, pro or amateur, who is not satisfactory from their point of view. I think the *amateur* coach should be required to pass a qualification test just the same as the professional.

But the reformers lost that one, too. The opposition's keynote voice from the past was that of Captain James Sutherland of Kingston, then in his late fifties, the wartime president who had come home from the trenches to become somewhat of an icon in the OHA.

"Let us remain true to the ideals of our late lamented life member, John Ross Robertson!" was his ringing declaration. "Let us go home with the amateur principle in our minds and in the government of our teams! Let us be a one hundred percent amateur association, which we will not be if we allow this amendment!"

You may be sure that when he sat down with the applause of the traditionalists booming in his ears, he had no idea that in less than ten years he would be supporting exactly the opposite principle: the pay-for-play revolution, George S. Dudley, prop. By that time, the middle 1930s, the burning issue that had prompted the lofty sentiments against pro coaches was long gone. Hewitt had brought it up again only two years after his earlier defeat, arguing tartly: "The original intention of this rule was to *control* the pro coach, not *exterminate* him." Dudley and Selke again were in strong support, Selke's contribution being the news that the rule was being abrogated anyway by several clubs hiring men who really were pro, and really did coach, but were listed as trainers. That time, Hewitt's constitutional amendment won in a breeze. Some of the old guard must have been surprised from time to time that W.A. Hewitt, once one of their own, often was to be found as an ally of George Dudley and others in the vanguard of change.

And so meeting after meeting – the annuals, the semi-annuals, acting as delegate to meetings of the NOHA, the CAHA, and other organizations, attending and sometimes running eleven or twelve executive or subcommittee meetings a year – Dudley's preparation progressed. He was becoming the quintessential hockey man. Sometimes he was double-crossed, even that being usually a valuable learning experience. Once in the late 1920s this was by Hewitt, in a meeting that – in its sheer lack of big issues – is covered here as a typical example of the genre.

At that meeting the OHA's brass hats received delegates from several Toronto senior clubs lamenting that Toronto's NHL team of that time, St. Patricks, had collared all the best dates in the Arena Gardens. The OHA's five-year contract with the Arena Gardens was up for renewal but the seniors wanted to move their act to the new Ravina Gardens, where they'd been told they could get 50 per cent of gate receipts instead of the Arena Gardens' usual 35 per cent.

Hewitt's preference for the Arena Gardens quickly showed. It could have been based on good business sense, friendship, tradition, whatever. His message was blunt enough: mainly to the effect that 35 per cent of the well-established Arena Gardens would be better than 50 per cent anywhere else in town, including the Ravina, which was still under construction. He somewhat placated the dissidents by offering to get a better deal for them from the Arena Gardens in a new contract. Still, he didn't jump for joy when Dudley, supported by the senior clubs' delegate – who included the fiery, thirtyish Conn Smythe, then the University of Toronto's hockey coach – moved that as a safeguard the new Arena Gardens contract should be restricted to one year, instead of five as in the past.

This motion was passed, followed by Conn Smythe's statement that his Varsity seniors would prefer to return to the system of having the Intercollegiate champion enter the Allan Cup playdowns directly, by-passing the OHA. As matters stood, if an Ontario university won the Intercollegiate championship, it still had to meet the OHA senior champions for a berth in the Allan Cup rounds. This had happened most recently that very spring, Varsity winning the Intercollegiate *and* the OHA before being beaten in the Allan Cup final by Port Arthur. Smythe wanted to eliminate the possibility that, another time, Varsity might win the Intercollegiate but lose to the OHA senior champions and not make it to Allan Cup play at all.

W.A. Fry of Dunnville: "Isn't it pride, Mr. Smythe, that makes the university desire Varsity to play directly into the Allan Cup round through the Intercollegiate?"

Smythe: "Yes."

Fry: "Well, the OHA has some pride, too. Had Varsity won the OHA championship last year but lost out in a subsequent Intercollegiate final (to, say, McGill) the OHA, the largest hockey body in Canada, would not have been represented in the Allan Cup playdowns."

Smythe's reply did not make it to W.A. Hewitt's minutes. He was never a polite loser.

The balance of that particular meeting provides other clues as to the well-rounded education of George Dudley. At the meeting mentioned above, after Smythe and the other senior poohbahs had disappeared, the OHA execs okayed playing certificates for seventy-one players, involving twenty-eight clubs. For another thirty players, involving thirteen clubs, playing certificates were withheld for one reason or another. On three disputed applications, more information was requested. And finally, the executive ruled that fourteen players whose talents were coveted by certain OHA clubs (eight in all) would require certified transfers from where they'd played last year, the list encompassing the Thunder Bay Amateur Hockey Association, Ottawa and District Amateur Hockey Association, Saskatchewan Amateur Hockey Association, Quebec Amateur Hockey Association, and Northern Ontario Hockey Association. If anyone is counting, all this means that 118 hockey players had their names and parts of their particulars trotted past the OHA executive gents in charge before the meeting adjourned, well past midnight. And in the next executive meeting, Hewitt had done enough lobbying to torpedo George Dudley's motion providing for a one-year contract with Arena Gardens. Another five-year deal was made, without renewed opposition from Dudley.

Maybe they'd made an arrangement involving something where Dudley needed Hewitt's vote, or his silence. Dudley could play the political game, too, and Hewitt was a hard man to beat on his home turf. Also, as a social history note – the kind of comparison one makes in coming across an advertisement offering a new car for $575 – that year the annual meeting was told that those clubs who insured their players might wish to consider a blanket group offer from an insurance company. Premiums would be $8 per senior player, $5 per junior, for which the company would cover accidents to the extent of $1,000 for death, $25 a week for injuries to seniors, and $15 a week for juniors. This was a good deal lower than clubs were paying on the open market, and some signed up; but within a few years, many OHA leagues set up their own insurance pools financed by 5 per cent deductions from each game's gross gate. What was left at the end of the season, after payouts, was divided equally among contributing clubs. Despite the occasional slow-pay club here and there that had to be threatened with the OHA's ultimate weapon, suspension, the system worked for several years, clubs coming to appreciate the springtime splitting of the insurance pot.

For some years by then, the OHA and the CAHA had established uniformity in playing rules and conduct of the game. This included forward passing in the neutral zone as well as the defending zone. The line that eventually was to become the blueline, but at that time was actually painted red, had been twenty feet from the goal line. In 1925 it was extended to forty feet from the end of the rink, meaning that in a rink, say, 160 feet long, the neutral zone in which players could pass ahead was eighty feet. However, in that zone forwards could not bodycheck. When that particular rule came to the OHA from the

CAHA for ratification, Frank Selke said referees wouldn't like it.

"A defenceman crosses the line and somehow he and a forward bump," he argued. "The rule says the forward then gets a penalty, but the contact might not have been his intention at all." Then he uttered what in later years would have been called a Selkeism; he wanted his objection on the record, but would support the rule becoming official for now. He was good at being able to distinguish between the forest and the trees. To him, standardization of playing rules was more important than scoring debating points. The fix could be argued at the next meeting of the CAHA, where the OHA already had a long-standing reputation for bullheadedness at least partly because the OHA's trickiest stickhandlers always were sent to carry the Ontario flag.

At such CAHA annuals, involving the hard talkers from Manitoba and farther west, as well as a few tricky tries from farther east, a certain amount of buddy-buddy hockey talk didn't hurt, but the meetings often involved wielding the OHA's big stick as the country's major hockey power. Of course, this attitude just confirmed what the rest of the country always had felt about Ontario, and still does, not only in hockey: too damn bossy. Sometimes when the others ganged up, the OHA had a fight on its hands before winning in the end.

P.J. Mulqueen, chairman of the Canadian Olympic Committee and an honorary non-voting member of the OHA executive, returned from one cross-Canada trip in 1926 to tell an OHA annual meeting exactly where the association stood across the country.

"Everywhere I went in the West," he said, "I heard the OHA mentioned many times." Applause. "You are not regarded as perfect." Incredulity and some laughter. "After telling me that the OHA wears horns longer than any other in the hockey world, however, when we were talking of some contentious matter they would ask me in the very next breath, 'Will you tell us how you think the OHA would deal with a case of this kind?' " Self-satisfied nods.

"That, I think, very well illustrates their attitude toward the OHA. They regard you as the parent body in hockey and are guided by your decisions." Cries of Hear, Hear! "This is something I think you should bear in mind the next time you receive some characteristically breezy Western criticism."

At the time, there happened to be one perfect illustration of the OHA going against the combined efforts of other CAHA affiliates, who wanted to raise the junior age limit to twenty-one from twenty. The underlying cause had much to do with NHL expansion to Boston (1924-25 season) and to Pittsburgh and New York (1925-26 season). The new U.S. teams were aggressively hunting for players and didn't care how old a player was if he was good enough. This was depleting junior ranks.

What was termed by Hewitt as "a very determined effort" had been made by the CAHA in its annual meeting in Montreal that spring, and again in its semi-annual meeting in Port Arthur in November, to raise the age limit by that one year. It had been "only with great difficulty," added Hewitt, "that we were able to have the matter put over until it could be considered by various branches. We [in the OHA] should have a very strong expression of opinion against that proposal."

He certainly got it. Delegate after delegate chimed in. Dunnville's William Fry pointed out that the OHA had more junior teams than all the other branches of the CAHA put together, and "there's no reason why we should allow the tail to wag the dog." One delegate then asked. "Well, what's the argument in favour of raising the limit?"

Hewitt: "The only argument I've heard advanced, and a very specious argument, was that it would help the CAHA clubs in their role as good feeders for the professionals."

Another delegate argued, however, that if the age limit

was raised, maybe along with it the pros would agree not to take a player until he was twenty-one, which was not then the case, the pros going for the most talented players of any age. This idea of a raised age limit maybe becoming a bargaining chip in dealing with the pros was shot down sharply by Frank Selke, on other grounds, i.e., humanitarian. "When you have boys drifting into the age of 21 and playing junior, would any father of a boy of 16 dare to send them against those older boys, up to age 21, and ask him to take his medicine?" he asked. "For my part, I would be ready to withdraw our teams from the CAHA if they are going to raise the age limit."

So the sense of the meeting was for the OHA to stick with the present limit and force the CAHA to do the same. But that was just a warmup for the main event: widespread lamenting about the way pros were pursuing Canadian juniors, whatever the age limit.

"American cities are offering our boys, of 17 to 19, contracts," said one East Toronto delegate, Charles Higginbottom, a power in the huge outdoor Toronto Hockey League. "These boys, in my mind, do not realize what they are doing. An offer of thirty five or forty dollars a week looks like a hundred to them and they are very tempted to sign the proffered contract. They fail to realize that they have not yet rounded out their hockey. We had two fellows from Boston down at the Beaches making these offers to boys playing hockey in the junior OHA. On the face of it, that's ridiculous, but that's what we're up against."

Captain Sutherland thought he had the answer: an amendment to the existing rule banning pros, extending it to anyone who signed a pro contract, even if he had not actually accepted money or played professionally. The Sutherland amendment proposed that "Any player who signs a professional contract automatically suspends himself from this association and cannot be reinstated inside of one year."

That real hardhat move roused sober second thoughts immediately. One delegate noted that a contract signed by a junior not yet of legal age could be vetoed by his parents, but under the Sutherland amendment just *signing* a contract would bar the boy from amateur hockey. "I'm not sure that you want to do that. I would suggest that Mr. Sutherland, in his motion that anyone who signed a pro contract was out, might change it to exempt junior players."

Higginbottom agreed. He knew kids who had been sought after and planned going to the U.S. to play, very shortly. But "there has always been a good deal of doubt in the minds of a majority of us as to just what constitutes professionalism," he said, urging caution, or more careful consideration, especially of the Sutherland motion.

He was backed up immediately by William Fry, who introduced a new element. The OHA was not the final word, he said. A player required an amateur card from the Amateur Athletic Union of Canada before he could play, or even before an amateur club could sign him. Higginbottom had more to add. The Ontario branch of the AAU, he said, "about three weeks ago sent a letter to the national AAU office in Montreal requesting definitions in three categories: What is the status of a man who signs a pro contract? What is the status of a man who accepts money and returns it? What is the status of a man who is just *anticipating* turning professional and [accepting] the various conditions [contract, pay, etc.] surrounding it?"

He thought that if the answers were stated clearly in black and white by the AAU, that would settle the matter. The AAU was the umbrella body for all amateur sport at the time. As Mr. Fry had said, without seeing an AAU amateur card, no team in the OHA or any other affiliates of the CAHA would issue a playing certificate. So with a definite statement of the AAU position, then there would be no need for further legislation by other organizations, such as the OHA.

Captain Sutherland persisted: a clarification was needed, and his amendment was an attempt at it. He remarked that he knew his OHA history as well as, and perhaps better than, anyone else in the room, and then went on to prove it.

"In our constitution," he stated, "an amateur is defined as, 'a person who has not, since December 14, 1883, competed in any open (i.e., with or against professionals) competition' and later, there is this following passage, 'and who has not made any offer which, if it had been accepted, would have made the recipient a professional.' That is ambiguous to a great many young players." (To say nothing of its ambiguity to practically anyone, of any age.) He felt that with sixty-five junior teams affiliated with the OHA, it was only fair to give due notice to each player of the consequences of signing a professional contract.

It then happened, almost too fortuitously, that Elwood Hughes, president of the Ontario branch of the AAU, was handy enough that he could be asked to address the meeting on this subject. He suggested that if the Sutherland amendment were accepted and put into effect, it might work a hardship. "In fact, during the past spring a boy signed a contract to play pro hockey this coming winter. I think that boy is still an amateur. Under what Captain Sutherland proposes, by the signing of that contract in the spring he automatically suspended himself [from the OHA] and every other sports governing body in the country would recognize your suspension . . . . A boy should not be placed in the position of not knowing exactly the trouble he's in, or getting into, by signing a professional contract. He's never made a mistake from an amateur standpoint. He's still a youngster. He probably has not read your rules carefully. Very few actually do. The final answer from the AAU, which will be thoroughly broadcast, will tell that boy and everybody else the exact position he's in, in such a case.

"Therefore, I suggest that you leave this over for three weeks, for the governing body of amateur sport in Canada to answer."

At this statement, Captain Sutherland withdrew his amendment. but that didn't end the discussion. Far from it. Former president D.L. Darroch immediately said he was very sorry that Sutherland had withdrawn his amendment. The OHA should place itself on record regardless of what other associations like the AAU said or did. The OHA's amateur rule "is as plain as words can make it," he said. Pecuniary benefit was the issue. Any boy of eighteen *did* know what he was doing. D.L. Darroch, it seemed, was pretty good at pouring gasoline on troubled water, for promptly he inserted and even twisted a knife. "We've had a wishbone in the OHA quite long enough!" he exclaimed. "What we want is a backbone! If we are to continue as an amateur association we must blaze our own trail!"

Several speakers waved at the chairman for the right to speak. Sutherland got the first nod. Sutherland did not like the insulting reference to wishbone and backbone. "All I have ever had is this piece of spine up here [pointing to his spine] that I thought constituted a backbone." There was more, all directed at Darroch, but Sutherland did say before sitting down that he now would reconsider whether to withdraw his amendment.

Then Selke jumped in. He, too, took offence at Darroch's statements in the backbone line. He made a veiled reference to people letting a man "cheat continually while annually the executive in this convention wink at such acts . . . . If any of us know of anything being done that the executive are supposed to be winking at [he was glaring at Darroch] he should bring evidence before this executive on which it can act! This past spring I was absolutely disgusted at the offers, contracts, and so on, with which our young hockey players were tempted.

"You could not send your players on the ice but so-

called scouts would call them aside and offer them contracts at $40 a week. They were going to put the thing
over big. I took occasion to call attention to it in no
uncertain terms. Now, if we think our executive are winking at any of these practices we should tell them so.
Personally I think the executive is okay. The trouble is,
we [club officials] don't tell them enough."

William Easson, OHA president that year and chairman
of this stormy meeting, thanked Selke for the way he'd
laid it on the line. "If we had the cooperation of the officers
of the different clubs our path would not be the thorny
path it is today. The OHA people are doing their utmost
to keep things clean but they can't get that cooperation
from the officers of the different clubs, which is necessary
to ensure complete success." So, he said, turning to Darroch, "Follow Mr. Selke's advice and lay your facts on the
table. Then you can rest assured that your executive will
take prompt and effective action."

At this point William Fry moved that the matter be left
in abeyance until after the AAU had met. Higginbottom
seconded. The motion seemed certain to carry. But if
anyone thought it was all over, they were wrong. Higginbottom stayed on his feet. He might have been a little
miffed at being the seconder instead of the mover of the
motion to leave it to the AAU, which had been his idea
originally. He drew that fact to the meeting's attention,
along with a remark apparently directed at people from
the boondocks, or even Kingston. "I don't think anyone
in the room has more experience than I in boys taking a
wrong step in these matters. In Toronto it is happening
pretty nearly every day in the winter. Do you men think
that the moment a boy signs a professional contract, he
should be professionalized?"

Darroch interjected, "Absolutely!"

Higginbottom: "I do not! Supposing a boy, having
signed a contract with a professional hockey club, talks
it over with his father and then realizes for the first time

the position he is placing himself in for the rest of his life. To my mind a man is not a professional until he plays on the ice and takes the money for the service he is rendering. I have adhered to that view all my life."

The debate might have gone on as long as the adversaries had life and breath, had not George Dudley intervened.

As he understood it, he said, under the *present* rule a man automatically became suspended when he signed a pro contract, and that the proposed amendment was simply to make the rule clearer.

Sutherland: "Yes!"

Dudley: "Then, instead of amending the rule as Captain Sutherland suggests, perhaps we should pass a resolution drawing the attention of hockey players throughout the association's jurisdiction to the effect of the rule already in place. This would get away from the idea that we are making a change in the rule, and would be a sufficient warning to any player. I am afraid that if we vote this amendment down we might create an impression among hockey players that we are *approving* of their signing professional contracts."

It was a method that became a Dudley trademark in later years: to listen a long time and then find a way to compromise, without anyone being actually forced to change his mind. Seconded and passed, however, the idea was still on the delegates' minds. Next up was an argument about whether suspension in one sport, such as hockey, actually did apply to all the others. A delegate from the Galt area said he didn't think so; someone he knew had signed a contract to play in the NHL for New York Americans the following winter, but had continued to play baseball all summer and fall.

Question from the floor: "Who was that?"

Answer: "Normie Himes."

Another delegate, also from Galt: "He made an agreement with the Americans but did not sign a contract. Normie Himes handled the matter quite frankly. When he made up his mind to become a professional, he so informed the Galt Athletic Association and later left Galt under very auspicious circumstances. He was given a good sendoff." (Normie Himes, a colourful figure who always wore a black baseball cap when he played hockey, was a high-scoring centre for Americans until the mid-thirties and also acted as fill-in goalkeeper from time to time.)

Elwood Hughes, who had stuck around to hear the fun, said he, too, knew a boy who had signed to play pro hockey but had stayed in Toronto and played football until the hockey camp opened. "No mention of this contract was brought to our [the AAU's] attention by any association. We have only the boy's word that he did sign a contract, that he has never received a copper for his services, intends to play pro hockey this winter, and because there is no rule to cover that situation the Ontario branch of the AAU allowed him to play football this fall. I think we were absolutely right, for I'm confident in my own mind that that boy is an amateur today."

There were no recorded rejoinders by the hardhats. In the end, Dudley's motion that players should be informed of the existing rule was seconded by Higginbottom, carried unanimously, and the meeting – as was usual – ended with odds and ends, some amusing.

Sutherland had one more shot, in a vastly different direction. He moved that goalposts be moved six inches wider apart! All former goalkeepers in the audience, or relatives of goalkeepers, managed to defeat that motion.

Sheriff Paxton then moved a rule amendment to make it clear that goalkeepers had to wear ice skates during games. He described this as a correction, rather than anything new. The matter had never come up, that he knew of, until that year: "A goalkeeper wanted to go into a game wearing rubbers instead of skates." There was no specific rule against it, but one was needed. No one disagreed.

Next up to bat was Hewitt, with a motion that the defence area on the ice should be enlarged to sixty feet, from the present forty. He made this motion, he said, as chairman of the rules committee of the CAHA. In this and other possible changes he had been directed by the CAHA to meet with Frank Calder, president of the NHL, and arrange a uniform set of rules. The first thing he and Calder had agreed, he said, was on the ice-marking of hockey rinks, to save public confusion. This agreement, which he now proposed as an amendment to the rules, would provide that on all rinks 200 feet or over in length, the line enclosing the defence area should be sixty feet from the goal line. In all smaller rinks the ice would be divided into three equal sections between the goal lines. The distance behind the goal lines had to be at least five feet, with the ideal distance ten feet. So the ice on a 200-foot rink would be divided along these lines: ten feet behind each goal line, totalling twenty, and three sixty-foot areas, totalling 180. In the new sixty-foot defence areas the old rule would apply – forward passes allowed for the defending team but not the attacking team. This agreement made obvious, officially, the extent to which the amateurs and pros were embarked on a form of stan-dardization to make the game consistent in the way it looked to the public.

When this particular, and fairly typical, marathon meeting was over, the members filed out to eat, drink, and go to an NHL game – two free tickets for each OHA delegate having been provided by the Arena Gardens and Toronto's NHL club at that time, the St. Patricks.

What none of those men realized was that the decades-long debate about the professionalism of amateur players was about to come to a head publicly and result in the most profound changes of attitude ever experienced in the game. With George Dudley front and centre.

Chapter Eleven

LEGALIZING THE BOOTLEG AMATEURS

"Last year the Montreal Amateur Athletic Association's collection of speed boys won the Allan Cup and displayed a good deal of strength in outclassing Port Arthur in the finals. There were those unkind enough to suggest that in the M.A.A.A. outfit one A. stood for Amateur and another for Almost, with the further suggestion that they were financed by the Montreal Maroons. At any rate practically all . . . are now in the lineup, on the bench, or at the Windsor farm of the aforesaid Maroons."
— TED REEVE,
Maclean's Magazine,
January 1, 1931

Although this was not primarily an OHA affair, it was the most flagrantly provable phoney amateur issue of the time. The background was that before the 1929-30 hockey season the MAAA team—one of Canada's earliest and most famous, first holders of the Stanley Cup in 1892, and known for decades as the Winged Wheelers because their crest showed a wheel from which sprouted two soaring wings—was in a precarious financial condition. Disbanding seemed a distinct possibility until a secret agreement was made with the Montreal Maroons of the NHL. In return for seeing that the talented MAAA "amateurs" wouldn't miss any paycheques that season, Maroons would get possession of all the Winged Wheelers they wanted as soon as the Allan Cup was over, which is exactly what happened.

The most publicized individual in the affair was John Gallagher, a big Kenora-born (January, 1909) defenceman who had been a standout in his home town and in Fort William before going to the Wheelers. After the 1930 Allan Cup, Maroons made preliminary preparations to exercise what they considered to be their pro rights to various MAAA players, including Gallagher. Then it turned out that to Conn Smythe of the Toronto Maple Leafs, any or all other Wheelers could go to Maroons. But not Gallagher.

Smythe said that more than a year earlier, not long after Gallagher turned twenty, Leafs had signed him. The deal had been negotiated by a Leafs' scout, helped by a Kenora storekeeper for whom Gallagher worked when he wasn't playing hockey. The scout had handed over two $100 bills to seal the deal. This, of course, was well before the Winged Wheelers had shown up in Gallagher's horoscope, or tea leaves, at all.

However, a few months after Gallagher signed with Leafs and the team was getting ready for the 1929-30 season, he had written to say that he had changed his mind and wished to keep on playing amateur hockey. Smythe said, in effect, "Nuts to that. You signed a contract and we paid you for it. You're legally bound." What happened next – why Smythe apparently relented and let Gallagher join the Winged Wheelers to play another year of amateur hockey – is a mystery not recorded in anybody's neat and tidy minutes and did not become public knowledge at the time. But the following spring with the Allan Cup in the bag, Maroons claiming Gallagher's pro rights, and Smythe hollering foul, details of the earlier Leafs-Gallagher dispute were part of the fallout. There were claims and counter-claims, along with name-calling.

The Toronto and Montreal papers were full of the verbal battle between Smythe and James F. Strachan, the Montreal boss, over who had done what to whom.

The answers to most points at issue came in *Maclean's* of November 1, 1930, under the byline of Frederick Edwards, a Montreal writer. He wrote that the battle over Gallagher's original refusal to honour his contract with the Leafs in the fall of 1929 had ended only after a meeting in Toronto's Royal York Hotel among Smythe, Gallagher, and some unnamed OHA and CAHA officials. Gallagher, supported by the amateur reps, insisted that he would remain amateur and play that season with the Winged Wheelers. Smythe wouldn't retreat an inch. Invoking the rules governing amateurs at the time, he said there really *was* no argument because Gallagher couldn't even get an amateur card any more; he was a pro, had signed as such, and had committed the real no-no, accepting money.

This showed that Smythe, for all his own skill at bending rules, wasn't quite up on the amateur breed of rule-benders any more. Wrote Edwards: "The amateur officials broke the deadlock by flatly declaring that, pro contract or no pro contract, if the player wished to turn out as an amateur they would give him an amateur card."

They did so, whereupon Gallagher promptly joined the Winged Wheelers for their Allan Cup season. One can only guess how much better a deal he got from the "amateur" Wheelers and their backers than he'd been offered by the pro Leafs. Some pro owners at the time contended that leading amateurs in the OHA and elsewhere were getting paid more than some pros. And some amateur league officials in the Maritimes had confided to friends that maybe they should turn pro and save money on salaries.

However, in the Gallagher case the you-know-what hit the fan after Winged Wheelers had celebrated their Allan Cup and Montreal Maroons claimed him as their own. Smythe could have made a public stink after the first turndown, but for whatever reason he had just been biding his time.

Now he immediately went public with chapter, verse, and the appropriate documents on the agreement Gallagher had signed with Leafs well before any deal he might have made with Maroons. NHL president Frank Calder, after checking the documentary evidence, supported Leafs' claim. Amazingly, that turned out to be not enough: a majority of NHL club owners sided with Maroons. It's impossible to determine now the exact details of the backroom compromise that ensued, which was basically that Maroons got Gallagher, but – and it was a big but – were ordered to repay any expenses Smythe had incurred, including what he paid to sign Gallagher originally.

Undoubtedly, Smythe himself decided to accept that deal, perhaps even, in the last resort, suggested it. He had just signed the Ottawa star defenceman, King Clancy. Besides making him feel a lot better about Leafs' defence situation, the deal had left him desperately short of cash. Even though a much publicized race-track win had helped him pay the Ottawa club for Clancy, he'd still had to give five post-dated $5,000 cheques to close the deal. Getting his Gallagher investment back, no doubt with something extra, would have done much to help Smythe's exchequer.

At any rate, Gallagher went to Maroons for three years, then bounced around the league to Detroit and Canadiens before finishing his career in 1939 with New York Americans, his brief time as 1930's most celebrated bootleg amateur a distant footnote in the eventual abolition of that breed.

It wasn't obvious at the time, but the Gallagher case was something like the final outraged finger pointing at "amateur" hockey and demanding reform. Although the vast majority of people playing amateur hockey were in it for the sport alone, the 5 to 10 per cent who were on the take in a major way were the highest-profile "amateur" players in the land. That's why they got paid.

At the same time, the practice of paying hockey's best players was so deeply rooted, as old as the game itself, that it was impossible to abolish. So it had to be dealt with. Someone once said that if you can't stop something, try to make a deal. That's what George Dudley and men who supported him had to make happen over the next few years – not by shooting everything that moved, but by negotiation and compromise.

This was tougher than it would have been in some kind of an autocracy, but when finally and resolutely tackled, it proved not impossible. Hypocrisy had a stink that nobody in hockey liked. Frank Selke's years-ago statement that he admired the man who could go out and get paid what he was worth had been widely agreed-with for one main reason: Selke was merely expressing in hockey terms one of life's imperatives in Canada and in many other countries. Even one of the last of the great defenders of the amateur concept, Captain James Sutherland, was coming around, slow but sure. The OHA had problems it had been trying to solve by flanking manoeuvres, instead of tackling them head-on. To serious men in the OHA and elsewhere in hockey, the part of the game that was pure hypocrisy was getting to be too big a load to carry.

A flurry of high-profile articles in several national magazines, loudly expressing the public concern, both bared the process and pointed the way to the only reasonable solution. In the winter of 1930-31 alone the twice-monthly *Maclean's*, not noted for coverage or even much interest in sport, was foremost among those suddenly paying attention. Details flooded into print. In one passage of his article "Bootleg Amateurs," Frederick Edwards told of being in the sports department of a major daily newspaper when a messenger delivered a telegram to the sports editor from the mayor of a city elsewhere.

My friend the sports editor passed the yellow sheet on to me. This is what I read: "Wire me collect can you send us reliable goaltender, defense man and left winger stop. Guarantee easy jobs forty a week."

Edwards quoted the sports editor as saying he got similar telegrams every season. He usually knew of players looking for a chance somewhere out of town and would answer with names, addresses, and phone numbers of likely prospects. The reaction to that and other revelations in the Edwards piece included many outraged letters, plus others saying in effect, "Tell us something we don't know." The team that the unnamed mayor was offering cash to recruit for, Edwards wrote, wound up in that season's Allan Cup playdowns.

Maclean's followed that article three issues later with a rather self-righteous retort called "That Bootleg Bogey" by W.A. Hewitt's long-time friend, a respected Toronto writer, Henry Roxborough. Roxborough said he agreed with Edwards's sports ideals, and that if his charges about the Winged Wheelers were true, the Wheelers should get the bum's rush, be expunged from memory forever, with their names "withdrawn from all 1929 records and their shields removed from the trophies."

Having got that pious sentiment out of the way, Roxborough said Edwards had gone too far in stating that "there is almost no letter-of-the-law amateur hockey in Canada today." For the rest of his article, he fought the good fight on that narrow front, as obvious and inconsequential as it was.

Sure, a large number of hockey players played for the fun of it – for a variety of reasons, including relative mediocrity. The public and media debate ran on for a few years, but the gist of it came in the first *Maclean's* issue following Roxborough's laundering job. That, on January 1, 1931, was a piece called "Hockey's Hard Task" by Ted Reeve. Later to become major figure among sports journalists, a man to laugh with on some days but to believe all the time, Reeve simply knew the score. He had played football and lacrosse for money or fun or both. His reprise on how quickly good hockey talent turns pro, or takes money to play "amateur" hockey, led to a simple wisdom: "There is no need to break down and deplore this situation," he wrote. "If a lad can make his living, or enough to help him get into business, through his speed and skill, there is no reason why he should not take the opportunity. But it does cut down on the class of our hockey militia . . . " Cutting down on the class of our hockey militia – that was the rub.

Part of Reeve's thesis was that as so many of the best Canadian players turned pro, the watering down of Canadian senior teams had become a flood that, with the 1932 Olympics looming, threatened to wash away our pre-eminence in the sport. Sheer numbers supported him. Besides the ten-team NHL of the time, there were four other operating pro leagues: eight teams in the International League, six in the American Association, five in the Canadian-American League, four in the Pacific Coast League. Those thirty-three teams were manned almost entirely by Canadians, meaning that more than 300 – possibly closer to 400 – good Canadians were gone if not forgotten. The main damage was to the quality of senior play. Many of them, if they'd been able to use their hockey ability to get jobs at home, never would have left.

Harking back to the great Ontario senior teams that had won the Olympics, Granites in 1924 and Varsity Grads in 1928, Reeve wrote that under existing conditions it was very unlikely that Canada could assemble teams of that calibre again. U.S. college players might soon rule the roost in the Olympics. He was a little previous in that judgement, but the pressure was on in Canada to *do* something.

What might be done didn't occur to Reeve when he was writing that straightforward assessment, but it did occur to others. Hockey men in the OHA and elsewhere in Canada began to face reality.

The OHA rebel contingent was led initially by George Dudley, the man from Midland with his spectacles and quiet suits and businesslike manner, an OHA vice-president by 1932 and president by 1934. The main problem seemed to be that good Canadian amateur hockey players were sitting ducks for all those offers to hire their talent and pay for it. Dudley came gradually to the opinion that the only way to keep those players from turning pro was to rewrite the definition of an amateur, even by resorting – as eventually happened – to a form of doublespeak. In fact, if the matter had been left entirely to hockey men without the implacable AAU standing on its old traditions, the revolution would have come a few years earlier.

There was plenty of motivation, fuelled almost daily. Minutes of OHA executive meetings indicated inexorably that in addition to the big problems, little ones were flourishing as well. Applications for player transfers within the OHA showed month after month the most vivid evidence of team-packing. Hockey's marketplace had some big spenders. Pay-for-play's very illegality made it impossible to control; how do you put a salary cap on anything when no money is supposed to change hands at all?   As a result, every OHA senior team trying to put together a contender had to vie for players with clubs in the Maritimes and northern Ontario and elsewhere, all trying to buy the Allan Cup or Memorial Cup. Chatham, Newmarket, Hamilton, Niagara Falls, Windsor, and others began applying for several transfers at once, obviously in aid of keeping up with the Joneses.

The stakes were high, even among junior clubs, all through the season but especially at playoff time. A front-page story in the *Toronto Star* on March 31, 1933, ran under the top-of-the-page headline,

CHARGE HOCKEY STARS
ARE BEING EXPLOITED
FOR SAKE OF BIG GATES

The story was about the junior Newmarket Reds asking postponement of their second Eastern final game against Montreal because of injuries suffered in playing three playoff series and part of the fourth, ten games, in less than a month. They had played four against Stratford, three going to overtime; three against Sudbury, two of them overtime; two against Ottawa; and the opening of the Eastern final against Montreal.

The *Star* backed up its use of the word "exploited" by stating that since entering the playoffs Newmarket had drawn 108,338 paid admissions – 38,000 in the three games with Sudbury alone. Now ten Newmarket regular players, including the later-pro Pep Kelly, were on their injury list. Of course, the OHA had a vested interest in such series – a percentage of each playoff gate – and so was listed, even if far down, among the exploiters. When the team management made the postponement request to the OHA, W.A. Hewitt replied that if the team did not play its next game with Montreal it would be out of hockey, not only for these playoffs, but for life. The players then went to the club executive and said they'd play, as scheduled. They did, and went on to win the Memorial Cup.

With such balance-sheet numbers at stake for any team with championship hopes, sheer inventiveness at getting around transfer regulations perhaps should have become a recognized Olympic event. Late in 1933 four players who had moved to Oshawa, but whose transfers had been refused in October by the OHA, enrolled in something called the Oshawa Missionary College (Seventh Day Adventist) to claim transfer eligibility as legitimate students. They were Leo Lamoureux, a star junior who later played six years with Montreal Canadiens, Henry Frost, Bill Morris, and Bill Morrison. Newspapers had a grand time poking fun at Lamoureux stating with a straight face that even if he never played for Oshawa he intended to stay at the Missionary College and finish his part-time studies in history of education and chemistry. This, called a pre-med course, involved nine hours a week of study, which naturally wouldn't impinge on his ice time.

NOHA teams in the player hunt had a major advantage: several big mines with a ready welcome for hockey players at the employment office. The country then was deep in the Great Depression of the early 1930s when jobs were increasingly hard or even impossible to find. Refusing to let a player move to where he could make a wage would have seemed cruel. As the OHA didn't want to seem cruel, this factor played a part in many OHA transfers. At a single OHA executive meeting just before the 1933-34 season began, the transfers okayed included twelve senior players going from southern Ontario to jobs in the north: three to Kirkland Lake (from Barrie, Sydenham, and Guelph); three to Falconbridge (from Toronto, Hamilton, and Trenton); three to South Porcupine (one from Newmarket and two from Niagara Falls); others to Dome Mines and Timmins.

The OHA did put its foot down, or part way down, on six junior transfers. All six were already in Sudbury. One Toronto newspaper stated the situation succinctly: "Sudbury just sent a big car south and came home with it loaded to the gunwales with OHA junior stars. The trafficking in juniors is certainly going to be stopped."

But it wasn't easy to stop. The northerners flatly refused to give up their booty. This caused the OHA to yield, but only a little, ruling that the players could play in the north but would be barred from playoffs outside of the NOHA.

Under such intense pressure, the old authoritarian system on transfers was on the point of breaking down entirely. The to-become-famous names involved told their own story: Ray Getliffe, Bill Durnan, Gordon Drillon, Leo Lamoureux, Jack Portland, Hank Goldup, Carl Liscombe, Fred Hunt, Art Child, Eddie Bush, Johnny Crawford, Johnny (Peanuts) O'Flaherty, and others, all with a high price in the marketplace. This transfer problem had become so pervasive right across the country that early in 1934 the CAHA ruled that *no* interbranch transfers whatever would be allowed for the coming season. That didn't work either. An OHA motion a few months later asked urgently that in view of that summer's migration of OHA players to other branches, the CAHA – which had forbidden such transfers – should get off the pot and enforce its rules. Any player who had moved illegally must return to his last year's club, the OHA argued, or be banned from national championships.

This had no appreciable effect. The following year the OHA acted drastically on its own. For years Ontario had been permissive in transfers to U.S. clubs "to assist in getting the game established in the U.S." Now, it decided: no more! One U.S. club alone had applied for twenty-one players! "If applications are to be granted in such wholesale quantities many of our clubs will be completely wrecked."

Many players made the move to the U.S. anyway. When suspended by the OHA, the U.S. clubs did not honour the suspensions. At the same time, the migration of Canadians to play in Britain and elsewhere in Europe was growing. OHA suspensions were being ignored there, too. While some of these matters were beyond the OHA's control, other changes could be made – and were. One, long overdue to help clear the logjam of disputed player transfers, was to loosen residence rules and allow each team in the senior and junior categories a certain number of imports as a matter of course, as long as each was linked to legitimate employment or family moves or educational opportunities. Each senior team was allowed four. Junior teams were allowed two. And these numbers could be expanded on appeal.

At the same time, to strengthen its weakening grip where it could, the OHA rescinded a rule banning commercial teams from OHA play. This ban dated back to 1912, when the Eaton Hockey Club won the OHA and eastern championship. Commercial and industrial leagues had been flourishing ever since, competing with OHA teams for players and gate money. Now the best teams from those leagues could move into the OHA, along with a cut of their gate receipts.

In the midst of such changes, the transformation of Captain Sutherland from a hardhat to a realist was one of the time's more striking features. His own town of Kingston, he said, "had been stripped of between fifty and sixty players" who had accepted hockey jobs in other countries, leaving local clubs staggering to survive. Indicating the totality of his conversion, he said in an interview that he had changed his mind about a belief he'd had for forty years—that "the amateur rules and laws were entirely satisfactory."

Now, he went on, "it would seem better if, under certain restrictions and conditions, a wandering player were given an opportunity to accept genuine working positions in an open and above-board manner without the fear that the association will debar him from competition because he has moved to another town and accepted a position secured through his hockey ability." In other words, he was lining up with Dudley and the other revolutionaries. His battle cry in subsequent OHA meetings was, "This is 1935, not 1890."

Not long after that interview, Sutherland sponsored a revolutionary proposal: that any pro who wanted to return to amateur hockey should be granted that right immediately, with no waiting period. "These experienced players could do much to bring color and excitement back into our game," said the man who once had even opposed the hiring of former pros as coaches. His instant-amateur idea did not get OHA approval, on the grounds that only the CAHA and the AAU could make such a drastic change.

It was also becoming obvious that some deal had to be worked out with the NHL about grabbing OHA players, anytime, without warning. The most flagrant example of this came on February 22, 1935, when Montreal Maroons plucked future NHL star player and coach Hector (Toe) Blake from the first-place Hamilton Tigers and had him playing for Maroons in Chicago within two days. That staggered the Tigers in their run for the Allan Cup and produced some bitterness that might have been a factor a few weeks later when, ostensibly in protest against being ordered to play an eastern senior final playoff game in Toronto instead of Hamilton, Tigers dropped out of the Allan Cup playdowns entirely. They felt they'd just been pushed around too much.

This was a blow to the OHA, allowing the NOHA's Sudbury Falcons, whom Tigers had beaten earlier, to play Montreal and eventually go on in the Cup playoffs (losing to Winnipeg, which Tigers might not have done). So things weren't going well on the ice. Nor at the bank. Income in all amateur hockey jurisdictions was dropping, seen as a reflection of the severe drain on the talent clubs could put on the ice.

The OHA was being hit harder than anyone. Its stalwarts (Dudley had just taken over as treasurer on the death of his predecessor, Whitby's Sheriff Paxton) felt that a few years of financial losses should not be taken as a definitive indication that an organization is running on empty. Also, the OHA was not the only outfit in Canada that dropped a bundle in the depression years of the 1930s. Still, the *way* the OHA bank account took a dive seemed significant. When the rest of the country seemed to be in the depths, in 1933, the OHA had a surplus of about $20,000 in cash and bonds, with team registrations hovering close to the 200 mark, a record. In the next three years, when many other organizations were on the road to recovery, the OHA sagged drastically.

At one point in the early thirties the *Toronto Star* had called the OHA "the strongest sports organization in the world." But as revenue fell and expenses climbed, the same newspaper, covering the annual meeting of November 28, 1936, called the treasurer's report "a classic in red ink," with the operating deficit for the year at $5,662, and noted that executive and subcommittee meetings alone cost more money than the OHA took in during the year. Then there were travel expenses (president George Dudley lived in Midland), honorariums (W.A. Hewitt as secretary was getting $1,500 a year by then), office expenses, entertainment for visiting CAHA delegates that took the form of tickets to an NHL game, and so on.

Actually, that year's expenses of about $7,500 for such a large organization – at the time all unsalaried volunteers – seem trifling by today's standards, but when the organization's total income for the year was about one-quarter of expenses, something had to give.

Money wasn't the whole issue. The *Star* also used such epithets as the Ontario Hurrah Association, referred to its veteran executives as The Family Compact, and noted that at the annual meeting at which the above bad news was made public, no more than four or five delegates out of 125 made suggestions, asked questions, or indeed spoke at all. Newspaper coverage in general strongly implied that some executive members took up so much debate time with set speeches that eventually everyone else, hungry and thirsty, decided to let it go at that and head for the bar and the food.

The troubles besetting the OHA in the mid-thirties had a pattern consistent with what was happening in the game elsewhere. The hockey world was changing. Something had to be done to keep the better players at home. The only way, as Dudley and the reformers saw it, would be to offer players financial opportunities competitive with what they could get elsewhere. Dudley had been elected OHA president in 1934. From that vantage point he helped change the face of hockey forever.

His main obstacle was that while such associations as

the OHA were self-governing in their own jurisdictions, every important sport in the country was tied to the apron strings of the Amateur Athletic Union. Without an AAU card, a man could not play organized hockey or almost any other team sport of consequence and could not compete in the Olympics or any other international event. At the same time the AAU insisted that hockey abide by the AAU definition of an amateur: "one who derives no financial advantage from playing a game."

What that meant was that the most skilled 10 to 15 per cent of all the hockey players in the country had to get their AAU cards by lying through their teeth. That meant the AAU had to be the main target of reformers. As Ralph Allen wrote a few years later in *Maclean's*, in spite of the AAU being a formidable hazard, hockey's growing band of reformers "kept right on groping toward some compromise . . . . The most determined gropers were a University of Alberta professor named Dr. George Hardy and a Midland, Ont., barrister named George S. Dudley."

Determined is the word. In the spring of 1935, Dudley and Hardy between them enlisted enough support to get the CAHA to pass what was to become practically a Magna Carta of the sport, known at the time (at least outside of the AAU) as "the famous four points." The hockey men were looking the AAU squarely in the eye and saying that henceforth, to the CAHA, the definition of a hockey amateur had changed. The four points were:

1. That payment to hockey players by their clubs or employers, for salary or wages deducted while playing hockey, shall be permitted.
2. That a hockey player shall be allowed to capitalize on his ability as a player to obtain legitimate employment, and if he obtains legitimate employment as a result of his ability as a hockey player he shall not lose his amateur status.

3. That exhibition games between professionals and amateurs shall be allowed at the discretion and judgement of the various branches.
4. That, so far as the CAHA is concerned, a professional in another sport may still play in amateur hockey.

Later in 1935, when Dudley and Hardy presented the AAU annual meeting with this rebellious hockey manifesto passed by the CAHA, the AAU refused to budge.

But within a year its position had caused a public scandal, and at the 1936 AAU annual meeting in Regina, as Ralph Allen wrote, "Professor Hardy and Lawyer Dudley bobbed up with the four points again. This time they had fire in all four eyes." The ammunition they now had was well known to the public through news stories, editorials, letters to the editor, and cartoons that depicted the AAU as relics of a bygone age.

Earlier that year, preparing for the Winter Olympics in Germany, Canada's Olympic hockey team had been put together as a merger of Port Arthur and Halifax players. Before sailing for Germany, four Halifax players went public with a statement that they couldn't afford to go unless some provision was made for their families. Most had regular jobs. By refusing to accept the lost-time payment clause in the CAHA's four points, the AAU was saying that these players, about to leave to represent Canada at the Olympics, could not be compensated *by anyone* for loss of their regular income while they were away.

In that case, the players asked, who would pay the grocery bills?

The AAU stood firm. The players were banished from the team and, Allen wrote, were "replaced by Toronto and Montreal players whose sense of propriety was stronger and whose children – the cynics remarked – perhaps had smaller appetites."

It didn't help the AAU's cause that when the makeshift Canadian team did get to Germany they were beaten for the 1936 Olympic gold by England, which iced a team made up almost entirely of Canadians – two of whom had been suspended by the OHA for migrating without permission. The suspensions had been acknowledged, but not enforced, by British hockey authorities.

All that was known when Professor Hardy rose to reintroduce the Hardy-Dudley four points and began by saying, "Unless we are sunk in decrepitude and senatorial moribundity . . . " But the AAU, nothing if not stubborn, still refused. As it turned out, that marked the spot where the CAHA and AAU parted company forever. By the time another year rolled around and the AAU *did* accept the four points, it was academic. By then, working on Dudley's initiative and through the CAHA, anti-raiding agreements had been reached with the British Ice Hockey Association, the AAU of the United States, and the NHL. Some transfers would be allowed. "It's going to happen," Dudley said. "We might as well try to regulate it." Regulate they did. No Canadian club could lose more than one player a year. Any British, U.S. amateur, or pro team intending to give a Canadian a tryout was obliged to give notice by September 20 and make a decision one way or another a few weeks later.

Because of the one overriding issue of pay-for-play that Dudley, Hardy, and the CAHA had dealt with, the CAHA decided it had had enough of the AAU and formally withdrew. Soon other team sports joined the revolt. And as it transpired, hockey must have done exactly the right thing. With clubs now safe from massive raids and jobs for hockey players completely acceptable – men receiving wages or salaries in their regular jobs and a little or a lot extra for playing hockey – interest in the game practically exploded.

Across the land, from Cape Breton to British Columbia, especially where mining or oil production or smelting or manufacturing could provide players with jobs, communities began producing famous hockey teams – Kirkland

Lake Blue Devils, Kimberley Dynamiters, Trail Smoke Eaters, and Flin Flon Bombers right up there in national esteem with the older Oshawa Generals, Hamilton Tigers, Chatham Maroons, and the rest. The OHA bank account began to recover along with hockey interest throughout the country. All this was due in large part to what George Dudley and George Hardy had done to bring hockey finally into tune with the times.

And it wasn't over. Near the end of the decade, when Hardy relinguished the presidency of the CAHA and Dudley replaced him, the CAHA convention passed with scarcely a ripple one of the strangest definitions of amateurism in the history of sport, one certainly not in the tradition of John Ross Robertson. "An amateur hockey player," the key sentence read, "is one who has not engaged in, or is not engaged in, organized professional hockey."

Testing this definition against the Olympic oath right then, and either winning the point or quitting the Olympics, would have made for some hectic times on the sports and editorial pages. When war in Europe caused the 1940 Olympics to be cancelled, the showdown was postponed. Nevertheless, it was still in some minds in 1940 when George Dudley, then the CAHA president as well as remaining high in the power structure of the OHA as past president and treasurer, addressed the issue.

"If the Olympics are revived after the war, Canada will want to send a team, of course," Dudley said. "But if our rules prove unacceptable to Olympic officials, I guess we'll stay at home."

GEORGE DUDLEY *as a young lawyer in the early twenties. Older and tougher, in 1936 he helped free the slaves.*

CYCLONE TAYLOR *was his era's greatest. But in 1904, when he refused to leave his home in Listowel and join Toronto Marlboros, the OHA barred him from hockey for a whole season.*

GOLDIE PRODGERS
*was an OHA amateur
playing pro under a
phony name when his
cover was blown. He
won Stanley Cups
after that.*

Rich and powerful
JOHN ROSS ROBERTSON
*the bane of fake
amateurs. He ran
the OHA partly by
dealing out
suspensions with
both iron hands.*

*In World War Two, many former OHA stars –
later to play in the NHL – wound up in
uniform. From left: Bob Goldham, Toronto
Marlboros; Johnny McCreedy, Lakeshore Blue
Devils; Frank Eddolls, Oshawa Generals; Lex
Chisholm, once an Oshawa intermediate.*

W.A. HEWITT, *an
OHA power for more
than fifty years was
responsible for
Cyclone Taylor's
one-season suspen-
sion. Cyclone never
forgave him.*

For many years Toronto Marlboros fed junior stars to the Leafs. **BOB GOLDHAM** *wears the 1940 crest . . .*

. . . which had changed by 1956 when **BOB PULFORD** *scored ten goals in five games as Marlboros won the Memorial Cup.*

This was not for the Stanley Cup – it was the Uxbridge Black Hawks winning the OHA intermediate B championship in 1963. Kids poured to the ice. Their parents stood along the frosty walls to cheer. For 100 years at all levels of the game in Ontario, hometown dreams have been made of this.

STAN MIKITA *of St. Catharines Teepees as an OHA junior all-star in 1959 – just before his great Chicago years.*

Tough and crusty **FRANK BUCKLAND** *moved from coaching and managing Peterborough teams to handling every major elected job in Ontario hockey. His high level of effectiveness and long volunteer record took him eventually to Hockey's Hall of Fame.*

MIKE RODDEN, *famous athlete, referee, and sportswriter, was a fiery presence when the OHA probed the 1951 Kingston fix.*

OTTAWA, OHA CHAMPIONS, 1891-93. *Top row, left to right. W.C. Young, F.M.S. Jenkins, H.Y. Russell, R. Bradley. Bottom row: A Morel, Dr. H.S. Kirby, C.T. Kirby, J. Kerr.*

BERLIN, OHA INTERMEDIATE CHAMPIONS, 1897. *Top row, left to right: L. Hueglin, trainer; J.H. Seagram, coverpoint; J. Gibson, point; H.F. Boehmer, goal. Sitting : P.J. Livingston, forward; E.F. Seagram, captain, forward; F.G. Oliver, secretary, manager; W.H. Dickson, forward; J.A. MacDonald, forward.*

KINGSTON FRONTENACS, OHA, 1899. *Top row, left to right: W.H. Waddell, wing; J.M. Shaw, president; A. McRae, point. Middle row: K. McDowell, coverpoint; D.J. Mc Dermott, sec. treas.; M. Murray, captain; J. Sutherland, manager; C. Clarke, wing. Bottom row: R. Hiscock, goal; S. Wilson, centre. Inset: H. Reyner, centre.*

OHA JUNIOR CHAMPIONS, 1900. *Top row, club executives J.W. Chowen, G. Caslake, W. Miller, C.R. Rankin. Middle row: C. Lightfoot, right wing; B. Gordon, coverpoint; D.M. Ferguson, president; R. Morrison, point; W. Hern, left wing. Bottom row: J.S. Rankin, rover; W. Woods, goal; F. Poland, centre.*

TORONTO ST. GEORGES, OHA INTERMEDIATE CHAMPIONS, 1901. *Top row: H.W. Bonnell, manager; J.G. Merrick, president; E.G. Platt, point; A.A. Wilson, secretary; J.L. Hynes, right wing. Middle row: A. Pardoe, centre; S.H. Henderson, honorary vice-president; A.B. Gillies, captain and rover; C.C. Temple, goal. Bottom row: J.C. Webster, left wing; A.E. Bish, cover point.*

PARIS, OHA INTERMEDIATE CHAMPIONS, 1903. *Top row: F. J. Murray, secretary; H. Munn; F.J. Nelson, president; A. Kuhlman; K. Harvey, manager. Middle row: E. Howell, D. Adams, W. Taylor, E. Gillard. Bottom row: R. Brown, A. Fraser.*

ST. MICHAEL'S COLLEGE, OHA SENIOR AND ALLAN CUP CHAMPIONS, 1910. *Top row: Herbert Matthews, right wing; E. Winnett Thompson, goal; W.J. (Jerry) LaFlamme, captain and centre; James Dissette, coverpoint; William Richardson, left wing. Middle row: Frank Dissette, manager; Rev. Father Henry Carr, president; James A. Murphy, coach. Bottom row: Peter Spratt, point; Charles Roche, rover.*

COLLINGWOOD, OHA INTERMEDIATE CHAMPIONS, 1910. *Clockwise from bottom left: executives H. Foulie, J.A. Gibb, H. Telfer, J. Patterson, M. Mitchell, W. Court, S. Bailey, M. Clark. On the ice: F. Cook, goal; W. Beattie; B. Cameron; H. Cain; E. Fryer, captain; J. Belcher; J. Burns; A. McLennan; M. Clark.*

ORILLA, OHA JUNIOR CHAMPIONS, 1913. *On the ice: N. Cooke, goal; R. Reid, point; K. McNab, coverpoint; Quinn Butterfield, rover; G. Moore, manager; A. Tudhope, centre; R. Jupp, right wing; P. Thornton, left wing. Bottom row: G. Perryman, spare; A.P. James, physical director; R.H. Jupp, honorary president; C.L. MacNab, president; J. Tudhope, treasurer; N. Johnston, spare.*

OTTAWA ALERTS, CANADIAN LADIES CHAMPIONS, 1923. *Top row: P. I. O'Connor, coach; Mrs. E. P. Day, chaperon; L. Vernon, G. Greer, Mrs. I. A. Burkholder, chaperon; C.L. McKinley, manager. Middle row: F. Dawson; E. Anderson; E. Ault; T. Turner, captain; L. Forward; B. Hagan; A. O'Connor. Bottom: S. Moulds; M. Giles.*

SAULT STE. MARIE GREYHOUNDS, OHA SENIOR AND ALLAN CUP CHAMPIONS, 1924.
Insets: executives James Gemmell, James Jones, W. J. Edwards. Back row: Fred Morgan, Arthur Nicholls, J.D. Tipton, Stan Brown, Fred (Bun) Cook, George McNamara, James (Flat) Walsh, Harry Wood. Front row: Frank (Dutch) Cain, Johnny Woodruff, Bill Philips, Babe Donnelly, Roy Lessard, Garnet (Wasp) Campbell, James Fahey.

MARLBORO ATHLETIC CLUB, OHA JUNIOR CHAMPIONS, 1929. *Top row: left defencemen Ellis Pringle and Harry Montgomery; honorary president Bert Cartan; goalie Laurie Moore; honorary vic-president Charles Coulter; right defencemen Red Horner and Alex Levinsky. Left, middle: Jim Darragh, left wing. Right, middle: Max Hackett, right wing. Bottom row: Harvey (Busher) Jackson, left wing; Clarence Christie, goal; Conn Smythe, vice-president; Frank J. Selke, honorary coach; Eddie Convey, centre; William J.D'Alesandro, manager; Bill Christie, vice-president; Bob Gamble, centre; Charlie Conacher, right wing, captain.*

TORONTO GRANITES, OHA SENIOR CHAMPIONS, 1923; OLYMPIC CHAMPIONS, 1924. *Left insets, top to bottom: W. A. Hewitt, manager; Frank Rankin, coach; Ernie Collett, goalie. On the ice: Harry Watson, Bert McCaffrey, Sig Slater, Beattie Ramsay, Hooley Smith, Dunc Munroe (captain), Harold McMunn, Jack Cameron.*

SUDBURY CUB WOLVES, OHA JUNIOR AND MEMORIAL CUP CHAMPIONS, 1932. *Players (circled) clockwise from left: Adelard LaFrance, Jr., Gordon Grant, A.J. Powell, Peter Fenton, Anthony Healey, Jack McInnes, Dalton (Nakina) Smith, Red Porter (captain), Hector (Toe) Blake, Max Bennett, Larry LaFrance, Donald Price, Ivan Fraser, Maurice Dabous, Robert McInnes, Borden Caswell. Middle row: Dr. H.C. Nash, Jack Dillon, coach Sam Rothschild, manager Max Silverman, J.J. Ferry, Adelard LaFrance, Sr. Bottom row: Dr. W. A. McCauley, W.J. Barager, Dr. W.R. Manchester, Ernest Craig, Ralph D. Parker.*

WEST TORONTO NATIONALS, OHA JUNIOR AND MEMORIAL CUP CHAMPIONS, 1936. *Top row: Jack Sinclair, Carl Gamble, Ted Robertson, F. Murray, Johnny Crawford, Reg Langford, Bert Conacher, D. Fritz, H. Newland (trainer), Roy Conacher, Red Heron, Alf Johnson. Bottom row: Bill Thompson, Bill Jennings, Johnny (Peanuts) O'Flaherty, W. Kerr, Dr. H. MacIntyre, manager Harold Ballard, G. Shill, Bobby Laurent, Torchy Hall.*

OSHAWA GENERALS, OHA JUNIOR AND MEMORIAL CUP CHAMPIONS, 1939. *Top row: trainer Sam Johnson, manager Matt Leyden, coach Tracy Shaw, vice-president C.E. McTavish, secretary Neil Hezzelwood, treasurer S.E. McTavish, executive W. Pearson. Middle row: Joe Delmonte, Don Daniels, Jim Drummond, George Ritchie, Gerry Kinsella, Nick Knott, Orville Smith, Jud McAtee. Bottom row: Dinny McManus, Norm McAtee, Billy Taylor (captain), president J.B. Highfield, Roy Sawyer, Gar Peters, Les Colvin, and stick boy Harry Tresise.*

COURTESY OHA ARCHIVES

PETERBOROUGH ARMY TRAINING CENTRE, OHA SENIOR B CHAMPIONS, 1942. *Top row: Frank Buckland, manager Fred Scates, Eddie Starr, Johnny Godfrey, Les Burton, Perce Nichols, coach Jim Ellis, Don Crowe, Joe Blewitt, Drake Jopling, Din Reilly, treasurer Max Glover, Lieut. W. Bowerman. Front row: trainer Shocky Mein, Doug Mortimer, Bun Kingdon, Ray Harding, Honey Tompkins, Johnny Johnston, Art Heal, Bruce Bennett, Corporal Spencer Kitchen.*

COURTESY OHA ARCHIVES

TORONTO MARLBOROS, OHA SENIOR AND ALLAN CUP CHAMPIONS, 1950. *Top row: trainer Art Marshall, Danny Lewicki, Howie Lee, Don Rope, Bobby Hassard, Frank Sullivan, Buck Gilhooly, assistant trainer Bobby Haggert. Middle row: statistician Joe Lamantia, Don Lockhart, Al Buchanan, Pat Boehmer, Scotty Mair, Charlie Blair, Gord Hannigan, public relations man Spencer Gaylord (Spiff) Evans. Front row: George (Chief) Armstrong, Red Johnson, manager Harold Ballard, Flash Hollett, coach Joe Primeau, Johnny McLellan, Hugh Bolton.*

Man, that was a hockey team! Celebrants above include Wren Blair, Harry Sinden, Charlie Burns, and many other Whitby Dunlops who later became household names across Canada. This night, however, they were far from world fame. They had just won the 1956 OHA senior B championship, losing the first two games to Woodstock and sweeping the next four. In 1957 it would be the OHA senior A championship and Allan Cup; in 1958, the world championship in Oslo; in 1959, another Allan Cup.

MONTREAL JUNIOR CANADIENS, OHA JUNIOR AND MEMORIAL CUP WINNERS, 1970. *Top row: Pierre Brind'amour, Ian Turnbull, Allan Globensky, Michel Latreille, Hartland Monahan, Paulin Bordeleau. Middle row: Bobby Stewart, Robert Lalonde, Richard Lemieux, Scott MacPhail, Serge Lajeunesse, Richard Martin, Claude Moreau, John Garrett, Phil Langlois. Front row: Michel Dion, Jocelyn Guevremont, Phil Wimmer, Gilbert Perreault, Normand Gratton, Roger Bedard, Robert Guidon, Wayne Wood.*

Chapter Twelve

THE FIX WAS ON IN KINGSTON

"I can't figure what was in that George Patterson's mind, to suggest such a thing."
— M.L. (TORY) GREGG
of Wingham,
with one eye open

When the OHA's fiftieth anniversary arrived in November of 1939, Canada was about ten weeks into World War Two, with the Canadian Army's famed First Division getting ready to sail for Europe. The OHA never was (and still is not) anxious for government intervention in its affairs but in this case did the loyal thing and asked, "Do we keep on playing, or what?" If there was a written reply it has not survived the ensuing fifty years, but the OHA recorded the outcome as: "In accordance with the expressed wish of the Government of Canada, the OHA has decided to operate its schedule and Cup playdowns as usual this season." As in World War One, residence rules were suspended for all players in the military. They could change teams any time they changed postings. Military teams could enter OHA leagues at any level. This led to a honeymoon situation that the military itself screwed up, but that was to come.

Meanwhile, although the *Globe and Mail*, for instance, led or echoed several other publications when it editorialized that young hockey players should be shooting rifles instead of pucks, and an Ontario judge declaimed,"When I read the sports pages I see great Goliaths of men in the wrong uniforms," the OHA ploughed on. Its fiftieth anniversary dinner in the Royal York Hotel on November 25, 1939, was attended by the bigdomes of every amateur hockey association in eastern Canada as well as presidents Frank Calder of the NHL and Tom Lockhart of the United States Amateur Hockey Association, plus local and provincial politicians. In the throng were all the long-time OHA stalwarts: Jim Sutherland from Kingston, W.A. Hewitt, secretary then for thirty-six years, George Dudley, and a host of others (not so well known) from all those Ontario hamlets, villages, towns, and cities where hockey was part of living and breathing.

The speeches were confidently warlike both in the matter of fighting the war and of launching the OHA into its second half-century. The thought was often expressed from the podium that the dedication and fighting spirit of hockey would help Canadians to be fighting men feared by any enemy, while at home continuance of the game would bolster the morale of their loved ones left behind. In the long and sometimes windy evening, there was no dearth of such brave and hopeful speeches.

As it happened, hockey did continue about as usual for the first winter of the war. Then the great blows began to batter the Allied cause. The German blitzkrieg overran much of western Europe in the spring and summer of 1940. Enlistments soared. Japan's devastating attack on Pearl Harbor on December 7, 1941, piled on the agony. Lacking enough men to fill lineups, hockey clubs began to fold. The number of OHA teams began a precipitous slide from 168 in 1940 to eighty-three by 1945, creating severe belt-tightening times for the two OHA presidents of that period, Ross Clemens of Hamilton and F.W. (Dinty) Moore of Port Colborne. Moore had been in goal for Canada at the 1936 Olympics. He also refereed for twenty years, including during his three years as president.

Despite the slide in team numbers during the war years, crowds were good, especially during playoffs – where the OHA traditionally scored much of its income. On Ross Clemens's initiative in 1940, urging OHA teams to help homefront organizations involved in the war effort, about $8,000 was raised in 1940, rising to $20,000 in 1941. Some of this came in direct donations from the OHA, made possible by deep cuts in its own spending. Travel allowances for executive members were reduced by 25 per cent. Executive meetings, normally running to a dozen or more a year, were cut to three. That put the heat on the busy few who could travel with minimum difficulty to the office at Maple Leaf Gardens. For long stretches only the president of the time – Ross Clemens, 1940-42, and Dinty Moore, 1942-45 – plus old warriors Hewitt as secretary, Dudley as treasurer, and a part-time typist, held the fort. They made the rulings, ordered the suspensions, spied out the fakes, kept the OHA's long mandate in good repair.

It was an irony during the middle part of the war that the armed services did more than any other single element to draw bad publicity for hockey. This criticism was not for the game itself. From the corner rinks on up, the sights and sounds of rough and tumble, speed and skill were there approximately as usual. But the armed services sometimes used hockey for power games of their own, the RCAF and Army the main offenders in what eventually was the undoing of service hockey entirely.

It happened in this sequence. After the first quiet winter of war, shock after shock hit home. Public and individual concern was heightened over battles that cost many lives. There was Dunkirk in 1940, the Battle of Britain later that year, the disaster of Dieppe in 1942 when more than 900 Canadians were killed or fatally wounded, many more wounded not fatally, and 1,944 taken prisoner. Partly because these events hastened call-ups and enlistments, putting thousands more young men in uniform, and partly because immigration officials got tough on Canadian NHLers crossing the border to play for U.S. teams, many professionals were enlisting.

With all that hockey talent getting into uniform either due to personal inclination or to anticipate the certainty of being drafted, several military commands began actively recruiting hockey stars for their own teams. In February of 1942, for instance, the entire so-called Kraut line from Boston Bruins – Milt Schmidt, Porky Dumart, and Bobby Bauer – enlisted in the RCAF and wound up in Ottawa.

"Why Ottawa?" people asked. "Why not their home town, Kitchener?" Ask the RCAF. Its big hockey team was in Ottawa.

And in Cornwall, where future NHL coaches and managers Punch Imlach and Tommy Ivan were in uniform and running the good Cornwall Army team, they wouldn't have minded having the Kraut line aboard along with their own assortment of ex-pros.

Anyway, having arrived in Air Force blue near playoff time and with all OHA residence requirements suspended for the duration as far as servicemen were concerned, the Krauts wound up playing alongside several other former pros for Ottawa RCAF. Major Conn Smythe, on wartime sabbatical from running the Leafs, once estimated that eighty former pro players were in uniform by that time. But nobody else had the Kraut line. Within weeks after their arrival in uniform, Ottawa RCAF was breezing past other excellent pro-stiffened teams and that spring won the Allan Cup.

In 1943 it was the Army's turn. That year Ottawa's Army team, called the Commandos, was almost entirely made up of ex-pros. Neil and Mac Colville and Alex Shibicky from New York Rangers were among them, as well as Bingo Kampman from Toronto Maple Leafs. The Commandos ran up big scores against everybody they met on the way to winning that year's Cup.

All this finagling, the RCAF one year and Army the

next, fuelled civilian resentment. Public criticism of the
Department of National Defence for fostering such a star
system, former pros wearing the uniform while seemingly
exempt from overseas drafts, was loud and getting louder.
Some games pitting NHL stars against run-of-the-mill
seniors were travesties. If some base officer in charge of
his unit's hockey team needed a centre, and a good NHL
centre enlisted somewhere, this event soon hitting the
papers, and before the guy's new boots stopped squeaking
he would be drafted to join other former pros on a service
team.

The OHA was torn. Its cancellation of residence and
other requirements for anyone in uniform was partly
responsible, but how could even the most canny OHA
executive have thought of inserting a rule that would bear
on enlistment decisions in the Army, Navy, or Air Force?
Yet, as it turned out, many such decisions obviously were
being made by some uniformed conniver looking for a
better hockey team.

Of course, the players themselves usually had little or
nothing to do with how they were being used. Many
enlisted and fought. Some were killed in action. Others
might have been lured to this team or that by promises
that they'd be kept as instructors in Canada with overseas
service unlikely, but if so that was unproved. Still, after
the bad-publicity seasons of 1942 and 1943 ended with
the public in full cry, that autumn Defence Headquarters,
in a belated onrush of common sense, withdrew these
all-star teams from competition entirely. Also, although
thirty-seven service teams competed in the OHA's lower
categories in the 1943-44 season, Defence Headquarters
barred them all from going on into championship playdowns. The idea obviously was to avoid drawing public
attention to the fact that such teams were still here, while
men who had been wounded three times "over there"
were being sent back into battle because of the shortage
of reinforcements.

Inevitably, the effect the war had on hockey caused some rapid revisions in hard-won deals between the amateurs and the pros. Dating from the rapprochement of 1936, before which amateurs and pros ran their shows from what George Dudley once called "two watertight compartments," their relationship had been friendly, even kindly. That was when the pros had agreed not to touch juniors at all and to compensate amateur teams on a sliding scale starting at $500 per player who made the NHL, less if he stayed in the minors. In 1941 this had amounted to $17,000 across Canada ($4,000 of it to the OHA), pieced out on a pro-rata basis to every team the new pro had played for as an amateur.

But war changed the rules. As the draft age in Canada went down to twenty and below (eventually to reach seventeen and a half) and seasoned pros enlisted either willingly or one jump ahead of their conscription notice, the pro teams were feeling hard done by, and with good reason. The original payments had dated from the minute a player signed a pro contract. Even if he didn't make the team, the payment had to be made. Sometimes a player would sign, the money would be paid, and within weeks or months the player would be called up. In 1943 the pros could produce evidence that 75 per cent of amateurs they had signed and paid for had wound up in the armed services. As a result, the pros proposed, and in 1943 the amateurs accepted, that instead of paying for each player, each NHL club would make a flat payment of $500 to the CAHA and each minor pro club $300.

This would total a good deal less than before but, as Dudley put it to the OHA in 1943, obviously the only players the pros could use to replace pros entering the armed services at the time were married men over thirty who were not affected by the draft or juniors not old enough to be affected. Something had to give.

"This being so," Dudley said, "we knew we'd have to make concessions to the pros and we did so readily. I think you'll acknowledge that it was absolutely essential. Had we not done so, the NHL could have said, 'Gentlemen, we are sorry but we cannot continue the agreement' and we would have been left with no protection or compensation at all." As part of the new deal, protection of juniors was suspended for the duration of the war, with some as young as sixteen and seventeen playing alongside gnarled old-timers in the NHL. As a natural extension of the junior teams losing many players to the pros, regulations against midget and juvenile players playing junior were also relaxed for the duration.

All this happened during the summer months before withdrawal of the armed services from advanced-stage hockey. This, although lack of clubs had caused senior B, intermediate B, and junior C categories to be abandoned, restored the senior field to players both young and old who, for reasons of age, marital status, or jobs in essential war work, were exempt from the draft. Still, in 1944 and 1945, there weren't enough good seniors to maintain the OHA's long tradition of excellence at that level. The shortage was the same across the country, so much so that when northern Ontario's Frood Mines beat Hamilton for the Ontario championship in 1945, that was all. The Allan Cup trustees decided to skip that year.

Yet in all the soul-searching and scrambling that went on in hockey between 1943 and 1945, one major rule change was made that would alter the game forever: introduction of the centre-ice red line. In the joint NHL-CAHA rules committee (W.A. Hewitt a member) the NHL originally had proposed a two-inch line. Hewitt and the CAHA managed to get it up to twelve inches, where it has remained.

The seniors did recover with some fine teams from the late 1940s to the early 1960s, but in 1945 the Memorial Cup was the only national championship still alive. St. Michael's College won it, drawing 65,000 to Maple Leaf Gardens for a good five-game final with Moose Jaw. Not only St. Michael's but other junior playoff teams along the way that spring were loaded with young future pros. Among the stars of St. Michael's Tod Sloan was then seventeen; Jim Thomson just turned eighteen; others included Gus Mortson and Johnny McCormack. Doug Harvey played with Montreal in the eastern junior play-offs and Bert Olmstead and Metro Prystai were on the Moose Jaw team beaten by St. Michael's.

Soon after that last wartime national playoff, the fighting men were coming home and the OHA was fully back in business, in a single year doubling its membership: 166 teams in 1945-46 from the previous season's eighty-three.

In the association at that time usually four men from the general membership were elected to the executive each year. Also, the president had the right to appoint three more. In the fall of 1946, when the outspoken George Panter of Gravenhurst replaced Dinty Moore as president, he appointed three executive members. Two were more or less expected, as they represented two major affiliates of the OHA – John Nelson of the gigantic Toronto Hockey League, which had signed a new agreement with the OHA that year to protect each other from player raids, and Maxie Silverman of the Northern Ontario Hockey Association, an OHA affiliate since 1919. The third Panter appointee was a tall, energetic, and commanding man, Frank Buckland of Peterborough, an executive at Canadian General Electric.

Anyone who has followed OHA history so far might agree that the outstanding personalities had been John Ross Robertson, W.A. Hewitt, and George Dudley. Frank Buckland belongs in that company. For Robertson, the role was leadership. For Hewitt, it was being the grey eminence who in his deceptively mild way knew where all the bodies were buried. George Dudley, in his prime as president of the OHA and then president and finally secretary-manager of the CAHA, ranked high among the

best men amateur hockey in Canada ever produced. Buckland really resembled none of them. He hewed his own
reputation. Of all the men whose part-time vocation for
significant periods of their lives was specifically the
Ontario Hockey Association, few have approached his
record of sheer time-consuming dedication.

For some years before the mid-1940s he had attended
OHA annual meetings as simply another foot soldier in
the throng of delegates representing individual clubs,
leagues, or associations. He made himself known as a
cogent, and sometimes pungent, debater, a delegate
increasingly noticed by the OHA brass, as witness Panter
appointing him to the executive. In the year following his
appointment, he was one of the four winning election.
From then on often he headed the poll, and in the 1950s
took the course that most presidents right back to John
Ross Robertson had followed – a term or two as a vice-
president, and then the presidency.

Meanwhile, he followed a herculean course that would
long outlast most presidencies. Besides rewriting the OHA
Constitution, Regulations and Rules of Competition as
set forth in the OHA manual, he set about compiling a
complete record of each OHA season back to its beginning
in 1890. These summaries, setting forth facts Buckland
garnered from OHA records as well as newspaper accounts,
expanded year by year from two or three single-spaced
typewritten pages covering the 1890-91 season to whatever number of pages were needed to record everything
that needed recording: executive lists; rule changes; major
crises, debates, or agreements with other hockey associations in Canada and abroad; OHA group standings year by
year.

His accounts of playoff series included scores of each
game and (in senior A and junior A) all who had scored,
plus how OHA champions fared in Allan Cup and Memorial Cup national playdowns, game by game, including
scorers on both sides. It is a record of archival significance,

too exhaustive to include here in full as it covers about 700 single-spaced typewritten pages. But without Frank Buckland's basic research, much of what is recorded in this book would have taken many more years to compile.

When Buckland became an OHA executive, the association for many years had been run from W.A. Hewitt's office in Maple Leaf Gardens. This office was a holdover from when Hewitt resigned the sports editorship of the *Star* in 1931 and accepted Conn Smythe's offer to become general manager of all attractions except hockey at the then brand-new Gardens. While Hewitt's involvement as a Gardens executive diminished and eventually ended over the years, his office along with all the OHA records stayed there. This didn't always sit well with other OHA people, who sometimes thought Hewitt was too close to the pros for comfort.

In January, 1948, Hewitt became seriously ill. Although he recovered, from then on he took it easier. With his illness, the volatile George Panter, then ending his term as OHA president, assumed the load of running the OHA's day-by-day affairs. But he and other OHA executives felt uneasy working in the temple of the pros. By May, when Hewitt's health was improving, he, Panter, and Dudley rented new quarters just across the street from the Gardens above a Bank of Commerce branch at 67 Carlton. Panter was named assistant secretary and then, when his presidency was over, took on the salaried role of running the OHA office as business manager for the next three years.

An account of what happened next comes mainly from Bill Hanley, a young Torontonian who had been hooked on hockey from boyhood and who eventually was to serve as the OHA's business manager for twenty-seven years, into the late 1970s, and in the late 1980s was inducted into the Builders' category of the Hockey Hall of Fame, to join other one-time OHA stalwarts John Ross Robertson,

Francis Nelson, W.A. Hewitt, P.D. Ross, James Sutherland, George Dudley, and Frank Buckland. How Hanley got his first foot into the door of the OHA is not untypical of the organization. Hewitt had taken on the secretaryship as a sideline to his newspaper job, never knowing it would last almost for life. Hanley's arrival and long-time service was equally due to happenstance.

As a boy on Toronto playgrounds and later a player with Oakwood Collegiate's hockey team, Hanley had been friends with another youngster, Spencer Gaylord (Spiff) Evans. After service overseas with Conn Smythe's 30th Battery during World War Two, Evans had been hired by Smythe at the Gardens for a variety of front-office jobs.

Hanley recounts what happened then. "One day just after the war I met Spiff on the street and we got talking. At the time I was working in our family's business, a chain of butcher shops, but I wasn't enjoying it. Spiff asked me, 'How'd you like to work on the penalty bench at the Gardens for amateur hockey?' So I worked the penalty bench for junior and senior games. At the time Ace Bailey, the old Leaf from the 1930s, was penalty timekeeper for Maple Leaf games and also coached the junior team at the University of Toronto.

"One time, this would be in the late 1940s, his team was going away to play over Christmas somewhere and I filled in for him as pro penalty timekeeper. Later, when he took a coaching job out of town for a while, I filled in again doing the penalty bench for the pros. So I was around, and one day Spiff asked if I'd take over as statistician for junior A and senior A games. I'd have to take these statistics across the street to the OHA office. That's how I got to know George Panter.

"One morning on the street I met him going for coffee. While we stood there chatting he said he was looking for an assistant to help him run the OHA office.

"I said, 'I'd be kind of interested in that.'

" 'Come and have coffee,' he said, and when he explained the job to me I took it on the spot.

"That's how I got started with the OHA. I loved it. That Church and Carlton office, and the later one we moved to a few years later a little farther north on Church Street across from the Gardens, were right in the middle of the hockey world. You'd walk out into the street and in one block you'd hear fifty different rumours."

One indication of how Hanley felt about his job was something of a throw-in during a 1987 interview about his OHA years. "For part of each year, the championship teams would keep the cups they'd won, but they had to turn them in at a certain date so they could be shined up and ready to present to the next winner," he said. "I was in that OHA job for a long time, but it never failed to thrill me to walk into the storage area where we kept the cups. We used to put everybody's name from each champion-ship team on the shields. I'd go there and spend an hour just walking around and looking at this one or that one, reading the names and thinking, 'Oh, what a hockey team!'

"I was just like a little kid in a candy shop, looking at the cups and seeing the names of some of those old teams, players I'd heard about, players I'd read about, players I'd seen. I could go there this week and again next week and I'd still have that same feeling."

For years the OHA had held its executive meetings at the Royal York Hotel free of charge, because when the hotel opened in the late 1920s Hewitt had been one of those invited to the opening reception. There he'd encountered the Canadian Pacific Railways boss at that time, Sir Edward Beattie, who, maybe having had a drink or two, said that as long as he was running things all those dedicated volunteers in the OHA could have meeting rooms at the CPR's Royal York free of charge. By the 1940s, with Sir Edward gone, the charges started out small but began to mount. "Eventually," Hanley said, "the executive decided to save the money and hold its meetings in this little room we had above the bank. Everybody would be practically sitting in everybody else's lap."

In 1951, Panter left to take a job running the hockey arena at Sudbury. Hanley was appointed his successor as business manager. His pay, including the raise he was given after the appointment, was $60 a week. He was new in that job when the OHA had to deal with one of the most hurtful situations in its long history. It is covered tersely in Frank Buckland's summary of the 1951-52 season. He wrote:

> Early in October (1951) a group that had broken away from the Kingston Nylons club tried to enter a second Senior B team from Kingston. The entry was opposed by the Nylons. When the executive refused to accept the second entry, it (the executive) was informed that the previous spring, the management and players of the Nylon team agreed to lose the group playoff series to Peterborough, who would then advance into the Senior A playoffs while Nylons would take their chance in the Senior B playdowns.

The first intimation of this situation was recorded unportentously in the minutes of the OHA's 692nd executive meeting, held in the OHA office above the bank at 67 Carlton Street on September 21, 1951. The office at first had consisted of two small rooms, originally separated by a dentist's office. When the dentist died, the bank knocked out some partitions to give the OHA more space, but it still wasn't big. President J.M. (Jack) Roxburgh of Simcoe, an affable farmer and long-time worker for teen-age hockey, was in the chair. The sixteen executive members crowded into the small office space, many of them former OHA presidents, including George Panter (who hadn't severed his OHA connection when he took his Sudbury job), Dudley, Hewitt, James T. Sutherland, Frank Buckland, and Bill Hanley. The agenda, as usual, was long.

By then, the OHA's junior A and senior A teams both did much of their own internal business through a council of clubs in each of those categories, with most decisions requiring OHA ratification. A minor agenda item involved Stafford Smythe of the Toronto Marlboros speaking for the junior A council's wish to allow three-game junior A tryouts for junior Bs during the league season. That was dealt with early. Then came the usual applications for player transfers, a plea (turned down) from Chatham Maroons for a bye into the OHA senior playoffs despite intending to play in the International League that year, a discussion on that year's traditional distribution of free hockey sticks and other routine items.

Finally, in mid-evening, agenda items #13 and #14 seemed to be somewhat related. Item #13 was an application from George Patterson, who had been a famous Kingston junior player and later a minor professional. He had coached the Kingston Nylons the previous season but now asked permission to form a new senior B team, the Kingston Pats. On motion of George Dudley, the decision was that if Patterson could guarantee ice time in Kingston, his application should be accepted.

Item #14 was an unusual appeal from six players who had been with the Nylons the previous season. They wanted their releases so they could play with the new Pats. One was Douglas Patterson, son of the Kingston Pats applicant. The others were Edward Plumb, Rawlind (Buddy) Aiken, Glen Udall, Robert Joyce, and Jack Stone. There was obviously more to this than met the eye, but local squabbles were part of the OHA's steady diet. Dudley moved that president Roxburgh, vice-president Stewart E. McTavish, and Frank Buckland should constitute a subcommittee to travel to Kingston four days later, September 25, and hear the players' appeal for releases.

At the next full executive meeting, held at the Empire Hotel in North Bay on September 29, Roxburgh reported on the Kingston meeting with the appealing players. The situation he had found was hinted at but not detailed in the minutes from that meeting, but many years later Hanley gave an overview.

"It was the only time it ever happened, or the only time it had been detected, but that senior B team in Kingston had tossed a whole series," he said. "We didn't have a very good senior setup that year and whoever won the championship of that Kingston area senior B group would have to go into the senior A playoffs. The Kingston team was leading the group and was favoured to win the group championship but apparently had figured out that they could make more money by going on into the senior B playoffs, staying home and packing the rink."

The situation boiled down to this: at the September 25 meeting former Nylon player Douglas Patterson and former Nylon coach George Patterson, his father, giving their reasons for wanting to form a new club, had confessed. They said that the previous spring, gathering in the Patterson home after the Nylons' final league game with Queen's University, the players had talked among themselves about the upcoming group championship series with Peterborough and had come to the conclusion that they'd prefer to lose, for the reasons Hanley summarized above: they probably wouldn't get far in senior A and would have a lot more chance for home gates playing off in senior B. This story, Roxburgh reported, had been confirmed to the subcommittee by two other former Nylons, Rawlind (Buddy) Aiken and Edward Plumb, who were among the six applying for their releases from Nylons.

After hearing Roxburgh's account, it was moved by Dudley and seconded by Hewitt that "the business manager [Bill Hanley] send registered letters to each and every player and each and every member of the executive and management of the Kingston Nylon senior B hockey team of 1950-51 requesting them to attend an OHA sub-committee meeting to be held in Kingston Oct. 10 to furnish reasons why they should not be suspended by the Association."

The subcommittee system at that time was generally understood to be the OHA's trouble-shooter, as it had been ever since Hewitt and John Ross Robertson had headed up the Three White Czars of 1905. However, the subcommittee that travelled by afternoon train from Toronto to Kingston on October 10 and set up shop in a meeting room at the LaSalle Hotel for a hearing to begin at 8 p.m. was considerably larger than the old Three White Czars. President Jack Roxburgh was accompanied by Stewart E. McTavish of Oshawa, M.L. (Tory) Gregg of Wingham, Dudley, Hewitt, Buckland, and Hanley. In Kingston they were joined by the venerable James T. Sutherland and OHA executive member Lorne Cook, who was head of the print shop at the local penitentiary. Also present was M.J. (Mike) Rodden, sports editor of the *Kingston Whig-Standard* and former sports editor of the *Toronto Globe*. It's not known who invited Rodden, but his presence displayed someone's shrewd understanding of the seriousness of the situation. Rodden was well respected throughout the Ontario sports world. The OHA obviously wanted this whole matter to be in the open, observed by a trusted reporter.

At 8 p.m. all those ordered to the meeting were in the hotel. In the hearing room, subcommittee members sat along one side of long table. The accused, waiting glumly in an anteroom, were called in one at a time. Doug Patterson was first. He repeated that the players, manager, and coach of the Nylons had agreed to throw the Peterborough series.

Next up were players Rawlind (Buddy) Aiken and Edward Plumb. They provided the first surprise. They had confirmed the fix at the original subcommittee meeting in September but now denied having done so. They were questioned closely on this reversal, but insisted they hadn't understood the seriousness of what they had said.

The feeling in the subcommittee was that they had taken a lot of heat from their teammates in the meantime.

The next ten players called – Jack Stone, Ken Murphy, Walter Gerow, Ken Partis, Jack McKeown, Fred Harrison, Joe Watts, Glen Udall, Robert Joyce, and Kenny Potts – all denied having been part of any agreement to throw that series. Players Joe Catlin and Robert Londry, up next, were able to prove that they hadn't been at the meeting and were allowed to leave. Player John Armstrong confirmed the Doug Patterson charges.

George Patterson, the coach as well as the father of Doug Patterson, admitted everything and said he was glad to get it off his chest, it had been bothering him all summer, he was ready to take his medicine. His appearance was particularly hard on one of his interlocutors, Tory Gregg, who had played hockey both with and against Patterson and considered him a friend. Manager D.L. McKnight was the final witness called. He denied being a party to any arrangement the others might have made.

It was a long, sometimes tearful, sometimes angry evening: the room full of cigarette smoke; the sometimes sheepish, sometimes truculent witnesses; the business-like questioners ranged along the table on which were jugs of water, glasses, pots of coffee, cups, ashtrays.

Hanley: "When everyone had been heard, Roxburgh asked Jim Sutherland and Lorne Cooke, the two Kingston men, to retire while the subcommittee discussed the case and eventually unanimously approved a decision, this being made as a motion by Dudley, seconded by W.A. By then it was getting close to midnight.

"Everybody was called in and I had to read out the decision. It said that the charges had been fully proven and that manager D.L. McKnight and coach George Patterson were suspended for life; players Rawlind Aiken and Edward Plumb were suspended for two years; and players Douglas Patterson, Jack Stone, Ken Murphy, Walter Gerow, Ken Partis, Jack McKeown, Fred Harrison, Joe

Watts, Glen Udall, Robert Joyce, Kenny Potts, and John Armstrong were suspended for one year each. It was explained that Aiken and Plumb were getting an extra year each because after confirming the charges on September 25, they had repudiated them at this meeting. It was also noted that the Peterborough club had no knowledge of Kingston's intention."

As eyewitness, Bill Hanley remembers two parts of the evening most vividly. One was having to read out the bad news to frowning young men with sagging shoulders, stricken or defiant eyes, some shaking their heads in dismay. The other part followed quickly on the heels of the first.

Mike Rodden then was just a few months past his sixtieth birthday, but his physical strength had changed very little and his spirit not at all from the days when he'd been a college football all-star four times at four different positions; a middle wing with Toronto Argos; a pro hockey player with the old Toronto St. Pats; coach of two Grey Cup winners and several collegiate champions; referee of 2,864 (he had kept track) hockey games in the OHA and NHL; and also a pugnacious sportswriter. In short, he was not a guy to be taken lightly.

"He was sitting across the table from me," Hanley said. "All through what was going on, the whole four hours of it, he always seemed to have a cigarette dangling from his lower lip, but apart from lighting a new one every so often and taking notes he hardly moved while he listened to man after man coming in and denying, admitting, pleading, whatever.

"After I'd read out the list of suspensions there was one fellow, he called the subcommittee every name he could think of, I had to hold my tongue at what he was saying, and at the end he jerked his head at Mike Rodden and said, 'Well, I see your sportswriter is here and we'll see tomorrow how he writes it up! If he writes it up the way you've said it, he's a damn liar!'

"Mike Rodden went right across the table and just lifted the guy right out of his seat like a dog with a cat and held him in the air, he was terrified, and then Mike put him down and said, 'I just don't like anybody talking about me that way. I'll write it however I write it.' "

When adjournment came at 12:05 the OHA people sat around and talked awhile, had more coffee, some sandwiches. "Sometimes we'd have a drink after we'd finished our business on a trip," Hanley said. "But not on this one." They had a couple of hours to wait before the overnight train from Montreal to Toronto came through, which they would board. Tory Gregg, normally one of the lively ones at any gathering, was as quiet as the others. In the black autumn night they taxied to the railway station.

When Bill Hanley had made the rail reservations for their return to Toronto, he'd arranged for a private car, thinking there'd be something in it where they could stretch out and grab a couple of hours' sleep. The railroad, instead, had put on a lounge car.

"There were lots of things like settees, little chesterfields," Hanley said, "but nothing really big enough to stretch out on—especially for Tory Gregg, who was six feet four or five. We flopped the best we could. A couple of hours later when the conductor came through calling 'Toronto Union, next stop' I was awake, and just happened to be across from Tory Gregg. He had his legs hanging over one end of this settee and otherwise was curled up like a pretzel, must have been the most uncomfortable night of his life.

"He opened one eye, just one. Didn't say good morning, Bill, or that was a hell of a night, or any other kind of a hello, he just looked at me with that one eye open and all he said was, 'I can't figure what the hell was in that George Patterson's mind to suggest such a thing.' "

Hanley was single at the time and living with his parents in Port Credit. He took a train from Union Station, then walked home thinking it all over and wondering, he said, "how the hell I wound up in that kind of a situation." A little later in the day he was back in the office above the bank, the phone ringing off the wall from wherever OHA hockey was played, with writers and radio reporters wanting comment on what had just come over the Canadian Press wire from Kingston, blowing the lid off the scandal.

Postscripts kept showing up in OHA minutes for more than a year. In a few weeks the OHA announced that appeals of the suspensions would be heard, if accompanied by statutory declarations from each individual who appealed, giving his sworn version of the events that had caused the suspensions. Nine did appeal, complete with statutory declarations, and appeared with their lawyers before the OHA executive in a meeting room at the King Edward Hotel. All appeals were denied.

In another few weeks another Kingston club asked permission to use the suspended players in an exhibition game. Refused.

Six months after the original suspensions, Kingston executive member Lorne Cooke, who had been taking a lot of angry criticism in his home town, requested that the suspensions be raised at the end of the current hockey season. Response: Let 'em apply individually, in person.

Manager D.L. McKnight engaged a lawyer, who jousted with George Dudley by mail and in person, saying he would take the matter to court. Dudley told him that was his privilege. This renewal of hostilities ended when Frank Buckland ("I've got something for you, Bill," he said to Hanley) produced affidavits from two Peterborough players that McKnight had offered them money to throw a game a year before the events of 1951. When these were shown to McKnight's lawyer he said simply to Dudley, "You won't hear from me again."

But in April, 1952, there was some relenting. Six of the suspended players, including the two we-changed-our-mind guys, Aiken and Plumb, asked that the suspensions be lifted so they could play softball that summer. Response: the OHA would pre-date the suspensions from October 10 to May 1, 1951, meaning that for four of the applicants their one-year suspensions would end May 1, 1952; that is, in time for the 1952 softball season; Aiken and Plumb would be free as birds again on May 1, 1953. With this partial success, all the others under one-year suspensions also applied and were pardoned.

In October, a year after the original suspensions, Lorne Cook asked for reconsideration of the Aiken and Plumb cases. Plumb subsequently came to Toronto, apologized to the executive, and his suspension was lifted as of December 1, 1952. With that encouragement, Aiken appeared in person at the OHA offices two weeks later, apologized, was severely reprimanded, and got the same break as Plumb.

In October, 1953, George Patterson asked in a heartfelt letter that his life suspension be lifted. The minute on that letter read: "Moved by Dudley and Buckland that the application be not considered."

Many years later, after a message to the OHA that Patterson was extremely ill, his suspension was lifted. At the same time, to clear those old books, McKnight's suspension was lifted as well. Letters were authorized to that effect. The one to Patterson was received and acknowledged, but McKnight was said to be not known at his old address and could not be traced.

Chapter Thirteen

LAST HURRAH FOR THE SENIORS

"We're better than most senior A teams."

— WREN BLAIR,
when his senior B Whitby Dunlops
were trying to make it into senior A
so they could go on and win the world championship

It's like a walk down memory lane to relive what happened to Ontario hockey in the 1950s. The post-war boom in artificial ice arenas was part of it – longer seasons, lots of teams, lots of people paying to get in, better pay for players, pressure from clubs for longer playoff series so they could make more money, and no shortage whatever of colourful characters both on the ice and behind the bench.

A few examples:

1. There were so many protests on player eligibility, especially during playoffs, that Bill Hanley did a little research on why protests tripled or quadrupled once a team was faced with elimination. He discovered that in many cases a club would know about an ineligible player long in advance but would keep quiet about it, like holding an ace in the hole in stud poker. Then, if threatened with lights out in the playoffs, they would play the hole card, protest the player it had known about all along. Dudley came up with the answer: twenty-one days before the end of the schedule Hanley

would present each club with a list of all registered players on any team it might meet, highlighting names of each player who had been imported or waived from another team (these being the categories causing most protests). If no protest was entered within fourteen days, teams were barred from protesting on import or waiver grounds.

2. Harold Ballard and Stafford Smythe represented both Marlboro senior and junior clubs at contentious OHA meetings. In one OHA debate Ballard expressed a concern for the game that would floor his critics forty years later. Faced with a motion that would have allowed OHA junior A teams to draw players from anywhere in the province, regardless of residence, Ballard foresaw the result as being a bidding war that would strengthen big clubs like Marlboros and weaken the smaller ones. "Doesn't that go against what we're trying to do, foster hockey in the communities?" he asked. "I'm against it all the way." His leadership helped defeat that proposal.

3. Further on the subject of free enterprise and the vanished amateur, one year the OHA ordered that all Owen Sound senior players who wanted releases *must* be released unless Owen Sound *matched the pay they'd been offered elsewhere.*

4. Rudy Pilous, then the St. Catharines coach, was suspended for a month in 1953 for ordering a player not to serve a penalty called by referee Frank Udvari. This is a coaching move that hasn't been seen lately.

5. In 1953 Wren Blair (later in the decade to win two Allan Cups and one world championship) applied for a senior A franchise in Oshawa and was turned down.

6. Leighton (Hap) Emms, owner, coach, and everything else of Barrie Flyers, having cited religious and moral grounds in refusing to play an Ontario junior final playoff game against Marlboros on a Sunday (this was just after Toronto had okayed Sunday sport), was

ordered to play anyway. George Dudley pointed out that Emms and Barrie "had compromised their position" (a nice Dudleyesque way of putting it) by playing a Sunday game earlier in the season in Rouyn.

7. Stafford Smythe of Marlboros, Hap Emms of Barrie, and Bob Duncan, a goal judge appointed by Smythe to work a November, 1953, game in Barrie, appeared before the OHA executive to debate what had caused the Barrie club to have goal judge Bob Duncan *handcuffed* and removed from the arena during that game. Decision: no action should be taken against Hap Emms, but Bill Hanley as business manager should send a directive to all arena managers that in future before any game official, such as a goal judge, was removed from the arena, the referee must be consulted!

This was even before the Charter of Rights and Freedoms.

And all that was before things really reached a climax in what eventually could be identified as the OHA's best decade ever, nationally, internationally, and financially. After the Kingston fix of 1951, the OHA's senior A and B categories, intermediate A and B, junior A, B, C, and D rolled along about as usual, except maybe the seniors were getting a little fat. If so, junior A was taking up all the slack. The roll call of those best junior teams in the 1950s reads like at least a partial who's who of pro hockey in the 1960s.

In 1950 George Armstrong and Danny Lewicki were with Marlboros, Andy Bathgate at Guelph. In 1951, Leo LaBine, Jerry Toppazzini, Réal Chevrefils, Doug Mohns, and Jim Morrison were winning the Memorial Cup with Barrie. In 1952, the powerhouse of Bathgate, Ron Stewart, Dean Prentice, Lou Fontinato, Harry Howell, Bep Guidolin, Bill McCreary, and Ken Laufman brought a national championship to Guelph. (Eddie Shack came along a little later.)

In 1953 Orval Tessier, Don McKenney, and Don Cherry helped win the Memorial Cup with Barrie, but to win their own league they had to beat a St. Michael's team including Dick and Les Duff, Bill Dineen, and Murray Costello. In 1954, Barry and Brian Cullen, Hugh Barlow, Hank Ciesla, and Ed Hoekstra had their Memorial Cup year with St. Catharines.

The 1955 and 1956 Cup winners, Toronto Marlboros, thrived on the likes of Gerry James, Billy Harris, Mike Nykoluk, Al MacNeil, Bob Nevin, and Bob Pulford (Pulford scored ten goals in the five games it took for Marlboros to beat Regina Pats in one Memorial Cup final). Bobby Hull was in St. Catharines and Frank Mahovlich at St. Mike's; Wayne Connelly about to arrive in Peterborough; Pat Stapleton, Vic Hadfield, and others taking over in St. Catharines; and at St. Mike's Dave Keon on the verge of his long years of being always one of the best.

The juniors carried a lot of the freight through that decade when OHA finances soared as never before. Strong men in the executive suite were part of the reason: the two long-time regulars, Dudley and Hewitt (even though by 1953, when a testimonial dinner celebrated his fiftieth year as secretary, Hewitt was reduced to about half speed), as well as presidents Jack Roxburgh, Stewart McTavish, Tory Gregg, Frank Buckland, and Lorne Cook. But a revival of OHA seniors was about to happen, too, and much of that was directly due to a dedicated maverick named Wren Blair.

The Russians had something to do with providing the impetus, as well. Early in the decade the competition for players who wanted good pay was exemplified by the Owen Sound experience, cited above. With salary levels what they were, to stay a couple of jumps ahead of the bank manager senior teams needed gate money they could depend on. Two or three league games a week usually did it, with help at the end from playoffs that in some leagues eventually grew to best-of-nine. Anything that would interrupt the cash flow was regarded with suspicion, which explains why, until early in 1954, such esoteric events as world championships enjoyed a very low priority, if any.

That was the problem faced by George Dudley in the last few months of 1953. As well as being OHA treasurer, he was secretary-manager of the CAHA and the main Canadian representative on the International Ice Hockey Federation. The next world championship was to be held in Stockholm early in 1954. Dudley's task was to arrange for a Canadian entry. Kitchener-Waterloo Dutchmen, one of the nation's dominant senior teams, had won the Allan Cup in 1953 and were the natural nominees. However, they flatly refused; they simply couldn't afford to lose several weeks of home gates in their own league while they gallivanted (as the common concept had it) around Europe.

Other senior A prospects felt the same. So did Kingston Goodyears, senior B champions. So did Woodstock, senior B runner-up. For a while, there seemed a chance that Canada would not enter a team at all that year. When England's Bunny Ahearne heard that, he immediately applied the pressure. Ahearne was the grand high maharajah of the International Ice Hockey Federation and had invented the world championships in 1930. He and Dudley were friends and colleagues in the IIHF, so when he argued that it wouldn't really be a world championship without Canada competing, Dudley kept on trying.

It's not known for sure how many teams across the country Dudley approached with his offer of board, room, travel fares, and $20 per player each week for spending money, but he finally came down to telephoning Greg Currie, coach of a senior B team called East York Lyndhurst Motors. Lyndhursts had made it into the OHA senior B semifinals that spring before losing to Kingston, which beat Woodstock in the final. This made Lyndhurst Motors something like the third or fourth best senior B team in Ontario.

Still, they were okay for that class of hockey – most senior B teams being made up of men with other jobs who just liked to play the game.

Currie's first question to Dudley was, "Are we good enough?" On being told that after they got to Europe, they'd be strengthened by a few players from senior A teams that didn't make the playoffs or were knocked out early, Currie asked his players what they thought. He wanted to go, and he convinced most of them that it would be a real experience. A free trip to France and Italy, just think of it. They set about getting time off, mostly without pay, from their day jobs.

Lyndhurst Motors came by its name because the team was sponsored by a Toronto area Nash dealer named Harry Crowder. His instructions to Greg Currie a couple of years earlier, on agreeing to be the team's financial angel, were, "My business's name is going to be on the sweaters, so I don't want a bunch of rangatangs giving me a bad name."

Rangatangs they weren't, but little did Harry Crowder know about other possibilities in the bad-name department.

Anyway, when the announcement was made late in October, 1953, that East York Lyndhurst Motors would represent Canada in Stockholm, the unspoken truth was that they were the very best Canadian team *that would go*. The idea of a senior B team, not a championship one at that, going out to do battle with the best of the rest of the world was virtually ignored. Canadian sports pages at the time were much more concerned with the Grey Cup, the new NHL season, and why Stafford Smythe's favourite goal judge had been handcuffed and conducted out of the rink at Barrie. Nobody even made much of the fact that by then Lyndhursts were even having trouble in their own league against the likes of the Stouffville Clippers, Lambton Lumbermen, Ravina Ki-Y Flyers, and Leaside Dynes.

Fans were not clamouring to support that particular Team Canada, either. They beat Lambton one night, with twenty paying customers in the stands. They won another 10–9, with 100 fans plus Dudley and other hockey big-wigs looking on. That one, coach Greg Currie described as "one of those 'pardon me' type games, my guys so afraid of getting hurt and missing the trip that they all skated around with one hand on their sticks and the other waving off guys who might try to check them."

When they set out January 22 by train for New York, where they would board ship for Europe, Lyndhursts bore no resemblance whatever to later international teams. Instead of today's cargo planeload of steaks, bottled water, toilet paper, oxygen tanks, girl friends, and so on, all Lyndhursts took were a supply of ear muffs, for playing outdoors, and Vaseline, to smear on their faces against windburn. Rex MacLeod, then with the *Globe and Mail*, observed in his sendoff story that the Lyndhursts might not be the best team Canada had ever sent abroad, but without doubt they would be the slipperiest.

Their first exhibition, in Paris, put them against a team of Canadian all-stars from the English league. Besides Lyndhursts being out of shape from nearly ten days with-out pulling on a skate, there was a certain amount of culture shock. After one penalized player came back to report that he'd been served a beer in the penalty box, there was rather heightened eagerness to own up to penalties. Lyndhursts lost that one 11–2. Finally, back home Dud-ley's phone began to ring. He assured newsmen and other anxious callers that help would be sent. Then Lyndhursts did begin to win. Soon after they reached Sweden, help was flown in from Canada, mainly from Niagara Falls Cataracts and Sarnia Sailors, whose seasons had ended. And when the world tournament got under way, Canada's by-then pretty good lineup won its first six games. They were better, actually, than all other teams in the tournament – except one. But their last game, a 7–2 loss to the Soviets, was what everyone later remembered.

Canadian newspapers, none of which had bothered to send a reporter to cover the tournament firsthand, greeted that loss with shocked headlines: *Black Eye for Canada!* And in a way you have to hand it to the Lyndhursts. Canada in international hockey was never the same again. From then on, world championships – especially anything involving the Soviets – were treated as matters of national honour. It's worth noting, too, that hockey people who remember that time, most of whose memories have become more sympathetic over the years, eventually took a second look at a comment from Don Lockhart, the good goalie who'd been added to the Lyndhursts from Niagara Falls.

Everywhere the Lyndhurst players went after leaving Stockholm there'd been swarms of reporters sending stories back to Canada. Lockhart was one of a few who flew home. In the accusatory atmosphere of the media throng that met those few at the airport, Lockhart wondered aloud, "Would we get this much attention if we'd won?"

The answer, of course, was no. The OHA's Lyndhursts had been Canadian hockey's sacrificial lambs. If they hadn't filled that role, however unintentionally, and had beaten the Russians that day – Greg Currie and others thought they would have, most days – quite possibly Canada would have sent a senior B team in 1955, too, instead of the loaded-for-bear Allan Cup champion Penticton Vees, who trounced the Soviets 5–0 and thus, as many a paper reported, restored Canada's hockey honour.

The OHA eventually was to redeem itself internationally, but before that time the 1956 Olympics at Cortina proved that perhaps Lyndhursts' loss hadn't been so scandalous after all. Kitchener-Waterloo Dutchmen won the Allan Cup in 1955 with former NHL star Bobby Bauer coaching, but at Cortina that team could have used a few veterans from Penticton and even East York who'd been on the real firing line and had a better idea of how to win internationally. The Dutchmen had five of the top point scorers in the Olympics, but couldn't do it when it counted – losing 4–1 to the United States, who won the silver medal, and 2–0 to the Soviets, who won the gold.

In 1957 Canada didn't compete (a protest against the Soviet putdown of the uprising in Hungary). And then, with Lyndhursts and Kitchener-Waterloo the unhappy benchmarks, Canada finally came up with people who really did know how to compete and in so doing restored to the OHA a lot of the glory that was its due.

Which brings us to Wren Blair, one of those, not a dying breed at all, of whom it is said they think hockey twenty-six hours a day. He'd been a milkman around Oshawa. When he first applied for senior A status in 1953 and was turned down, it was with a senior B team called the Oshawa Truckmen – who beat Lyndhursts in an exhibition just before they left for Europe early in 1954. By then he'd changed jobs and was a National Housing Act appraiser in the Oshawa area, running his hockey team out of his basement recreation room.

At the time his team didn't even have a rink to play in. The Oshawa arena had burned down, all the Truckmen's equipment going up in the flames. He'd hustled around and found someone who'd give him $5,000 credit to get started again.

In the traumatic post-Lyndhursts hockey spring of 1954 when some people were debating whether even the new Allan Cup champion Pentictons were good enough to send against the Russians the following year, Blair was winning the OHA senior B championship over Simcoe even though, because of the Oshawa rink disaster, all games in the final had to be played in Simcoe. Blair piped up brashly right after that series to say that if Penticton didn't go, he'd be glad to fill in with the Truckmen. "We're better than most senior A teams," he'd tell anyone who would listen, and he might have been right. But the OHA still didn't think so, even though Hamilton's senior A team had distinguished itself in the 1952-53 season by losing its first twenty-eight hockey games before it finally won one. In overtime.

An oddity in 1953-54 was that all OHA senior A hockey was based in western Ontario – Owen Sound, Kitchener, Windsor, Hamilton, Stratford, Chatham, Niagara Falls, and Sarnia. The same was true in 1955, except with two fewer teams (Hamilton and Sarnia dropped out). Blair applied to enter senior A that year and was turned down again. In the 1955-56 season, it was the same once again – five senior A teams, all in western Ontario (Niagara Falls was out).

Meanwhile, Wren Blair, Oshawa still without a rink, had changed his team's name from Oshawa Truckmen to Whitby Seniors and was looking for a sponsor who'd help the team's finances by paying to have its company name on his team's sweaters.

Listening to Blair in full flight gives one an idea of the style that was to become famous in the hockey world, including in the United States after he became an executive with Minnesota and later Pittsburgh in the NHL. The following is from a taped interview in which he recalled his 1955 Whitby Seniors, née Oshawa Truckmen.

> When I moved the team to Whitby it was about the same time that the Dunlop Rubber Company opened their big plant there. We needed money. I went to the mayor and said there is no reason why that company can't join us, we're both arriving at the same time, we're both good for Whitby. So the mayor wrote Anderson, the top guy at Dunlop, a letter. I'll never forget it! I got back a cheque from Dunlop for $100! Anderson was over from England. He must have thought we were a bantam hockey club or something. I sent him back the cheque and wrote, "Dear Mr. Anderson: I'm sure that a cheap bunch of Englishmen like the Dunlop

Rubber Company need this $100 more than we do. Keep your goddamn money and I'll buy Goodyear," or some bloody thing.

It really upset him. He got on the phone to the mayor and said, "Who does this person think he is?"

The mayor explained that we'd correspond to a second-division soccer team, all men with jobs, and that $100 wouldn't do much. To give Anderson credit he got upset enough to send twenty men from the Dunlop company, top executives, to see us play our next game. It was December of 1955. It just happened that we were playing Kingston Goodyears that night. The Dunlop guys had dinner up where they could watch the game through glass there at the Whitby arena. After the second period those Dunlop guys came down with $200 in ten-dollar bills. Ten bucks each, they'd shelled out. It was a 2–2 tie then and they're so goddamned worked up, most of them were English, they hadn't even seen hockey hardly. They were saying, "Give these to your boys and tell them it's a great show. We've got to win, beat those goddamn Goodyears."

So I went into the room with this fistful of $10 bills and said, "Jesus Christ, you win this game and we'll split this up." Our guys came out and had a hell of a third period. We beat Goodyears 4–3.

The Dunlop guys must have been impressed. Anderson got in touch with me and asked what I was looking for, really. I said, "I want the right to call this team the Whitby Dunlops and I want $2,500 for that name on the sweater for the rest of the year." They had a meeting and sent me a cheque . . .

So that's how the later world-famous Whitby Dunlops were born, and went on that year, 1956, to win the senior B championship, losing the first two games of the final to Woodstock and then winning four straight. But . . . that was still senior B, and Blair wasn't through yet. In his mind, although hazily, was the idea that he would really like to play in the world championship. And if that ever was going to happen it probably had to be as Allan

Cup champion. So the first step was to be accepted in senior A.

He had two or three meetings with rather amused, but fairly polite, OHA executive members that spring and early summer of 1956. The final one came at a hotel in Stratford operated by a long-time OHA executive member, hockey coach, and eventually OHA president, Dave Pinkney. Blair made his pitch. They asked him to leave the room while they discussed it. When they brought him back in they said they admired his fight, and so on, "but you know, Whitby, what the hell, you can't play senior A."

The entry in the OHA minutes covering that situation read merely that Whitby Dunlops had applied for senior A status. Refused. Blair's account is somewhat more lively:

> I was livid. I said to them, "I'll tell you what I'm going to do! I'm going back home and get a meeting called of the eastern Ontario senior B league and I'm going to go senior A one way or the other! Either that league turns senior A or I'm going to turn my team senior A all by itself and I'll play exhibition games all year, and then you're going to have to play me in the playoffs. And when I turn senior A you guys will never see another Allan Cup!"
>
> I say this to Ernie Goman of Kitchener, just back from the Cortina Olympics, and Dutch Meier of Stratford, all those veteran hockey men, and they say, "Poor Wren, nice kid but he gets all huffed up."

Blair then went back to his eastern senior B colleagues. There he had another fight on his hands. None of the others wanted to turn senior A. The salaries were higher. The commitments were greater. They were filling their rinks with senior B, anyway. Things began to swing his way when he announced flatly that if they were going to stay in senior B, it would be without the censored-deleted Whitby Dunlops, their best draw at the box office. Then Pembroke Lumber Kings, who had been playing in another senior A league and were looking for a change, said they'd go with Blair. That helped. Cornwall, Brockville, Kingston said they'd go along, leaving only the most reluctant convert of all, Belleville. Blair only got Belleville in by going to see the manager, a city official named Drury Denyes, and offering to help him muster a team of senior A calibre.

In the end he did so well getting players for Belleville that at the end of that first Whitby Dunlop senior A season (with the Dunlop company paying $4,000 that year to have its name of the sweaters), Whitby wound up having to beat Belleville for the league championship and the right to go on to play for the OHA title.

"We then met Kitchener and put them out. You know, the same guys who'd said the previous summer that Whitby couldn't play senior A. The seventh and deciding game was played on their ice and we beat them 3–2."

Whitby, the hottest hockey ticket around by then, went on to draw huge crowds against North Bay Trappers in the all-Ontario final. With interest so great, OHA president Frank Buckland insisted the Whitby rink wasn't big enough and ordered the Whitby home games played in Maple Leaf Gardens. It took seven games for Dunlops to win that series before going on to demolish the western champion Spokane Comets, the first U.S. team to play for the Allan Cup.

Frank Buckland had won no popularity contests in Whitby by ordering those all-Ontario final games to be played in Toronto, but in his summary of that year's events he wrote with uncharacteristic fervour of "the amazing Whitby Dunlops, who last year won the senior B championship and this year captured the senior A honors and gave major hockey in Ontario the greatest boost it has had in years."

Well, what had Blair been telling them, so loudly, all along?

Naturally, there was more to Blair than non-stop talking, threatening, and cajoling, both in the committee room and behind the bench. What he had assembled was a team including some of the finest players outside of the NHL – among them Harry Sinden, Tom and Ted O'Connor, Bus Gagnon, Bobby Attersley, Fred Etcher, Charlie Burns, Alf Treen. But front and centre always was Blair, the noisiest and most provocative coach in all hockey.

That designation comes from Hugh McLean, who played OHA junior and senior hockey, refereed in the NHL and in Canadian national championships, Olympics, and world championships, and who once ran a school for referees in Moscow. He eventually became referee-in-chief of the CAHA and president of the OHA. The first time he refereed Wren Blair's Dunlops was in that 1957 OHA senior final against Kitchener-Waterloo.

His memory of Blair in that series is that, "He was the greatest guy for yelling from behind the bench and then ducking down or getting behind the players so I couldn't see who was yelling. But I knew. I put up with it a couple of times, then threw him out. I just stood in front of him and said, 'Okay, that's it, good-bye.' It didn't change him much. He'd be screaming and yelling. I'd say to Bobby Attersley, 'Bobby, try and shut him up.' Bobby would say, 'You can't! Forget it!' But when I did many more of his games I had to realize he was a good hockey man. He got a lot of mileage out of a lot of guys."

Winning the Allan Cup that year, Blair knew exactly what he wanted next. He immediately applied for permission to take the Dunlops, with a few additions, to represent Canada at the world championships of 1958 in Oslo. His additions were shrewdly hand-picked, with Blair using all his noise and eloquence to get the ones he wanted. He was looking for speed, checking strength, toughness, experience, all the elements that would count when the crunch came. The heart of the club he already had, in the Dunlops. Then he added Roy Edwards of Windsor in goal; Jean-Paul Lamirande, a thirty-five-year-old reinstated ex-pro on defence; Jack McKenzie (Kitchener-Waterloo veteran of Cortina); speedy Connie Broden, who later played with Montreal Canadiens; tough-checking left wing Goose Gosselin from North Bay; and Sid Smith, thirty-three, a veteran Toronto Maple Leaf and one of hockey's fastest skaters.

Getting Smith was a particularly Blair-promoted coup. He hadn't been seeing much action that autumn with the Leafs. Blair said he had to screw up his courage before he could bring himself to phone Stafford Smythe of the Leafs and ask if he could have Smith.

A few days later, Blair called back to check.

Smythe said tersely, "You got him."

Blair knew that Smythe would have had to get Smith waived by all other NHL clubs to give him his release. That must have been costly, he figured, either in money or players. So he asked, "Well, for how much? What do we have to do?"

Smythe barked, "What do you mean, for how much? For nothing! You think you're the only goddamn Canadian, for Christ sake, you stupid bastard?"

Smith already was with the Dunlops that November when they played the first-ever touring Soviet team an exhibition in Toronto. Blair always felt that game helped, plenty. The Soviets scored two goals in the first seventy seconds. Blair was swearing a blue streak in his head, thinking, *A goal a minute! At this rate we'll lose 60–0!* The whole rink was in dead silence. "Then I looked at our guys," he said:

> They were busy being spectators! It was like, "Look at that! Right in the net! Just like we do! Did you see that?" I got mad. I walked along behind the bench. I said, "Look, for Christ sake, what is going on here? We got fifteen thousand people who paid an average of five or six dollars a head to watch these bastards and you seventeen other guys are doing the same thing. That's fine with me but there is one thing wrong. At least have the decency to get up off this goddamn

bench, go out to the box office and pay your admission, and we'll all watch the goddamn game and say, "Just look at them! Aren't they great? But what would happen if you got so silly as to run into some of those red-shirt bastards a couple of times?"

And they sat there like, "What the hell do you mean?"

I said to Alf Treen, "Jesus Christ, Alfie, go out there and cream a couple." So he went out there and boom, Alfie got a penalty. Next guy came down, wham! We knocked the shit out of them. We took two or three penalties, killed the penalties off. The minute we started to hit we broke their whole concentration.

That was, at the time, the conventional wisdom on how to deal with Soviet teams: get physical and they folded. Penticton had done it in 1955; Kitchener-Waterloo had failed to do it in 1956. Now Dunlops did it in 1957, went out hitting and scored the next seven goals to win 7–2.

But it was a whole new situation by the time both the Dunlops and the Soviets got to Oslo for the world tournament beginning in late February. Blair had foreseen that the Soviets didn't need anybody to draw them a map – they would know they'd have to improve. But Blair also had done that improving of his own, as detailed above.

Both Canada and the U.S.S.R. were unbeaten when they finally met on March 9, 1958, with the gold medal at stake. Not only from Whitby and elsewhere in Ontario but from across Canada bags of telegrams, letters, and good-luck charms piled into the Canadian dressing room. By late in the third period the score was 2–2. With their goal average higher than the Soviets, Canada could have won the gold with a tie (the Soviets had been tied earlier by Sweden). Blair explained what happened next.

But playing for a tie we'd only be one fluke goal away from losing it anytime. Anyway, we didn't want to win any damn thing on a tie. But it stayed 2–2 right down to about three minutes to go. It was brutal. The pressure was godawful. Late in the period – doesn't Alexandrov break in the clear from our blueline! Right in! I can't watch! I turn my head away. All of a sudden I hear our guys yelling. I know somehow they haven't scored. I said, "What the hell happened?" and someone said, "Jesus Christ, he pulled Roy right out flat on his ass and hit the top cross bar." The puck bounced free and Bobby Attersley took off down the ice, right down the rink and scored, to make it 3–2. We come back to centre and face off and Bobby goes right in the clear again and Bus Gagnon comes roaring in from the left side and Bobby pulled the defenceman and threw it across and Bus took it . . . Bang! Into the net. And our team went nuts.

Many times later in Canada, when Blair was much in demand at banquets to tell how Dunlops won, he'd start by talking about the cheers, the acclaim, the national status his Dunlops had attained as hockey heroes. Then he would tell about that instant when Alexandrov broke in and beat Roy Edwards and hit the crossbar. "We were no more than an inch right then from being one goal down. If they'd scored that one, I couldn't be sure now or ever that we would have won." He kept making that point, hockey's oh-so-narrow line between being a hero and a bum.

That short stretch of highway 401 between Whitby and Belleville produced the top amateur hockey in the country in those years from 1957 to 1959. While Whitby was winning the world in 1958, Belleville McFarlands took the Allan Cup and immediately – as Whitby had done the previous year – applied for permission to wear the Canada sweaters in the next year's world championship in Prague. Got it. And won, beating the Soviets 3–1, losing 5–3 to the hometown Czechs on the final day, but winning the gold narrowly on goal averages. While they were away Blair's Dunlops, transformed so miraculously from the OHA's most troublesome mavericks to hockey's kings of the hill, were winning the 1959 Allan Cup.

Which takes us forward one more year to when a few Whitby stars and others had been added to Bobby Bauer's Kitchener-Waterloo team to represent Canada at the Squaw Valley Olympics of 1960. Again, as in Prague in 1959 when Canada's tunnel vision was focused so much on the Soviets that the players were sitting ducks for the Czechs, the unexpected happened. They beat the Russians 8–5 but lost 2–1 to the U.S. In that amazing game Canada widely outplayed the Americans but was virtually stonewalled by Jack McCartan in one of the greatest goalkeeping displays of that or any age, and many of those present were to recall Blair's oft-repeated story about Alexandrov beating the goalie and hitting the crossbar in 1958. It recalls the saying that what goes around comes around.

Canada had the sharpshooters in that U.S. game. The shots on goal were 15–8 for the U.S. in the first period, with one U.S. goal, but two of the Canadian shots, by Fred Etcher and Ken Laufman, were point-blank – McCartan making what seemed like impossible saves. In the second period the shots were 20–6 for Canada, with no goals for Canada and one for the U.S. In the third Canada had the shots edge, 11–4, many of them dangerous, but only one goal, by Jim Connelly.

It is worth recalling here what referee Hugh McLean had said about Wren Blair as a world-class troublemaker the first time they encountered one another a few years earlier. It is also worth recalling something else about hockey, how the heat of the moment does not necessarily obscure later, saner judgements, such as the fact that the original Blair-McLean feud was one of those that would continue every time they faced one another in combat, but not when a game was over and real values were being considered. After that Squaw Valley game, Blair and the few Whitby players who'd been on the Canadian team were looking for a place where they could suffer in privacy.

"Blair called my room and asked if he could come up," McLean said. "The Whitby players came with him and

I've never seen hockey players like that, Bobby Attersley
and some others . . . crying like babies. They'd outplayed
and outshot the Americans by a mile, but it was one
of those games. The feeling of letting Canada down is
something that anyone who has experienced it never
wants to again."

Chapter Fourteen

THE OHA AND THE NHL

"What's that kid's name?"

– Scout BOB WILSON of Chicago,
when he first saw
eleven-year-old BOBBY HULL

From the founding of the OHA until the NHL's 1967 expansion changed the process forever, the discovery, development, training, and ultimate destination of any hockey player had a fairly logical, even comfortable pattern. Seventy-seven years of OHA minute books tell the long, often niggling, story. At first clubs picked players off the ponds or outdoor rinks and simply brought them along, not even a free twenty-five-cent hockey stick part of the deal. Once having decided he liked the game even if big-deal scouts were never going to pester him with their pens out, the player might be a Dunnville Mudcat or Lindsay Meteor or Toronto Marlboro up through the age groups from childhood on. Then he might go on to coach or referee or become a club volunteer, take tickets, clean the ice, or in comfortable middle age be chosen a delegate to the mighty OHA. That was hockey for the masses. The fun and excitement of playing was the first reward, the one that hooked some people for life.

At the upper end of the proficiency scale and on a few years, when a youngster showed early star potential, scouts from higher clubs would be on his trail. Because of strict OHA rules that a player must get one club's release before signing with another, once signed with even an amateur hockey organization, the player became, quite simply, a human chattel – although the OHA's appeal procedures (a family move, school enrolment, change of job) did leave some room for change.

No such partial elasticity carried over once a player became a pro. At that point the chattel factor was total, sometimes from childhood on up (as with Bobby Hull, among hundreds). Being sold or traded simply changed one master for another. That was the system, understood and in most cases accepted by players and public alike.

The farm system in hockey came early. Dating from the early 1890s, one of the earliest flashes of forward-thinking in the OHA was that each senior hockey team must sponsor a junior team. This was to give the less proficient a place to play, besides keeping on tap a steady supply of reserves for the "big" team, men who, called up in an emergency, were a lot better than an empty sweater.

When the OHA invented intermediates around 1896, that took care of providing a robust place to play for those great skaters who couldn't score, great scorers who couldn't skate, and a lot of men in between who played the game pretty well. Junior hockey then became an age-limit game, the age requirement changing from time to time but rarely far off the present system: restricted to men not older than twenty on January 1 of the season being played. From then on junior was where kids played to see if they were good enough, or liked the game enough, to go on to senior or turn pro. Stemming from the original narrow village, town, or city district framework came years of changing relationships between all classes of amateur hockey, and eventually between amateurs and pros.

As we've seen, the focus wasn't always necessarily for the good of the game or even the individual player. Despite tough controls to enforce the OHA's eleventh commandment, "Thou shalt not covet thy neighbour's meal ticket," the promoters, amateur and pro alike, were free-enterprisers, and players were their product. The first pro executives, having started out as amateurs, didn't need any instructions on how to get around the rules.

And if there was no meal ticket available to covet, sometimes almost any warm body would do. In the 1920s and early 1930s, well before the Ontario Minor Hockey Association was formed and for its own protection joined the OHA, it sometimes seemed to be open season on youngsters. One favourite target was the old Toronto Hockey League, established in 1912 by a legendary hockey man, Frank D. Smith, who was later elected to the Hockey Hall of Fame but whose sole aim at the start was only to give anybody of either sex a place to play. At first, the THL functioned mainly on outdoor rinks. Under OHA rules of the time, if a player appeared even once in an OHA game, he couldn't play for any other OHA team without that first club's release. This was the essential OHA red tape that prevented players flying from one team to another like snowbirds. But signing such neophytes was also a great way to stockpile: fill the kid's head full of rosy dreams, put him in one game where he couldn't do any harm, and if he didn't make the team just tell him, "Don't call us, we'll call you." But the team still owned his rights until it gave them up voluntarily. One junior club's scout, apparently a world champion at standing in snowbanks, signed forty players from these THL clubs in a single year! Eventually the THL (which later changed its name to Metropolitan Toronto Hockey League) affiliated with the OHA to protect both organizations against raids as well as bringing order to such matters as competition for ice time, especially during playoffs.

But that was a time of OHA pre-history, at least in relationship to the agreements that eventually regularized amateur-pro relations. Until then there had been two phases. One encompassed years of anarchy, up to 1935, when the pros grabbed whoever they wanted, never mind the harm done to senior and junior teams. The second phase began with agreements in the mid-1930s that would be built upon for more than three decades until amateurs and pros achieved more or less peaceful coexistence.

The beginning of modern times in player control began at the OHA's 1934 annual meeting when George Dudley was pressing for OHA ratification of amateur hockey's first agreement with the NHL. His best unintentional comedy line came when he said that as a welcome part of the agreement, the NHL would not touch a junior "unless his club consents." Hilarity ensued, one delegate terming that as "bordering on the ridiculous, because there's no club in Canada would stand in a player's way if he had a chance to sign with an NHL team." And that would be without compensation to the amateur club that brought the player along, although that provision was soon to come.

When one considers how robust junior hockey has become, it is rather amusing that another part of that first NHL-amateur agreement called for the OHA to abide by all NHL playing rules, including allowing bodychecking in the centre ice area – even in junior hockey, where it had been banned. Dudley obviously anticipated a trouble spot there. On the matter of standardizing the rules, already fairly standard, he noted that "the only thing of any importance at all to us is the matter of bodychecking in centre ice." But, he said, to get the concessions the NHL had made on player-grabs, the amateurs had to give up something; bodychecking was it.

This precipitated a long and passionate argument. The opposition included horror stories about what would happen, say, to a sixteen-year-old junior facing husky twenty-year-olds in small rinks where he'd have nowhere to hide – "sheer murder!"

A rejoinder: "Ah-h-h-h! If a kid can take a bodycheck in the attacking zone, he can take it anywhere on the ice."

One delegate argued that if bodychecking was allowed everywhere in Canada except in Ontario – that is, if all other branches of the CAHA signed and the OHA didn't – OHA teams would be at a disadvantage in national championships.

Father Lynch of St. Michael's College strongly rejected that as an argument. "Instead of adjusting the boy to the game, the game should be adjusted to the boy!" he exclaimed. "We're not playing hockey to get into the Memorial Cup playdowns! I'd rather see the playdowns eliminated than hockey eliminated!"

George Panter, then a mere delegate from Gravenhurst, retorted angrily: "The players are not pansies! The game was not made for pansies!"

Voice from back in the room: "With bodychecking in small rinks we'll raise town feelings to such an extent that we'll have a riot at every game!"

Another: "When you think of mothers and sisters watching the boys being knocked all over the ice, with the knee up in the groin . . . "

A delegate named Bill Christie, of the Marlboros, sardonically: "Oh, dear! Oh dear!"

Dudley: "Now, gentlemen . . . "

There were cries of "No! No!" and "Yes! Yes!" and "Vote! Vote!" before James Sutherland moved that the OHA try to get the CAHA and NHL to agree to maintain the ban on bodychecking for intermediates and juniors.

When this motion passed, Sutherland remarked, "This shows there is still wisdom in the OHA."

Christie, dying hard, replied: "Not necessarily!"

Sutherland's rather conciliatory motion didn't go far in the big world of hockey, as anyone who has watched junior hockey would agree. Opposition to bodychecking, of course, is a never-say-die issue and always will be, connected as it sometimes is to boarding and charging infractions that cause injuries, some serious, some for life. But at the time other aspects of relationships with the pros were the controlling factor. None of the higher echelons, CAHA or NHL, had any time for Sutherland's plea. Bodychecking in centre ice it was.

The hold that pros had on potential hockey stars from the cradle on up was practically total. Farm systems had become an integral part of the scene. As we've seen, the Montreal Winged Wheelers, Allan Cup winners in 1930, had been a Montreal Maroons farm team. Toronto Maple Leafs had controlling links with the Marlboros, senior, junior, and below, as well as (later) with St. Michael's College. Canadiens had their feeder system, including first call on any French-Canadian player. Besides arrangements to sponsor junior teams, Boston Bruins had a senior team called the Olympics in the old Eastern U.S. Amateur Hockey League, another team in that league being the Rangers' New York Rovers.

Most of these controlled players came originally from what was called the negotiation list, kept in the NHL's Montreal headquarters. It worked this way: if an NHL scout spotted a promising player *of any age* anywhere in the U.S. or Canada, he could telegraph NHL headquarters and put that prospect's name on his team's negotiation list. The player need not even be informed until the pro club was ready to do so. But from then on, as long as the listing club wanted, it had the exclusive right to bargain with that player.

The next stage usually was to offer the player what was called a C-form. The player, on signing, was given a small payment, maybe a hundred dollars or not much more. The C-form was really a tryout contract, but it bound the player to that club until he was found not good enough and was released, or was traded or sold. If he refused to sign the C-form, he could be (and some were) left on the negotiation list while the club tried to wear him down. He could continue to play amateur but was that club's pro property until the club removed his name from the list. The only edge the player had was that each club's negotiation list, at least by the late 1940s, was restricted to four names. If he persistently turned down the club's offers, eventually it might make room for someone more tractable. That sort of giving up, especially on a talented prospect, did not happen often.

Perhaps pro hockey's hold on OHA amateurs in those days is best illustrated by a real-life example. One winter Saturday in 1950 when Bobby Hull was eleven, a Chicago Black Hawks scout named Bob Wilson traveled to Belleville to watch some prospects in an OHA junior game. He got there many hours early but went to the rink anyway, where he knew that bantam, midget, and other minor teams would be on the ice. There Wilson noticed a stocky fair-haired boy, not tall, but obviously very strong, and a great skater. Nobody could get the puck away from him. Whack! It was in the goal.

"What's that kid's name?" he asked a bystander.

"Bobby Hull," he was told. "Some kid! There are days around here when he starts with the bantams, then gets into a midget game if he can, and if somebody doesn't show up for a juvenile game he gets into that, too. I've seen Saturdays when I'll bet he scores twenty goals in four different leagues."

Even in those days when there were only six teams in the NHL, pro scouts had to move fast. Bob Wilson had heard enough. He went to a pay phone and dictated a telegram to NHL headquarters putting eleven-year-old Robert Marvin Hull on Chicago's negotiation list.

After the call he hunted around the rink for the youngster's father, a mill worker, burly, built like an older version of the boy. Wilson approached him and said what he had done. Mr. Hull approved. He had even hoped this would happen, but never dreamed it would come this soon. He did make one provision: "Don't let Robert know right away, it might give him a big head."

It's not certain exactly when the news did get to Bobby Hull that he belonged to Chicago, but some believe it wasn't for two years.

The scout had been back often. On one trip, Wilson went to the boy's parents and told them their son was ready for better competition, better coaching. He wanted Bobby, thirteen, to move to a juvenile (seventeen and under) team that Chicago had an agreement with at Hespeler, promising that Bobby would be placed in a good home, Chicago paying for his room, board, laundry, and school books, and that he'd also get $5 a week spending money and would not miss any school. Bobby's mother thought he was too young to be away from home like that but relented in face of her husband's strong feeling that "This is Robert's big chance." That winter, Bobby has since confessed, he was lonesome, homesick. His mother and sometimes his father went by bus almost every weekend to see him play. He was on his way.

At fourteen, Chicago moved him to its junior B team (players up to age twenty) at Woodstock, where he helped win the OHA junior B championship. His next move was to St. Catharines' junior A team, where he spent two years before, at eighteen in 1957, he worked out with the Black Hawks under Coach Tommy Ivan in their St. Catharines training camp. When Chicago broke camp, Hull was with them beginning his NHL career.

A somewhat similar illustration from almost the same time involved Frank Mahovlich, born in Timmins a year earlier than Hull (who was born at Point Anne, near Belleville). When Mahovlich was thirteen or fourteen, scouts were jockeying to get him on one of their farm teams. In those days if an NHL team put money into a team or even a league, it had first call on all players involved. Detroit Red Wings set up a sponsorship for a whole league in Schumacher, just to get Mahovlich. But Toronto Maple Leafs got there first. They convinced Frank and his parents, devout Roman Catholics, that he should move to Toronto and attend school at St. Michael's College. That meant Leafs had first call on him when he was ready for pro.

That's how it *could* happen in the days of the negotiation list, the C-form, and the possibility of playing in one hockey organization for life. Although by today's standards such a system would not be acceptable, veterans of those times can become warmly nostalgic. To many of them, the sponsorship system's disadvantages – loss of a player's control of his own life, except within the prescribed boundaries – were outweighed by advantages. A group of talented youngsters in one NHL farm system might play together for years, growing up in the same system before some or all hit the big time. That provided a continuity, almost like an extended family. Throughout the system all coaches taught the techniques used by their NHL masters in the old six-team league, so that moving up the ladder involved little or no culture shock.

In the OHA at the time, besides Chicago's top farm at St. Catharines, New York Rangers sent their best juniors to Guelph, Boston worked with Barrie and later (before Bobby Orr broke in) Oshawa, Detroit was in Hamilton and Windsor, Montreal had all of Quebec, and Maple Leafs had their great feeder system in Toronto and environs.

At the same time, senior hockey was on the decline. There were no more Whitby Dunlops or Belleville McFarlands with their eyes on world championships. In 1962 the OHA had to loan $6,000 to the senior league to persuade it to continue. But the juniors never stopped blossoming. All this added up to a setup that had to disappear, never to exist again, when the six-team NHL doubled its size to twelve in 1967. Abolishing pro sponsorship of amateurs and supplanting it with the universal amateur

draft were the main moves designed to give the six new
NHL teams in 1967 a chance to improve on the castoffs
acquired for their $2 million entry fees to the NHL. For the
OHA, this brought the most profound structural change in
its history.

The main impact – really a blessing in disguise – was
on junior A. The long years of the best junior clubs being
stocked and supported by NHL owners were gone. In their
place, what? In some cases the NHL clubs were magnani-
mous, turning over their junior franchises for nominal
sums. In others, junior clubs had to pay back any money
their NHL sponsors had advanced. Although this caused
major shakeups in junior management, at ice level the
changes were almost invisible. Nine junior A teams operated before they lost their NHL angels, nine remained for
the next season, and the number has kept growing since.
The OHA juniors not only survived but flourished as privately owned businesses when the pro sponsorships were
gone.

Many junior A clubs in the past had had, in effect, their
own farm systems. These usually remained: the junior A
team developing its better prospects in its own junior B
club, sometimes two, and others in the lower echelons.
There were different management philosophies, of
course: most of the junior As were paid something, the
junior Bs rarely so. Most years there were roughly three
times as many junior B clubs as junior A. Some indepen-
dent junior B teams had links with others in junior C or
junior D ranks and in general the junior age group was
healthier than any other in the OHA. In 1967, as an example, there were nine teams in junior A, thirty-one in junior
B, thirty in junior C, twenty-three in junior D, for a total
of ninety-three junior teams dominating the OHA's entire
registration of 132 teams (a figure that doesn't count the
age-group legions of the OMHA and MTHL).

Meanwhile, the structure of the OHA remained healthier than ever in spite of having lost two if its best-known

executive stalwarts. The first to go was George Dudley. Only eight days after the OHA annual meeting of 1960, when he had been treasurer for twenty-four years as well as being the CAHA's secretary-manager, he died of a stroke. At first George Panter succeeded him as treasurer, but another year later Frank Buckland took on the task.

In the first few years of the 1960s leading to the major restructuring of 1967 there had been other changes. One was establishment of an Emergency Fund. For years some individual clubs had carried insurance, but nothing had been built into the OHA to meet the drastically unforeseen. In 1959 the OHA wanted to help financially after the Listowel rink collapsed, killing eight and injuring others, but found that nothing in the constitution authorized such payments. They were made anyway, but the OHA didn't want to be scrambling every time an emergency arose. The Emergency Fund was set up in 1963 at about $4,000, getting that sum by transferring $3,000 in bank interest earned by the OHA surplus in 1962, plus about $1,000 in unspent funds the OHA had set aside to support what treasurer and straight-talker Buckland called "a half-baked CAHA scheme to establish a hockey magazine, [which] sank into oblivion in less than a year." Various means were tried to keep the fund growing, but nothing much happened until Harold Ballard of the Toronto Marlboros was put in charge. Within a few years of Ballard's combination of chutzpah and arm-twisting, the fund had grown to $30,000 even though $14,300 had been paid out for reasons that cast a long shadow into the future: the pressing need for much better face and head protection. Between 1965 and 1969 grants of $1,000 each were made to twelve OHA players, each of whom had lost an eye in a game accident.

Meanwhile, exciting times in the committee room included two battling intermediate clubs, Walkerton and Elmira, hiring private detectives (from the same agency!) to obtain sworn evidence on the residential qualifications of four Elmira players. From Frank Buckland's summary of that year: "The affidavits contradicted one another in every instance. The protest was disallowed and Elmira went on to win the intermediate A championship."

In 1965 the OHA celebrated its seventy-fifth anniversary with a lavish birthday banquet. Those present were among the most famous in OHA hockey. Ontario Mines Minister George C. Wardrope, a balding long-time hockey man from Thunder Bay, brought the Ontario government's cheque for part of the tab in recognition of the association's lively role in the province's social history.

Chairman was one of the OHA's most famous coaches and managers, Matt Leyden. At the time Leyden was the incoming president, but through the hockey world he was known better as the General Motors worker who had guided the Oshawa Generals for so long, including an amazing seven junior A championship years from 1938 to 1944. (In the late 1960s, while still the OHA's immediate past president, he returned to the Generals as manager.)

Rudy Pilous, the coach who once had been suspended a month for instructing one of his players not to serve a penalty imposed by referee Frank Udvari, was master of ceremonies. He was full of hockey jokes about his time with the great St. Catharines junior teams of the 1950s and how fast the rink emptied at each intermission as the crowd bolted across the lane to a nearby beer parlour, where every table would be laden with full glasses of draft in readiness. Later Pilous had followed his stars Bobby Hull, Stan Mikita, Chico Maki, Johnny McKenzie, Elmer Vasko, and others to become coach of the Chicago Black Hawks, getting laughs from his accounts of how he was now among the mighty who had fallen. (By then he was coaching in OHA junior A again, with Hamilton Red Wings.) Conn Smythe proposed the toast to the OHA in an anecdote-spiced speech going back to his earliest days as an OHA coach and all-round gadfly. NHL president Clarence Campbell, not one for jokes, pleaded for a cessation of new hostilities that had developed in the 1960s between pros and amateurs.

Through the entire evening, the room was full of a sense of the high points and low points of the game and the volunteers from all walks of life – some still around, some long gone – who had guided it through three-quarters of a century. Smythe and Frank Buckland then were presented with the OHA's highest honour, the Gold Stick, for service to the game.

Present at that anniversary dinner, too, was W.A. Hewitt, becoming old and frail and who by then had lived for some years in the home of his famous broadcasting son, Foster. One year later, in 1966, at a testimonial dinner honouring his OHA years from 1903 on, Hewitt was named the OHA's Honorary Life Secretary; later that year he died in a home for seniors in the city where he had spent his life, except for those troubleshooting trips to wherever OHA hockey was played. As Frank Buckland wrote in his summary of that period, "in the span of six years the OHA lost two men who more than anyone else, with the possible exception of John Ross Robertson, had shaped the destiny of the OHA."

There's a mention above of Clarence Campbell deploring new hostilities between amateurs and pros. Smythe had thrown a few barbs in that direction as well. What they were referring to was amateur hockey's grand project of the 1960s: Canada's national team, which Jim Coleman in his book, *Hockey Is Our Game* (1987), called "the most nobly conceived of all Canadian hockey enterprises." Many in the OHA who had been involved in Olympics and world championships would support Coleman's judgement, but the NHL opposed the idea from day one.

Almost forever, except for a few young Canadians who opted for hockey scholarships in the United States, the NHL had enjoyed the status of being the *only* destination for talented young players. In the 1960s Father David

Bauer, a Basilian priest who had been a teacher and hockey coach at St. Michael's College, provided, for a while, an alternative. His idea was to assemble and somehow keep together a team of talented young players who would represent the country in international competition and get an education at the same time. Obviously he would be trying to attract the same talented players that in normal times would be heading to the NHL. The NHL did not like that at all.

Hockey was in the Bauer family's blood; one brother, Bobby, was an NHL all-star with Boston; another, Ray, was a good senior and later executive with Kitchener-Waterloo area teams. As a student at St. Michael's in the early 1940s, David Bauer had played on the school's OHA junior teams, helped Oshawa win the Memorial Cup in 1943, and was considered an excellent pro-calibre prospect. Instead, he chose the priesthood. After being ordained in the early 1950s he taught at St. Michael's and coached hockey – including the Memorial Cup winners of 1961. Dozens of players he coached over the years went to the NHL, Frank Mahovlich, Gerry Cheevers, and Dave Keon among them. In short, he was much better than a green hand when, after being assigned by the Basilian fathers to St. Mark's College at the University of British Columbia, he travelled to the world tournament at Colorado Springs in 1962. There he watched the Allan Cup champion Galt Terriers lose in rather mediocre fashion even though the world tournament that year did not include the U.S.S.R. or Czechoslovakia (those teams stayed away in protest because the U.S. government refused visas to the East Germany team).

It was at Colorado Springs in long evening discussions with other Canadian hockey men, including Jack Roxburgh, by then president of the CAHA, that Father Bauer (Father Dave, everybody called him) developed his idea for a national team. He saw it being based on university students who, for international competitions, could be strengthened by the best seniors available. To make it work, to get the core of his team, he'd have to compete for the hearts, minds, and hockey ability of players who normally would have gone straight to the NHL. This automatically meant that the pros would fight him at every turn. However, the amateurs were on his side, especially those of the OHA. With the passing of Whitby Dunlops, Belleville McFarlands, and that ilk, every time there was an Olympic or world tournament, the OHA was prime candidate either to put a team together or help someone else do it. Father Bauer's idea of assuring continuity, with the matter always in hand, was attractive to almost everyone except the pros.

The CAHA annual meeting was in Toronto that year, 1962, with all provincial branches represented. The OHA, still by far the largest and most powerful, worked hard on any doubters. Father Bauer's plan was endorsed unanimously. That was the beginning of an eight-year odyssey. The CAHA came up with some start-up money and agreed to provide university fees and something toward board and lodging for the team to be assembled at UBC. But then or later, there was never enough money. Private donors, including Father Bauer's mother in Kitchener, helped. The government contributed nothing until in the mid-1960s the federal Fitness Council, stirred by Montreal journalist Andy O'Brien's impassioned tales of how Team Canada's dedicated young men had to scrounge housing, furniture, equipment, and even food, put up $25,000.

The Nationals became a warming part of Canada's hockey history in everything but medals. They came close a few times but never did manage to beat the Russians and usually lost to someone else along the line as well. It was to the credit of the OHA and CAHA that the Nationals never did run out of moral and player support from amateur hockey. In contrast, the paranoid opposition of the NHL is a matter of history. The old days were long gone when Stafford Smythe had made Sid Smith available to

Whitby Dunlops and, when asked the cost, told Wren Blair angrily, "You think you're the only goddamn Canadian . . . ?"

There were Canadians in NHL offices in the Father Bauer years who must (or at least should) have reflected later with shame on the implacability with which they fought the idea. With another attitude from Leafs and Canadiens at the beginning, for instance, figuring out which of their young prospects would benefit from the pressure of international experience, Canada might have beaten the Soviets in the Innsbruck Olympics of 1964, instead of losing 3–2. Father Bauer dropped out of direct control after that, but the national team moved to Winnipeg under Jackie McLeod and continued to grow.

At the 1968 Olympics in Grenoble, the Nationals came closest. When Canada met the Soviets in the final game, the gold medal was the prize. The game ended 5–0 for the Soviets. The writing on the wall that day was clear: Goodbye, Father Bauer. Even though for four years he'd been in the background, the team in many ways was still philosophically his, and internationally it had not worked out.

With that experience and a sudden onrush of practical interest, the Canadian government set up an umbrella group, Hockey Canada. Its avowed aim was to make Canada count again in international hockey. Formation of Hockey Canada owed much to federal Sports Minister John Munro, as well as to consultant, journalist, and former MP Douglas Fisher, financial whiz Chris Lang, and others, among whom NHL Players Association director Alan Eagleson, eventually to become the world's most powerful hockey figure, filled the essential role of sharp edge. The CAHA, with OHA support, was cool to the new plan. In effect it pre-empted the CAHA's half-century of building international hockey relationships. Much of the income generated by Hockey Canada's exhibition tours and tournaments would go to Europeans, the CAHA seeing little of it for amateur hockey development in Canada.

The CAHA naturally was outvoted time and again by other Hockey Canada principals, including Eagleson's NHL Players Association as well as Montreal Canadiens and Toronto Maple Leafs, the two organizations that – having prospered for many years off Canada's fascination with hockey, and having feared Father Bauer's competition the most – originally had worked the hardest against his idealistic dream.

While that hockey force was developing just over the horizon of the 1960s, the OHA had become more prosperous than at any time in its history. To some extent this was due to the new arrangement for drafting former juniors into pro ranks. The NHL, its sponsorship expenses ended, was paying $3,000 for each over-age junior taken in the first two rounds of the draft and $2,000 per player for those drafted in later rounds. In 1968 Frank Buckland's report as treasurer included a bank balance of nearly $60,000, which helped influence the OHA to decide to buy a building to house its central office.

In April, 1969, the building, at 24 Merton Street in central Toronto, was opened, paid for out of current funds without entirely wiping out the bank balance. And in 1970 the OHA won the Memorial Cup for the eighth time in ten years.

The list in that decade went back to Father Bauer's St. Michael's team in 1961, Hamilton Red Wings (Paul Henderson, Pit Martin) in 1962, Toronto Marlboros (Pete Stemkowski, Ron Ellis, Brit Selby, Mike Walton, Wayne Carleton, Rod Seiling, Jim McKenny) in 1964, Niagara Falls (Derek Sanderson, Jim Lorentz) in 1965, Marlboros again (Brian Glennie, Gerry Meehan) in 1967, Niagara Falls (Tom Webster) again in 1968, Montreal Junior Canadiens in 1969 and 1970.

Montreal Junior Canadiens? Twice OHA and Memorial Cup champions? With, one year or the other or both, Gilbert Perreault, Richard Martin, Jocelyn Guevremont, Ian Turnbull, Guy Charron, Marc Tardif, Réjean Houle?

It was an anomaly, but Montreal had been playing OHA junior A since 1962, a strong natural drawing card both in Montreal and Ontario. Without a strong Quebec league in 1962, Canadiens had been persuaded into the Ontario Provincial junior A group by Hamilton, St. Catharines, Niagara Falls, Guelph, and Peterborough. This was done to fill a gap when the two teams sponsored by Toronto Maple Leafs, Marlboros and St. Michael's Majors, withdrew from the strong Provincial group in a dispute over the number of games to be played, which was especially troubling St. Michael's. The two Leaf farms then wound up forming a Metro group with three much weaker teams, Whitby, Brampton, and Unionville. Hamilton from the Provincial group had little trouble beating St. Michael's in the OHA final and went on to win that year's Memorial Cup. Montreal kept building steadily for seven years before achieving its 1969 and 1970 powerhouses.

Chapter Fifteen

THE OHA AND THE LAW

"I verily believe that Mark will suffer
irreparable harm if he is not allowed to play
for the team of his choice . . ."

— from an affidavit presented by
a nine-year-old hockey player's father
in the Supreme Court of Ontario

For most of the years that Bill Hanley ran the OHA office, there was lots of interesting action but little of it got to court. Once when Bus Gagnon's Kingston team and Wren Blair's Whitby Dunlops could not agree on playoff dates, and Frank Buckland and Bill Hanley finally ordered dates that Kingston did not agree with, nobody sued but a *Whig-Standard* column stated flatly, "The best thing that could happen with Frank Buckland and Bill Hanley would be to take them to a mine in northern Ontario and drop them down a shaft, about 2,000 feet."

Then there was the time when four teams in the Niagara Peninsula were engaged in a fiery debate about rights to one player, and the Crowland team lost out. Nobody sued but the local uproar was such that Dinty Moore of Welland asked OHA president Stewart McTavish and Hanley to meet the dissidents one night and explain the decision. The meeting was in the Crowland fire station. When it was called to order, a tall and burly man in the front row rose. "Before we go any farther," he said, "I'd

251

just like to say I admire Mr. McTavish and Mr. Hanley's courage in coming. If the people of Crowland knew you were here, you wouldn't get out of Crowland alive."

But sometimes there were laughs, as once when Cobourg and Port Hope were at daggers-drawn as to who had the rights to a player named Richie Evans. Evans worked in Cobourg but had married someone from Port Hope. Hockey teams from both towns claimed him, but again nobody sued. Instead, Hanley and another executive member or two journeyed to the site of the argument to listen to both sides. There were glares and an extension of the general annoyance, certainly no laughs, until up rose the first speaker, for Cobourg, who began: "Gentlemen, Richie Evans is a Cobourg boy who made the mistake of marrying a Port Hope girl . . ."

And once a fight during a game between Midland and Newmarket left a Newmarket player cut for a dozen stitches. Newmarket lodged a protest—not about the fight, but because the Midland battler had been wearing a big signet ring, like a one-knuckle knuckle-duster. It could, of course, have been taken to court as assault with a dangerous weapon (suits have been launched for less), but this was just a complaint. The OHA ruling: from then on, the Midland player must remove his ring before each game.

Also, there was an OHA commandment (which still exists, although unwritten) that when a game was over and the referees were as thirsty as everybody else, they shalt not go for a beer in the vicinity of where the game had been played. This was a precaution against officials being attacked by grudge-bearing players or fans who happened to be having a drink in the same place. After one game in Walkerton the on-ice officials duly drove a few miles down the road before they stopped for a beer. However, it turned out that players from the losing team drove down the same road and showed up at the same place. Nothing occurred until one referee went to the washroom.

Two of the losing players followed and roughed him up. The referee phoned the OHA to complain. Could have led to an assault charge, would have made nice headlines, but nobody thought of it.

"We got a dandy this morning!" Hanley told another executive member the next day, while he pored over the law books and found that no specific rule covered a fight between officials and players in a bar well removed from the rink. So a rule was invented on the spot. Both sides being somewhat in error, one of hockey's eternal verities is that in case of a tie, the win goes to the referee. One player was suspended for three games and the refs were told to for Heaven's sake drive farther the next time before stopping for a beer.

Hanley, well into retirement by 1989, said he always felt lucky in his job because while serving under fifteen presidents, they all were happy to have him run his own show: "They all could see the advantage of one person in the office doing all the interpreting of the rules when disputes came up. That way there'd be less chance of getting a cockeyed answer – like one decision one day and a different one the next." He never wanted to sit on a disciplinary committee because he preferred to keep a detached attitude in major matters, but his recollections sometimes are spiced by hockey's own particular sort of value judgements, such as, about a known bad guy: "He was one of those players who are happiest when there's no puck on the ice."

Still, amazingly enough by today's litigious standards, before Hanley's retirement in 1976 only rarely did anyone take a beef beyond the OHA's own appeal procedures and subcommittee judgements. The extent to which change came about may be seen in more recent files. Very large and commodious ring folders labelled "Legal Cases," plus supporting material, trail on for hundreds of thousands of words, perhaps into the millions

Amateur hockey today in Ontario has come a long way

from little kids skating on their ankles and dreaming of glorious goals to come. The image might be more accurate if the little kids skating on their ankles were dreaming of becoming lawyers. Affidavits, statements of claim, applications for injunctions, hearings seeking leave to appeal, actual appeals, examinations for discovery, Ontario Supreme Court judgements . . . you name it, the OHA has been there.

The tip of the litigation iceberg came into view a year or two before Hanley's retirement, but at first it showed on the horizon no bigger than an ice cube. A case in 1971, one in 1973, a couple in 1974, one in 1975, then rising: six in 1978, more in 1979, and the flood was on. They had a profound effect, including on the OHA presidency. For ninety years, the presidency had arrived on doorstep after doorstep in an orderly fashion: men from the individual clubs might become delegates to the annual convention, might be appointed or elected to the executive, and after fifteen or twenty years of hockey administration experience (more, in some cases) might make vice-president and then president. By the time a man became president, an elected and unpaid position, he often was retired or free enough at his work that he could be available to the OHA office when required. Partly because of legal involvements, by the late 1970s the OHA presidency had become impossible to handle properly on that basis. For one thing, every two years, no matter what problems remained unsolved, there was a new man in the president's chair. Something had to give. In 1980, the switch was made to a full-time salaried president. The top elected official – still changed every two years – would be called chairman of the board. But the president would make the day-by-day decisions, hand out suspensions, deal with legal hassles, talk to the media, represent the OHA in dealings with government, open rinks, speak at banquets, and try to get home for dinner once in a while.

Which brings us to Brent Ladds, who is about the size of Toronto Maple Leafs' goalie Allan Bester—five feet seven, 150 pounds. Ladds, a one-time goalie himself (Loyola College, Orillia Terriers), was born in Noranda, Quebec, and at twenty-five was married and making his living from a carpet-laying partnership with a brother-in-law, Bill Wilson. Hearing that the OHA was looking for someone to work in its Merton Street office in Toronto, he applied.

Dave Branch, who had attended the University of Massachusetts on a hockey scholarship and had been a counsellor at Hockey Haven, a hockey camp owned by Wren Blair and Toronto Maple Leafs manager Jim Gregory, had succeeded Bill Hanley as OHA secretary-manager. Cliffe Phillips, then in his retirement year as president, recalls that when he offered Ladds the OHA office job he asked, "When can you start?"

"Tomorrow," Ladds said.

He didn't know much about the operation of the OHA, having grown up and played most of his hockey in Quebec. "I remember after about a week and a half being there—there was the office upstairs and another room downstairs where we had the board meetings—I said to Dave Branch one day, 'When does everyone else come in to work?' and he said, 'It's just you and me!' I couldn't believe it. From what I understood of the OHA and the magnitude of its operation I couldn't believe there was just the two of us."

Then, less than two years later, Ladds came back from vacation one day. "Dave said, 'Have you seen the paper this morning?' I said I hadn't, and he showed me a story announcing that he was going to the CAHA as executive director. I said, 'Congratulations,' and then he told me that I would be offered his job as secretary-manager.

"It was incredible. I had just come to grips with my own job, putting in, I'm not exaggerating, a lot of fifteen-hour days, seven days a week, trying to get a handle on it and trying to understand what Dave was doing, too, so I could take some of the load off him . . ."

But when the secretary-manager job was offered by Larry Bellisle of Penetanguishene, then the OHA president, Ladds took it. "There was no alternative. If I didn't do it, who would?" He hired another brother-in-law, Garey Wilson, a teacher, as referee co-ordinator, and did the job well enough that when the OHA decided to hire its first full-time president, he was a prime candidate. This decision to make the top operating official a salaried employee did not come easily after ninety years of elected presidents. The issue was swung by long-time executive member Bill Ruddock. About to become president, Ruddock unselfishly plumped for what he saw as essential change. That swung the vote. At twenty-nine, Ladds was it.

At the time one employee also was added to the office secretarial staff. With the president and referee co-ordinator, this made five in all to run an organization directly responsible for 5,900 to 6,000 OHA games each winter, hundreds of hockey teams, approximately 140,000 registered players (a total of those in the OHA and its various divisions), nearly 400 referees, and a vastly increased workload due to much-expanded training programs for coaches, players, referees, and trainers.

To say nothing of all the court cases.

Ladds's hockey background and friendly but decisive personality helped greatly in his job of ruling on hockey problems, from suspensions and investigations of excessive violence to playoff dates. He could call on long-time OHA executive members and past presidents for opinions or guidance when he needed it. But in the beginning, his background in the law as it affected hockey was virtually non-existent. In this he got a very quick education. Bryan Finlay, of the Toronto law firm Weir and Foulds, had handled most OHA cases since 1974 and in so doing developed a probably unequalled expertise in the legal

niceties (and otherwise) of hockey and its relationship to
OHA rules and regulations, players, their families, the laws
of liability, other organizations such as the CAHA and
Sport Canada, the Ontario Human Rights Code, and the
Canadian Charter of Rights and Freedoms, plus studies
and research on sports injuries.

After Ladds was named president, for a while neither
he nor Finlay kept regular office hours. "My full-time job
was supposed to be development of hockey," Ladds said.
"I would deal with that all day in the office, a pretty full
workload, and then I'd go down at night to Bryan's office
and sometimes we'd be there until midnight, going over
stuff we were dealing with in court."

At first this didn't involve much travel, but the year he
became president, the OHA sold its building on Merton
Street and bought another in Toronto's northwestern outskirts (easier for hockey people from out of the city to get
to). By the time the OHA sold that building and moved in
the mid-1980s to comfortable rented quarters in Cambridge, closer again to amateur hockey's heartland, Ladds
had spent a great deal of time on the road getting to court,
and in court. In the process, he has become as close as a
layman can to being expert on the law and public attitudes
as they apply to hockey.

The importance of these capabilities is that in common
with all hockey leagues and associations from minor
atom up, the OHA lives with a great deal of quiet and
rarely expressed public approval, but also must endure its
opposite: often emotional criticism of the game by the
media and the public. Why does hockey inspire such
strong emotions, sometimes running to the quite ir-
rational? *Hockey Is Our Game* is the name of a book by
Jim Coleman; *The Game Of Our Lives* is the name of
another by Peter Gzowski. Those works by distinguished
writers join hundreds of books, past, present, and future,
that detail a Canadian mind-set about hockey that, if
we were a more pretentious nation, would be called a

mystique. It is because Canadians *care* so much about the game that the OHA has to deal on a daily and very public basis with both the good and the bad. It has done so for lo, these 100 years, but never as often in court as has been the case in the Ladds-Finlay era.

Some cases, superficially, are relatively inconsequential, it being rather difficult for the average innocent bystander to take seriously that a boy of nine or ten can suffer "irreparable harm" by being refused permission to break the OHA-OMHA-MTHL residential rules in his choice of what team he'd like to play on. That happened in 1975, incidentally – to Wayne Gretzky. His father, Walter, tried and failed to get an injunction allowing his fourteen-year-old son to play in the MTHL. The refusal didn't seem to do Gretzky irreparable harm.

Much more serious are the cases involving lifelong injuries, players who wind up paralysed or partially so and who sue for damages running into hundreds of thousands of dollars, and in a few cases, millions. It is even possible that the 1966 decision of the OHA to incorporate under the laws of Ontario was prompted by some executive member's nightmare – namely, that a seriously injured player, or even someone claiming that a lifetime suspension for punching a referee had ruined his chances of becoming the federal sports minister, would sue individual OHA officers for substantial sums.

The number of eye injuries cited in the previous chapter, covered by the Emergency Fund's payments of $1,000 per damaged eye, would seem reason enough to seek whatever legal protection for individual OHA people might be provided by incorporation under the Companies Act. In the same year, 1966, perhaps with some of the same motivation, the OHA argued for and won unanimous consent of the CAHA to make the wearing of hockey helmets mandatory in minor hockey. (Eye and other head injuries have dropped dramatically in numbers since.)

But rarely did an on-ice accident or committee-room

decision lead to litigation. Now that possibility hovers over every dispute large and small. Because hockey is a physical contact sport in which injuries do occur, and some parents of young players seem prone to challenging the rule system in court, the number of cases in which the OHA and its affiliates have had to defend themselves in the Ontario Supreme Court add up to much more than those of all other amateur sports combined.

"At first the whole swing to taking things to court was a moral and mental problem with me," Ladds said in a 1989 interview. "I resented the fact that money as well as time that should have been going into the essentials of our hockey program had to be spent on court cases. Especially for cases that seemed to me simply people trying to break our rules for purely self-centred motives." He hasn't changed his mind on that point over the years. But he's managed to live with it and learn from it. He's pretty good in court.

His resentment is natural, from his standpoint: however nutty a legal action might be, lawyers are hired to argue both sides in court, motions are made, affidavits are sworn, the defendant hockey organizations make their depositions, Supreme Court judges listen, pronounce, and justice is done—while funds designated for hockey development have to be spent in this manner even when the OHA wins, which is overwhelmingly the case.

A document Ladds swore to in one case of a child's parents trying to break the OHA's residence rules in effect applies to all of the many such disputes. One part of this affidavit seems worth posting up somewhere, or being circulated to hockey parents. After introducing in a separate document the OHA's constitution, rules, and regulations and the affiliative relationship of the OMHA and MTHL in regulating all minor hockey below junior, the Ladds affidavit stated:

Each of the OMHA and MTHL requires a player to be resident

within its geographical area as a condition of membership in its organization. The purpose served by the residency rule is to ensure even competition between teams and to provide opportunity and incentive for advancement of players. If a boy is free to play for the team of his choice, the best players will be attracted to a very few teams. This would result in an imbalance between teams. The rule results in the best young players being required to stay and provide a nucleus for a team and an incentive around which to build that team, resulting in more clubs and more opportunities for other boys to play.

That seems straightforward enough. In such cases, of course, only one side can win – and almost invariably it is not the plaintiff. This line of litigation has even developed its own bundle of landmark precedents, one of these being the outcome of a 1974 case brought by a fifteen-year-old named Tom Boduch and his father, Ted, plaintiffs, against the OHA and one of minor hockey's more aggressive recruiters, Toronto Red Wings, and their manager, Jack Harper, defendants.

Ian Scott, who was later to become Ontario's Attorney-General, represented the Boduchs, with Bryan Finlay for the defence, one of his first for the OHA. As the judgement by Mr. Justice T.G. Zuber of the Ontario Supreme Court was to be cited in many cases later and embodies most of the plaintiff-characteristics that Ladds calls self-centred (and use up money and time), it seems worth reporting in some length.

The Boduchs were seeking an interlocutory injunction forcing Tom Boduch's release by the Toronto Red Wings so he could play with another team. In his judgement, Mr. Justice Zuber outlined the role of the OHA in hockey as follows:

All the amateur teams in Ontario, or at least most of them, are grouped together under the Ontario Hockey Association and have for themselves laid down a series of rules with respect to the hierarchy of the leagues, the ages of the boys who will play and so forth. The bylaws of this association have been filed and go into great detail. As part of the detail there are rules concerning the movement of players from one team to another and it's said in the rules, in general terms, that one team will not accept a boy who has played under the auspices of another team without the team from whom he moves consenting to that move.

The words "consenting to that move" were the rub. Tom Boduch had been playing for a team in the Toronto Red Wings organization whose home base, King City, involved more travel than he would like. Playing for that team was still open to him, the alternative being to play for another Red Wings team of slightly lesser calibre that was closer to home. In short, observed the judge, in the Red Wings' refusal to give Boduch a release, "he is not being put out of hockey." The judge termed the OHA "a private and voluntary association which has very success-fully organized amateur hockey in Ontario and this asso-ciation has prescribed . . . certain rules."

What the Boduchs were asking, he said, posed this question for the court's decision: "Should the rules of the OHA in effect be struck down?" He felt that an interim injunction to that end would be justifiable "only if the plaintiff demonstrates a strong prima facie case and that irreparable damage will be suffered, or in some excep-tional cases, if the plaintiff demonstrates an arguable case and a strong balance of convenience."

He thought the Boduchs had not demonstrated such a strong prima facie case regarding irreparable damage and that on the balance of convenience, while the Boduchs had an arguable case, "the inconvenience to the defen-dants (OHA and affiliates) would be very great. An injunc-tion forcing a departure from the rules that govern the activities of, I gather, some 70,000 young hockey players in the city of Toronto would seriously impair the organi-zational structure which presently exists."

Application for the injunction: dismissed.

Six years after that 1974 judgement, and with several more or less related cases between, the case of nine-year-old Mark LoPresti came to court. Mark's father was seeking a Supreme Court of Ontario injunction that would order the OHA, the OMHA, and the MTHL to allow Mark to play on a Toronto team outside of his home residential area, suburban Thornhill. In the father's affidavit it was claimed: "I verily believe that Mark will suffer irreparable harm if he is not allowed to play for the team of his choice and at a level of competition that will best develop his hockey talents." The background was partly the usual, and partly very unusual.

Mark LoPresti had been playing hockey since age six in the Thornhill Minor Hockey Association at the house league (meaning recreational) level. When he was eight, he was given a tryout with a team of higher calibre, the Thornhill Thunderbirds (players under ten) in the category known as Minor Atom AA. In mid-November he was cut by the Thunderbirds and, according to his father's affidavit, "was extremely upset . . . and required the moral support of his family to stand up under the emotional distress caused by his release . . . ."

Most families with children are familiar with such parental backstopping for a wide variety of reasons other than the disappointment of a young hockey player, but mercifully few of those cases get to court, as this one did. Mark LoPresti's father had applied for, and subsequently got, a written release from the Thunderbirds, believing that the release would allow Mark to play elsewhere. Mark finished the season back in the house league, but in May of 1980, when he was nine, he tried out for Toronto Nationals in the Metropolitan Toronto Hockey League's Major Minor Atom series (higher than Thunderbirds' Minor Atom AA).

Nationals apparently did not check if he was eligible from a residential standpoint. By the agreed-upon boundaries that separate the OMHA and the MTHL areas of operation (in this case, Steeles Avenue), he was not. The boundaries are designed to limit raiding from one organization or the other and save both untold arguments and even litigation on these very points. Still, he had been working out with the Nationals for some weeks when his father was told of this ineligibility ruling. The father then asked the OMHA to let Mark continue with the Nationals. The OMHA refused. This refusal was echoed by the MTHL, for the same reasons.

Mark, a year older and presumably a year better than when Thunderbirds had released him, then was asked back by the Thunderbirds and did play for them – but now felt uncomfortable with the club that earlier had been his heart's desire. He told his parents that other players kidded him, the coach had implied that his main trouble was his parents, and all-round he would rather not play hockey at all than with the Thunderbirds. At that stage the matter went before the Supreme Court and was heard before Mr. Justice Arthur Maloney.

The boy's parents, in a letter to OMHA president Tony Bloomfield that became Exhibit "C" among documents considered by the court, cited all these circumstances as being part of "the damaging effect this has had on both Mark's self-confidence and self-worth. He was robbed of both at only eight years of age." They had tried to persuade him to be comfortable playing with the Thunderbirds, they said, "but unfortunately, the psychological damage has been done."

Mr. Justice Maloney, in refusing (with costs, if demanded) the LoPresti application for an injunction that would rescue him from this psychological damage, cited two previous judgements. One was the 1974 Boduch case. The other was a 1978 case: that of Daniel Coady, age ten, vs. the Ontario Hockey Association *et al.* Coady, like LoPresti a resident of Thornhill and therefore in OMHA territory, had been registered with an MTHL team, the Toronto Red Wings, as living at an address within MTHL territory but which actually was the residence of someone else. He was playing with the Red Wings and hoping to make a hockey trip with that team to Boston when the ineligibility blow fell. At that point his father, Ronald Coady, took the matter to the Ontario Supreme Court.

The case, somewhat of a journalistic tear-jerker because young Coady had been counting on the trip with the team to Boston and had been selling tickets to help finance it, made for sympathetic coverage in the *Toronto Star, Globe and Mail,* and other sports pages. It also didn't hurt the headline writers' feelings that Mr. Coady's twelve-page affidavit included the nicely quotable line, "I verily believe that the OHA and MTHL and in particular the OMHA act as almighty rulers over the lives of young people."

So the case was heard. In the MTHL's defence for barring Coady, one precedent cited was from 1975, when Walter Gretzky tried unsuccessfully to have his "infant" (as legal documents use the term) son Wayne play in the MTHL for the same reasons cited by Boduch, LoPresti, and Coady: better competition.

The Coady judgement was delivered by Mr. Justice E. Saunders on December 22, 1978. As in previous cases, he gave an overview of what the OMHA and MTHL were all about: "Voluntary organizations which provide an opportunity for boys to play hockey." Such organizations had rules, one being the residence rule, and to grant the injunction requested "would require the MTHL to act contrary to its own rules . . ." He added that the Coady argument had not established that he had a right the court might enforce, so the injunction could not be granted. The judgement also pointed out, with careful judicial acerbity:

It should be noted that the applicant's father in completing the MTHL card for his son, inserted a Toronto residence address which he knew was not the residence of his son. He also purported to appoint his secretary who resided within the defined boundary of the MTHL as the guardian of his son.

On the basis of the deliberate misrepresentation of the father, the applicant played 12 games this season with an MTHL team although he was ineligible to do so. The actions of the father at the very least cast a shadow on the ability of the son to seek equitable relief in this court. The application is dismissed with costs.

It might seem excessive to cite three cases, all including almost the same parental arguments and almost the same defendants, the MTHL, OMHA, OHA and their rules. However, that was the point of including them: the time-consuming effort, the fact that the OHA with good reason is unbending on the principle involved, and that agreement with that principle came from court after court (and in many more cases as well).

As we've seen, the residence-rule examples cited have a lot of similarities. All bring out charges and responses as predictable as the lines of a Gilbert and Sullivan operetta: the tenor or perhaps soprano litany of charges by the parents and their lawyers, answered by the civil and rather liturgical – he's been handling OHA cases for fifteen years – baritone of Bryan Finlay, and finally ruled upon by the distinguished basso profundo on the bench. If any gambling man had been consulted in any of these cases, he would have given staggering odds against success by the plaintiffs.

But the OHA didn't always win. Two of the rare losses, closely related and perhaps better described as technical rather than real knockouts, came in 1984 and fell in the realm of the OHA-affiliated Northern Ontario Hockey Association.

In one, a boy named James Sheldon Petras from Green Bay, Wisconsin, was moved to Sault Ste. Marie in 1984 because the boy, his parents, whoever, felt that playing with the Soo Legion's triple A midget hockey team was better suited to the boy's talents and hockey hopes for the future than anything available in Green Bay.

At the same time a boy named Jacques Serge Beaulieu moved to Sault Ste. Marie from Long Lac, where there was no hockey up to his skills. Beaulieu first tried out for the junior A Soo Greyhounds and didn't make that team, but he enrolled in school, lived with family friends, and made the same midget team as Petras of Green Bay.

However, under residence rules, playing certificates were denied both players. They and the hockey club took the matter to the Ontario Supreme Court in their home district of Algoma. In the Beaulieu case one document was an affidavit by Terry Crisp, then coaching junior A in the Sault, later to coach Calgary in the NHL. Crisp called Beaulieu an excellent player, with a good chance to go far.

When both cases went to court simultaneously in October, 1984, the players won an injunction allowing them to play with the midget team, this being greeted with joy that might well be imagined – as both had left their own homes to have a go at the brass ring. Within a few days the OHA, NOHA, and CAHA got (from another judge) the right to appeal that injunction. Then, enter the factor of Ontario's crowded courts: the earliest date for hearing the appeal was April!

By mid-winter, months had gone by with both boys happily playing with the Soo Legion midgets, the team of their choice. By the time the appeal could be heard the season would be over. Overturning the original injunction wouldn't mean much and would cost money. Ladds, dropping the appeal, decided to accept the consolation prize: by allowing even the right to appeal in the first place, the court had acknowledged that the original injunction was open to challenge.

Indeed, the high rate of OHA success in residence cases probably is attributable to the fact that one of the more appealing social aims in the OHA and all its affiliates and divisions is to keep a boy, until a certain age, within range of his own home and school. This is part of the "greatest good for the greatest number" argument.

Still, despite the wide public and court support for the OHA's stay-near-home rules for young players, that concept often is depicted as its opposite: cold and arbitrary, paying no attention to individuals. In almost every case that the OHA wins, the losers allege that other players have beaten the system and do play outside of the boundaries imposed. As Ladds concedes, this is possibly true. For one thing, the OHA itself will hear and sometimes allow appeals stating exceptional circumstances. But the circumstances have to be more than simply a family's annoyance or their perhaps prematurely overheated ambition for their son's future. As well, a few may slip through the system by misrepresentation. False residence addresses are not unknown in other cases. Some parents and some hockey clubs try to get away with it if they can and take the heat if found out.

If such rules had been in effect years earlier, of course, Bobby Hull, as an OHA-registered player, would not have been allowed to leave home in Point Anne to play hockey in Hespeler at age thirteen. Still, there must be considerable doubt that Hull would have suffered "irreparable harm" had such a restriction been in force at the time. It might even have made him a happier person in those early teen years, because the Hulls are a big and loving family. And no such rule would have stopped him from becoming one of the all-time greats of hockey.

The parent-oriented examples given here have been chosen for a variety of reasons. One is that such attempts to use the courts, the media, public opinion, and loopholes real or created are reflections of a darker side to hockey. Affluent, well-dressed, cool-looking suburbanites of normally exemplary social behaviour may turn into furious screamers or even physical attackers of referees, opposing players, and anyone handy among the thousands of unpaid and largely unsung volunteer officials who give up a great deal of spare time to do the actual work of organizing the vastnesses of minor hockey.

The kids themselves, as well as more composed parents, may be embarrassed by a mother or father who acts like a jerk. Boys have been known to ask their parents *not* to attend games.

Chapter Sixteen

BOYS AND GIRLS TOGETHER?

"We feel sorry for her, just sad . . . she was manipulated by the media, the radical feminists, and the politicians."

— FRAN RIDER, president of the
Ontario Women's Hockey Association,
on the subject of Justine Blainey

As in residence cases, predictability of content is also the norm when hockey's highest-profile, most media-conscious issue is getting yet another airing in the courts. This is – or was – the issue of discrimination on grounds of sex, when the OHA defended what it saw as its inalienable right to bar girls from boys' teams.

The first of these cases began in 1978. A ten-year-old named Gail Cummings registered with a house league team in Huntsville and was taken on as a goalie. That, at the house-league level (not being eligible for OMHA playoffs), didn't raise much, if any, opposition. But Gail was specially talented. When tryouts were held for an all-star team that *would* compete in OMHA playoffs, Gail got that goalie job as well. Then the trouble started.

The OHA constitution states that it is in business to "promote, encourage and govern . . . hockey for *boys* in the province of Ontario." By that rule, the OMHA and other OHA affiliates may grant playing certificates only to males.

In an atmosphere of rising public interest, an inquiry by Professor Mary A. Eberts was ordered under the Ontario Human Rights Code, which in most instances bans discrimination on the grounds of sex. Gail won that one, Professor Eberts upholding her right to play on the boys' team.

The case for keeping the sexes separate in hockey was not helped much with the court when one male witness, asked what mixed male and female sports he was interested in, answered, with what has been described as a leer, "Sex." But that isolated distraction aside, the OHA and OMHA lost the case and then felt obligated, by their constitutions and overwhelming support of members, to launch an appeal. Some clubs thought they could handle mixed teams in the youngest age groups, but most felt that beyond puberty they didn't want the extra difficulties – including, at the most mundane level, such matters as separate dressing-room facilities. Gail Cummings had solved that by dressing in her hockey gear at home. That was okay in Huntsville, with a short trip to the rink, but obviously would not be workable everywhere.

So in due course the OMHA, with OHA support, appealed Professor Eberts's ruling to the Ontario Supreme Court. A panel of three justices heard the arguments at length, after which Chief Justice Gregory Evans set aside the earlier decision by Professor Eberts and allowed the OHA's appeal. He ruled that because "the services or facilities of the OMHA are not open to be made use of by the public at large, but are accessible only to those who qualify under the rules and regulations of the OMHA and as girls do not qualify, the refusal to grant Gail Cummings a registration card in order to compete in competitions supervised by the OMHA does not breach" the Human Rights Code.

That decision still rankles in some quarters. Widely respected sports columnist Milt Dunnell of the *Toronto Star* harked back to the case ten years later, in 1988, lambasting the OMHA's "arrogance and autocracy" in the Cummings case.

However, his flashback column included a huge silver lining. When Gail was barred from playing hockey with her male peers she had turned to lacrosse (with mainly the same boys she'd played hockey with) and at age fifteen was a member of the Canadian women's team in the World Cup of field lacrosse in Britain. Her performance there brought many scholarship offers from major U.S. universities with women's lacrosse programs. Eventually, she chose Temple University in Philadelphia, starred with Temple's powerful team, graduated in 1988, and went on for a master's degree in sports administration.

Asked by Dunnell what her reaction would be if a male showed up to try for a women's lacrosse team under her jurisdiction, she said the first thing she would do would be to find out if there were enough male players available to make up an all-male team. If not, "I would have to make it possible for them to play."

It is worth noting here that the Ontario Women's Hockey Association, not at the time affiliated with the OHA, supported Gail Cummings in that 1978 case not because it wanted to share its game, women's hockey, with men, but because without any team specifically for girls in Gail's home town she had to play with the boys or not at all. The OWHA position at that time, taken by the head of the OWHA, lawyer Kaye Cartwright of Kingston, seemed fair. As one OWHA official later noted, "We just want every kid to play."

However, the 1978 ruling on the Cummings case had echoes nine years later in a much-publicized action by a Toronto-area girl, Justine Blainey, thirteen.

The Blainey case occupied the courts, and the media, through several ups and downs for two years until another three-judge panel of the Ontario Supreme Court ruled 2–1 in her favour. The fifty-page dissenting opinion was written by Mr. Justice Charles Dubin, who later investigated the situation vis-à-vis drug use by Canadian Olympic athletes. The matter of pursuing the case into a final appeal to the Supreme Court of Canada was still an option. This course was strongly opposed by some on the OHA executive, including chairman Larry Clark, whose position was to accept the way the wind was blowing and avoid further legal expense. However, the opponents were outvoted – in retrospect, unwisely. On the basis of the strong Dubin dissent, the OHA did go to the Supreme Court of Canada seeking permission to appeal, was refused, and abided by that ruling. Finally losing that permission to appeal, and with it the case, with costs (about the costs award, Justine Blainey remarked, "My mother will be pleased"), presented the OHA with a legal bill for about $150,000.

The Blainey ruling meant little in a practical sense. The fundamental truth remained that while girls may not be banned from boys' teams because of sex, they still have to qualify on the basis of ability, a challenge that, as many female athletes in hockey and other sports told the court and the media, is somewhere between unlikely and impossible, because when strength is involved – as in hockey – it would be a rare girl who could match the boys. Justine played for several boys' teams subsequently and was cut by at least one. So that part of the challenge has gone virtually nowhere. In most instances, after all, a girl will be a marginal player on any first-rate boys' team in her age group. Meanwhile, Canadian women's hockey teams compete in national and world championships. More than twenty Canadian women in the last few years have accepted hockey scholarships in U.S. universities, which scout Canadian women's hockey tournaments.

There is no gloating from the OWHA. Fran Rider, the organization's president, said in 1989, "We feel sorry for her, just sad." Justine had played originally with a girls' team in Leaside, a Toronto district, until her mother, not satisfied with the quality of the team, had taken her out and started the events that led to the discrimination case. "After that," Fran Rider said, "she was manipulated by the media, radical feminists, and politicians." That is what put her where she is today . . . hung up somewhere between justification and actuality.

As a side effect, women's teams now routinely say no to tryout applicants who are male. Their situation is not similar to the one that faced Gail Cummings: there is no place in Canada where a man can't find a male team to play for. One of the Blainey lawyers forecast in her moment of triumph that now women's teams would have to make room for male players. But there have been no court cases on the matter, apparently there being no male equivalent to the forces that took up arms for Blainey.

At the same time, thanks to the Blainey ruling, there are hundreds of girls playing house-league and church-league hockey with boys. No one knows how many. At the time the Blainey case began, the OWHA had okayed about fifty girls to play on boys' teams where all-girl teams did not exist; once integration became law there was neither a method nor inclination to keep track.

It is also a fact that women's hockey, first documented in Barrie in 1890, has never been as strong a factor in the game as it is now – and some of the fault, and credit, goes to the OHA. "What the Gail Cummings case taught us," Brent Ladds said in 1989, "was that there was a void in our program. There were a heck of a lot of women out there who wanted to play the game, and who we had more or less ignored. We realized our mistake. The women already had their own organization. We just got in touch and offered to help."

At the time, the OWHA's first inclination was to tell the OHA, "Thanks, but no thanks." The idea of joining a male organization raised fears of once again being lost in the shuffle. "The feeling was that we were going into the unknown," said Fran Rider, who operates her own courier

business and now is the OWHA divisional director on the
OHA board. In the end, the decision to go for it was by no
means unanimous. But they did join and in the next
eleven years the number of OWHA teams rose from sixty-
five to 273, with provincial and national championships
and world tournaments now a matter of course, admission to the next Canada Winter Games assured, and a
feeling that maybe women's hockey will make it to the
Winter Olympics in the 1990s.

The long and short of the matter is a strong feeling
among the best female hockey players that women's
hockey is quite able to stand on its own feet—and that
for women to play with male teams simply weakens the
all-female hockey clubs. The OWHA's intent to give every
woman who so desires a chance to play the game has also
brought some surprises, one being what is called senior
recreational hockey, played by older women, some in their
sixties. Many of them say they always wanted to play but
didn't have the nerve. Now they borrow kids' equipment
and get out and give it a try.

It's probably true to say that Gail Cummings would
approve.

Chapter Seventeen

HOCKEY INJURIES

"... a neat kid, in the language of today."
— lawyer TOM MARSHALL of Oakville,
describing David Hawkins

The saddest cases brought to court against the OHA and its affiliates are those concerning a player who has suffered a crippling accident during a game. Most often such injuries happen accidentally, but that is very little solace for anyone who is limited to a wheelchair for life. One of those on-ice tragedies took place in a junior B exhibition game between Oakville and Stratford on September 14, 1980. An Oakville defenceman, David Robert Hawkins, seventeen at the time, had played organized hockey for about ten years and in 1979-80 as a midget was rated above average, being chosen his team's most valuable player. Now he was trying out for the Oakville junior B team, hoping that success at that level might attract a hockey scholarship offer. Junior B being considered by the National Collegiate Athletic Association in the United States to be amateur (unlike Major Junior), its players thus are eligible for U.S. college hockey. As a result, junior B is the category of Canadian hockey most often scouted by U.S. universities.

In the moments leading up to the accident that ended such hopes forever, an Oakville rush on the Stratford goal had failed and a Stratford player broke out with the puck.

The only player between him and the Oakville goal was David Hawkins, near the Oakville blueline. Hawkins is five feet ten inches, of average build. As Hawkins got ready to intercept the puck-carrier from in front, head on, another Oakville player, Craig Kowalchuk, about six feet three and weighing about 200 pounds, was closing in on the puck-carrier from behind. All this was in the centre area near the Oakville blueline, well out from the boards. At the last instant the Stratford player managed to elude both checks and Kowalchuk crashed heavily into Hawkins, knocking him to the ice.

While he lay helpless, the Oakville trainer ran out and kneeled beside him, decided quickly that David had suffered a spine or neck injury, and called for the type of stretcher called a spinal board. He was taken from the ice by ambulance attendants and then to hospital, where in subsequent days he was diagnosed as having a spinal injury that would leave him paralysed from the chest down, limited to partial use of his arms, and in a physical state requiring medical treatment and assistance for life.

Almost exactly two years later, in September of 1982, after many months of fund-raising to help with his medical expenses (the OHA and many of its member clubs, some having arranged benefit games, contributed to this fund), David and his parents filed suit for a total of about $2.3 million. In such cases, the statement of claim invariably casts a wide net. Named in the suit were his hockey club, the Oakville Blades, and the Blades' coaches, who were said not to have trained him properly for the vicissitudes of the game; the Stratford hockey club, which really had very little to do with the matter except having one of its players get out from between his two potential checkers. Also named was David's former teammate Craig Kowalchuk, who had been attempting an entirely legal check; the Oakville trainer, on the grounds that he might have compounded the injury by removing David's helmet (later it was found that an ambulance attendant had removed the helmet); Cooper Canada Ltd., manufacturers of the helmet and faceguard David had been wearing at the time of the accident; and the OHA, on grounds that subsequently will be discussed in more detail.

Without going deeply into the legal processes, examinations for discovery of all principals, and debates on details that took up nearly five years, the defendants denied all charges and took a position supported by precedents from lawsuits involving several sports: that when an individual chooses to engage in a pursuit, including hockey, known to have a history of injuries, he was consenting to that possibility.

Over the years after the suit was filed certain compromises were suggested by the plaintiffs' legal counsel. One was that the damages be limited to the $1 million liability insurance carried by the OHA. A later one dropped a possible settlement to a sum well below that figure. In 1987, just before the case was scheduled to go to trial, the suit was settled by the insurance company out of court. Part of the settlement agreement was that the terms would not be made public by either side. This secrecy is usual in such cases, to avoid what the insurance industry terms "copycat" claims.

At the time of the settlement, David Hawkins was described by his lawyer, Tom Marshall of Oakville, as "remarkable, humble, a very erudite young man. Over the years you can see his strength and maturity coming through – a neat kid, in the language of today."

David's use of his arms does not include his fingers, but he still is able to drive a specially equipped Ford van. Beginning in 1982 he attended Sheridan College, earned a degree in computer programming, and upon graduating soon found work. The van, Lois Kalchman of the *Toronto Star* reported, has a device allowing him to steer and a lever which, when pushed, puts on the brakes, and pulled, activates the accelerator. In 1987 he was working at Canadian Tire from 9 a.m. to 2 p.m., after which he would go home to rest until dinner.

Some of the charges originally levelled against the OHA in its part of this suit were that it not only condoned but encouraged violence in hockey and that this contributed to the kind of play that resulted in the injury to Hawkins. The evidence mustered against those charges is considerable. Part of this will be examined in a later chapter in details of mandatory and substantial suspensions it imposes against players who are penalized for acts known to be likely to cause injury. High-sticking, cross-checking from behind, spearing, butt-ending, head-butting, and grabbing a face mask are among them. The numbers of players suspended each season for these infractions will surprise those OHA detractors who feel that the OHA is soft on violence. Also, in concert with the CAHA and doctors who specialize in sports injuries, including those in hockey, there is a constant effort – largely unfunded by governments, despite detailed urgent submissions – to find new rules, better protective equipment.

Still, there are cases where defence is difficult, due to the nature of the game, its speed, animosities between individual players, crowd reactions that sometimes spur violence; all of these, to be sure, have been present in hockey since its beginnings. Referees, coaches, managers, and trainers – all responsible to varying degrees for controlling the action on the ice – are by no means perfect. When a game gets out of control some or all may be held to share responsibility, although even in a flawlessly refereed game, or for individual factors almost impossible to control, serious injuries may occur.

In the OHA, regular clinics have been set up for years to improve the calibre of coaches and the efficiency of trainers (especially in first aid). There are routinely scheduled instructional clinics for the OHA's nearly 400 referees and men hoping to join the referee force in the future.

As further backing for the officiating part of the game, performances of referees in games are checked regularly and assessed in writing by experienced former referees who do not make public in advance when they are monitoring a game. Grading of referees on a scale from one to six (the higher the number the more efficient and experienced) and assigning the best referees to the most important or most emotion-fraught games or playoff series is a system that is not always infallible, but it seems the best possible. All factors are taken into account when the referee-in-chief (the incumbent until 1989, when he was appointed co-ordinator of development for NHL officials, being Will Norris – in earlier years an NHL official) decides on his hundreds of referee and linesmen assignments each week not only for all OHA games but for Intercollegiate league games as well as those in the senior OWHA.

Changes in refereeing staff are made each year to keep officiating at the highest possible level. Young persons wishing to take up refereeing must pass tests on knowledge of the rules and how to react under stress (including fights), as well as basics such as skating. Then they start out as level-one officials in minor games and move up the ladder on merit alone, those who excel as linesmen in higher company being moved into refereeing at the lower levels when they earn it.

This process has qualified many OHA officials for steady work at the highest hockey levels. These have included the late John McCauley, NHL director of officiating, and Bryan Lewis, the NHL's co-ordinator of officials' development, as well as such well-regarded past and present whistle-blowers and big-league bear-wrestlers as Neil Armstrong, John Ashley, John D'Amico, Leon Stickle, Ron Finn, George Hayes, Bruce Hood, Scotty Morrison, Frank Udvari, Bob Myers, and Ray Scapinello, and dozens more currently calling games in the pro leagues.

All OHA on-ice and club officials are kept up to date on new injury statistics – some of which have a direct bearing on the way hockey seems to have changed because certain injury categories have risen alarmingly. One is the relatively recent proliferation of neck and spinal injuries, the main concern of the volunteer Ontario Committee for the Prevention of Spinal Cord Injuries due to Hockey.

In 1989 Bob MacKinnon, the OHA's past chairman, was a member of this committee along with the CAHA's Rick Parayre. Dr. Charles Tator, chief of neurosurgery at Toronto Western Hospital, was chairman. Other members included Dr. Tom Pashby, a pioneer in the design and effectiveness of helmets and face masks; Dr. Joanne Bugaresti, a rehabilitation specialist; physiotherapists Lucy Scarbo and Virginia Edmonds, RN; Pat Bishop, head of kinesiology at the University of Waterloo; Bob Firth, head of sports medicine for Ontario in the Canadian Paraplegic Association; and Lois Kalchman, the contact with the media.

The statistics that concern them most had a rather striking starting point. In 1973 a study of sports injuries in two major Toronto hospitals over a period of twenty-five years found that not a single spinal cord injury due to hockey was seen in that span. It is since 1976 that these injuries have reached nearly epidemic proportions. One 1985 figure given by Dr. Tator was that spinal cord injuries from hockey were occurring at the rate of about one a month; about one in three of those injured wound up in a wheelchair.

Yet, while spinal injuries increased in the late 1970s and into the 1980s, the *total* number of hockey injuries declined in one period that was studied in records of Toronto's Hospital for Sick Children: from 491 in 1973 to 346 in 1982. That's only one hospital, but the trend has been confirmed elsewhere. Part of this decline may be credited to hockey helmets, whose first mandatory use in minor hockey across Canada stemmed from OHA initiative in 1966. The later vastly growing use of face masks has helped as well, especially in reducing the once-heavy toll on eyes.

There is a team called the Ice Owls whose organization is the Canadian Blind Hockey Association. They play a version of the game by listening for the rattle of the "puck" and by vocal guidance from sighted friends. They are naturally the most eloquent advocates of face masks. Once when some player-categories in the OHA voted against face masks, a member of the Canadian Blind Hockey Association remarked acidly, "Your decision probably will provide us with a few more hockey players."

Thanks to both helmets and face masks, concussions and other eye and face injuries have declined dramatically. But neither piece of equipment does anything to protect the neck. That is the major current injury problem throughout Canadian hockey, with the answer so far eluding the best efforts of those most concerned. Considerably increased penalties and new suspensions for checking from behind or blindsiding an opponent into the boards might in time cool the kind of goon hockey that has led to some of these injuries, but there is no sign of an improvement yet.

And none of this prevents the totally unforeseen, which can occasionally result in tragic accidents such as the one that put David Hawkins, a neat kid, into a wheelchair and a specially equipped van for life.

Chapter Eighteen

WHO'S TO BLAME WHEN THE RIOT STARTS?

" . . . Very few people (4%) expressed a desire for more control by government."

– from a 1985 research report issued
by Sports and Fitness Ontario, based on asking
1,000 adults across the province
for their attitudes toward organized amateur hockey

" When it comes to hockey, politicians get on and off bandwagons faster than anybody."

– JACK DEVINE,
former OHA and CAHA
president, in a 1988 interview

This is a large subject and bears to some extent on the April 16, 1974, first game of the OHA's junior B championship playoff between the Bramalea Blues and the Hamilton Finochio-Cupido Red Wings (for short, Fincups). The game was won 3–2 by Bramalea in the kind of contest hated by those people who really care about hockey. This led to (a) Bramalea refusing to continue the series on the grounds of excessive violence and (b) a wide-ranging investigation and inquiry into the manners and mores of amateur hockey conducted for the Ontario government by Toronto lawyer William McMurtry. In McMurtry's report, issued four months later, he wrote:

This clearly was a violent game, 189 minutes in penalties were assessed, yet nearly all the witnesses who were present at the game believed more penalties should have been called. Several vicious fights resulted in only minor penalties, and at least three players admitted to participating in fights where no penalties were awarded.

Injuries were received by five players and one team official as a direct result of the fighting and brawling. On one occasion a Hamilton player left the penalty box to resume his fight, and two players sent to the dressing room engaged in an altercation in the hallway where they were joined by other players, officials and fans. The fans who were approximately 750 in number were orderly until the game became violent, and by the end of the second period large numbers of them were out of control. The two policemen on duty were forced to call in reinforcements. At one time 14 police officers were present in the Arena. The referee himself termed it the most difficult game he had personally ever handled.

That sets the scene, but McMurtry concluded that the game's violence couldn't be blamed on a single team, group, or cause, but was "symptomatic of a trend in amateur hockey which threatens to become much worse if remedial steps are not taken." He also found it "more than significant that the OHA executive in refusing to find justification for Bramalea's withdrawal from the series" did so on the grounds that the game was not as violent as some, "in which case it does not speak well for the state of amateur hockey."

He acknowledged that during his investigation, "reviewing accounts of countless games," he found that "there are hundreds if not thousands of games played each year which bear no resemblance to the Hamilton-Bramalea fiasco." Nevertheless there was a substantial increase in amateur hockey's violence, "and, more alarming, the use of violence as a tactical instrument to assert superiority over an opponent." (In hockey parlance later to become common, this tactical use of violence is called "gooning." Usage: a manager years later, defending his team's tactics in a playoff game before an OHA disciplinary tribunal, asked, more in sorrow than in anger, "Why would we goon them? We were away ahead anyway.")

McMurtry found in the gooning aspect of the Bramalea-Hamilton series, "an aftermath of emotion, confusion and even hysteria" compounded by the fact that the second game of the series was supposed to be played in Hamilton twenty-four hours after the first game. It was in that situation that Bramalea pulled out.

As it happened, and as does happen in an organization depending almost entirely on volunteers to do its business, the head of the OHA at the time was Frank Doherty of Thorold, a paper company executive who was intensely involved in union negotiations. This left the matter on the plate of Cliffe Phillips of Newmarket, a business executive who was due to be installed as OHA president in a few weeks. Phillips has said since that what happened next brought him "more pressure than I'd ever had in my life."

He had not seen the game in question, but from years of other OHA crises as a referee, executive member, and four years as vice-president, his first reaction was that if Bramalea was pulling out of the playoff and therefore *under the OHA constitution* must automatically be suspended, the championship series still should be played. Too quickly, he said later, he decided that a previously eliminated semifinalist from Owen Sound should replace Bramalea as Hamilton's opponent.

"That was a bad decision," he said in a 1989 interview. "It made it look as if I didn't care about the violence as much as making sure that the show should go on."

With that realization being hammered home by the media and the public, he quickly abandoned the Owen Sound idea but in a sense had opened up another can of worms: that about 47 per cent of the OHA's operating budget at the time depended on revenue from playoffs.

This was seized upon by McMurtry as being evidence of what he called "an unintentional conflict of interest" in the OHA: that being dependent on playoff revenues, as the individual clubs were as well, called into question the OHA's motives in dealing with events that might call for suspension of a playoff participant. During McMurtry's public inquiry, involving forty-two witnesses in all from the OHA, Bramalea, Hamilton, and the National Hockey League (the NHL being called for reasons that will follow), he urged that a compromise be worked out that would "ameliorate the harsh effect of the original suspensions." Those views did have effect. On June 17, only midway in the inquiry, the OHA executive decided that while Bramalea would remain on probation, the team, trainer, and coach were reinstated, although the suspension of the club president would remain unchanged.

Meanwhile, McMurtry was still hunting for the causes of excessive violence in all of amateur hockey, not just this one game, and considering what he might recommend to improve the situation. The first of these aims, the hunt for causes, he sought partly by questioning NHL president Clarence Campbell. At the time, the NHL's Philadelphia Flyers, popularly known as the Broad Street Bullies, dominated professional hockey while habitually using intimidation as a tactic. At the end of a then just-completed series in which the Flyers had manhandled New York Rangers, all-star New York defenceman Brad Park had commented: "Until this series I always considered a hockey fight to be something that happened after a flareup. As to this team [the Flyers] we find that fights are started deliberately."

This was later confirmed by Philadelphia's Dave Schultz in his frankly confessional book, *The Hammer: Confessions of a Hockey Enforcer* (1981). Actually, it was no secret. The more people knew about it, the more they might be intimidated. Dennis Hull, Chicago Black Hawks star, once told this book's author, "When you go into a corner with Schultz, sometimes he'll take a shot and not retaliate. And sometimes he doesn't even need provocation. Right out there with nothing unusual going on he'll

come out and start swinging. I'm convinced on those
occasions that's what he'd been sent out to do."

It was on the role-model line that McMurtry questioned
the NHL's Clarence Campbell. Many hockey players had
a natural ambition to make it to the NHL. Therefore they
were inclined to copy the way the currently most successful NHL team went about its business. The McMurtry-
Campbell debate, as it soon became, zeroed in on why
the NHL did not ban fights altogether by giving game
misconducts to anyone who fought on the ice. Campbell
made no concessions, retorting sharply to *any* suggestion
of NHL wrongdoing. In fact, McMurtry right then was
about as popular with the NHL as Father David Bauer had
been a decade earlier, for some of the same reasons.

A matter not noted in the inquiry, and possibly not
known at the time it was written, was that OHA president
Cliffe Phillips also was a strong opponent of fighting in
hockey games. A few days after the McMurtry report was
issued, Phillips led the OHA executive to recommend game
misconducts for fighters. This was passed at an OHA board
meeting held in the Walkerton hotel of OHA past president
Clarence (Tubby) Schmaltz.

"Our first idea was to make it apply only to teams
below senior and junior, those being the leagues that
competed for national championships," Phillips said.
"The board wouldn't accept that, so in the end we made
it apply to *all* hockey in Ontario." This decision was
announced at a subsequent meeting that Phillips and a
few other OHA brass had with Ontario Premier William
Davis. But under the OHA system of having all major
decisions ratified by the membership, it was not a final
word. Phillips said, "we always knew that if a certain
number of clubs demanded a meeting on the subject they
could get it, and maybe turn us over. They did just that.
It was the only extra whole-membership meeting that
we had that year. One hundred and six teams showed
up to vote, as well as the eighteen members of the

OHA executive. The vote against the no-fight rule was 102–22.

"All the same, there was a feeling in the membership that even if we're not banning fighting, let's change things. That's where some good new anti-violence rules came from: the ten-minute aggressor penalty, some stiffer rules on high-sticking, and another good one – for verbal abuse. It used to be that some loudmouth would call the referees names and get a misconduct, but it didn't mean the team had to play shorthanded. The new verbal-abuse penalty called for a two-minute minor as well as the misconduct. What we were doing was dump some rules back on the coach – if he couldn't control his players, he'd be playing short."

He saw the exercise as being like what sometimes happens in politics: proposal of a drastic change runs into strong opposition and is withdrawn, but the resultant relief makes the opponents more or less amenable to something less drastic.

Everyone who follows the game is aware of hockey's widely accepted rationale on fist fights: that, one-on-one, it's a way players get rid of frustration caused by infractions not seen by the referee, or seen and not called. The argument goes that outlawing fights, which almost always are broken up quickly and without injury, would merely result in players taking out their spleen on one another with potentially more dangerous high-sticking, slashing, cross-checking, butt-ending, spearing. A more cynical view is that the blood-and-thunder aspects of hockey are part of what draws crowds. The debate on fighting goes on, pretty well as it has for a hundred years.

McMurtry's report, while critical of the OHA on several grounds, also showed a certain sympathy: "It is perhaps an unfortunate aspect [of the Bramalea-Hamilton game] that the news media focused most of the blame on the Hamilton team and the OHA executive, when this particular game was only symptomatic of a trend prevalent in amateur hockey, caused for the most part by reasons beyond the present control of either an individual team or the OHA executive."

He noted, "in fairness to the present officials of the OHA," that, while responsible for the huge task of regulating hundreds of thousands of players and teams, coaches, and officials, they were *all* volunteers, handicapped by lack of funds, shortage of manpower, and undergoing constant criticism from coaches, parents, and the media. Without OHA volunteers and their rules and regulations, he said flatly, "there would be a chaotic hockey jungle . . . the only solution will be to work within the present army of volunteers because no government could possibly replace the vast reservoir of energy and goodwill now participating in amateur hockey." (Cliffe Phillips still keeps handy on a bookshelf a copy of the McMurtry report – with its cover inscription reading, "To Cliffe Phillips. Kindest personal regards, Bill McMurtry.")

The McMurtry recommendations included increased government financing (for the game, not specifically the OHA) in several areas: training coaches and referees; educating fans and parents as to what amateur hockey *should* be all about; supporting further research in the field of sports psychology and coaching methods. The recommendations were definitely good for the game. Most objectives have subsequently been pursued by the OHA to the point that little, if any, of what McMurtry wanted has been left undone. Mainly because the OHA prefers to make its own decisions and government money by definition always has strings attached, while funding for the sport has multiplied, little or none of it has gone directly to the OHA.

McMurtry's real blockbuster was to recommend establishment of an Ontario Hockey Council to help his reforms come about and to act as a final appeal tribunal. However, having a Hockey Council act as a court of last resort was recognized at the time as unlikely to fly. The idea was that such a council would have representation from the various hockey associations, as well as academics and others concerned with sports psychology, and would be answerable directly to a government ministry and yet be "separate from the government." How this could be achieved – answerable but separate – is the rub. If such a council is answerable to a government department, there is no way its most high-profile and controversial hassles could be kept from the floor of the legislature. To make a government agency responsible for making the hard decisions on hockey would plunk down right in the laps of the legislators the element they now can sound off about without taking any of the responsibility.

Cliffe Phillips put the matter in a nutshell to a government official during the Bramalea-Fincups debate. "If you guys want to run hockey," he said, "appoint the referees!" Imagine a winter session of the legislature in that event.

But naturally, there was no response. "No guts!" Phillips said.

How many years ago should the OHA have foreseen the possibility of direct government intervention in its affairs, and not only in the matter of curbing violence? The answer is: more years, the majority of them successful, than you might imagine. A tiny tip of the iceberg poked up virtually unnoticed in the McMurtry report's observation that nearly half of the OHA's annual income came from its percentage of playoff gates. In the headline-generated and violence-oriented fuss of the time, the short view held sway: that such dependence on playoff money might lead to decisions not inherently for the benefit of the game. The long view, that the OHA's financial structure eventually would require change, was ignored. Senior hockey, which once had provided a major portion of playoff take, was on a collision course with oblivion. Its long-time financial support for the OHA was going with it. No replacement was in sight.

In hindsight, some origins of the OHA's need for change

are a good deal less than specifically attributable to any previous errors. Volunteers, as a poet once put it, march to an unseen hazard. Volunteers started the OHA and operated it, usually with success, for much of its first 100 years. But being run by volunteers imposed its own penalties – one being that the bigger and more successful the OHA became, the heavier the pressure on those volunteers charged with running things. At a guess, by the 1940s when the OHA signed affiliation agreements with the MTHL and the OMHA, there just wasn't anyone among the busiest and most able volunteers – Dudley, Buckland, Panter among them – who peered into a crystal ball and acted accordingly. The MTHL, with its enduring (since 1912) mix of every form of hockey known to man, including many women's teams, wanted to join because its operation would be simpler without having to compete with the OHA for players, ice time, and so on. The OMHA had grown out of a group led by Simcoe's Jack Roxburgh who were convinced that the OHA's senior, junior, and intermediate categories were not enough, that the OHA also should extend its historic savvy to players under junior age – juveniles, midgets, bantams, peewees. (There were no atoms in those days; at least, no hockey players *called* atoms.)

Taking both minor organizations under direct dues-paying control would have been one way of handling the situation, if anyone had been able to see many years down the road. Instead, the OHA directors took the easy way out, signing affiliation agreements with the two organizations while saying, in effect, "We've got our hands full – Allan Cup, Memorial Cup, all the hockey we want. You guys go ahead and run your minor hockey." They even threw in an annual grant to both organizations to help them handle the minor side.

This seemed sensible enough at the time, but forty years later the reasons were vanishing rapidly. The minors grew while the OHA shrank. (By the 1989 annual

meeting, when about 100 OHA delegates showed up, in
the same hotel the OMHA annual meeting had nearly ten
times as many.) The MTHL and OMHA had two special-
ties – good hockey for the young, and border wars. From
about 1975 to 1985 jurisdictional problems between the
two main minor hockey divisions meant that too often
OHA directors' meetings were spending more time sorting
out MTHL-OMHA problems than their own.

Only then did the realization come that the boundary
problems, lawsuits, and other difficulties involving the
two minor hockey organizations, almost all drawing a
bad press for the OHA, would never have reached anything
like epidemic proportions if a single organization had
been running the whole show from the beginning. It must
be mentioned that the minors certainly didn't lack
money, or players, even if that didn't do the OHA much
good at the bank.

Meanwhile, senior hockey, for the OHA meaning a once-
considerable *raison d'être*, not to mention income, had
all but disappeared. Playoffs leading to the Allan Cup
slowly drooped into little more than old-timers' nostalgic
memories of the last great senior teams – Hamilton,
Kitchener, Chatham, Marlboros, Whitby, Belleville,
Windsor, Galt, Orillia, and a few others.

The senior decline was easy enough to delineate. Men
who in earlier years would have been playing senior
hockey were sought to fill rosters for the NHL's 1967
and subsequent expansions and then to collect the big
paycheques of the World Hockey Association. As a result
the Allan Cup as a force in hockey was kaput, finished,
gone forever, along with its one-time importance in help-
ing the OHA maintain its position as *the* major hockey
organization in Ontario and the country as a whole. The
last year an OHA Major Senior league operated, three of
the teams were from OHA territory, one from Thunder
Bay. Part of the arrangement with Thunder Bay was
that every time an OHA team had a game scheduled

there, Thunder Bay must provide twenty-two return air tickets.

"They're wonderful people in Thunder Bay and draw good crowds," one OHA past president said, "but they couldn't keep that up."

Next to go, for different reasons, was income from junior A. Following the 1967 abolition of NHL sponsorship of junior clubs, by the late 1970s all the old hockey men who had operated junior A teams in the past — Hap Emms, Matt Leyden, Lloyd Pollock, Dave Pinkney, and others — were gone. The new franchise holders, although hiring coaches and managers who'd learned their skills in the OHA, basically were businessmen accustomed to regular business practices, such as calling their own shots.

Their investments in franchises were worth close to $300,000 at the time (more since) and their team budgets were in roughly the same range, but their businesses ultimately were under the OHA's control. So in junior A hockey what one saw were businessmen at the club level being overseen by a changing array of volunteers, with a new president to deal with every two years. Decisions directly affecting club owners' investments were being made by OHA volunteers meeting in rooms to which the owners didn't really have total access.

To make the situation harder to bear for club owners fretting over their own bank balances, many looking to the playoffs to get them out of hock, the OHA took 7.5 per cent of playoff gates up to the richest series, the championship final, at which point the OHA share doubled to 15 per cent. In 1980, the OHA was operating on an annual budget of close to $400,000. Revenue from the junior A league was approximately $125,000, or nearly one-third of the total. As a man familiar with both sides said, "The junior owners just thought they were paying too much for the licence plate." Despite the long and honourable familial relationship between the juniors and the OHA, something had to give. That something was a real turning point for the OHA. The junior A clubs took the plunge, deciding that they would break away and run their own show.

Shortly before this decision was made public, but was very much in the air, Dave Branch, after two years as executive director of the CAHA, telephoned Brent Ladds, his friend and former assistant in the OHA office, by then OHA president. His call was to say that he was coming back to Toronto to be the junior A league's new commissioner. Both knew what that would mean, besides renewing old friendships.

Ladds referred to it. "You know, Dave, things aren't exactly smooth asphalt here. We might find ourselves on opposite sides of the table sooner than we expect."

Both knew the battle was looming and that, somewhat ironically, Dave Branch would be negotiating against the organization that had given him his start as a hockey administrator. Whatever happened, he and Ladds agreed, it would be done professionally, which it was.

Luckily, both sides had before them an example of how *not* to orchestrate such a breakaway. Earlier, Western Hockey League junior teams had left their various provincial associations to run their own show. This caused bitter chaos for a while. In Ontario both the junior A clubs and the OHA took tough lines, but the closest they came to open battle was when the OHA maintained that if the juniors broke away entirely, without maintaining some kind of OHA link, they would not be eligible for the major junior hockey event of each year, the Canadian championship series for the OHA Memorial Cup.

The meetings went on and on, but real rancour usually was held in check. Both sides wanted a settlement that wouldn't be a public relations disaster or damage hockey as a whole. Accordingly, both worked toward a settlement, but in the end it was not without turmoil. As Brent Ladds put it, "It was like knocking the house down and putting it together again."

For a year before the negotiations were completed, the newly named Ontario Hockey League paid the OHA nothing. But when the agreement was struck, it included that the OHL would pay the OHA an annual $30,000 as a straight affiliation fee, the connection being maintained but now at arm's length, and with no sharing of playoff gates. That done, the OHL paid its arrears and has made the same $30,000 payment each year since.

One result bore on the fact that for what seemed forever in Ontario, the OHA and top-drawer junior hockey had been synonymous. It took a few years before the public came to accept that the best junior hockey in the province was no longer part of the OHA, but was called the OHL. More drastic for the OHA was that, left with about 155 member clubs – mostly in the junior B, C, and D categories – it had lost fully one-quarter of its operating budget. This was met at first by assessing individual clubs to meet the shortfall. Next, in 1983, the OMHA, MTHL, and NOHA were made jointly responsible for a portion of the OHA's affiliation fee to the CAHA, and the membership agreed to a drastic raise to a flat $250 (up from $50 in some intermediate categories) for the annual registration fees paid to the OHA by its individual clubs.

All those arrangements were still in force in 1989. Many OHL teams work with farm systems (junior B and lower) that are directly under OHA rules and control. The OHL's player source is mainly based on what is called the midget draft, in which OHL teams annually pick and chose about 150 from each year's crop of the more talented young OHA players. Some move up to fill holes caused by the OHL's losses through age-limit rules, as well as players moving to NHL teams. Others among the drafted are assigned to various lower categories of OHA junior hockey, meaning basically that the age-old road up hockey's ladder still prevails. Not many players refuse if some OHL club calls and says, "How would you like a tryout in the big time?"

This occasionally does cause pain in the lower echelons, but without the OHA affiliation an OHL club wouldn't even be obliged to call a junior B club's manager to ask if they could have this or that player. That way would be chaos, a modern version of 1935, when the NHL could pluck players anytime from senior or junior, and the OHA couldn't do a thing.

Chapter Nineteen

PORT ELGIN, HANOVER, AND OTTO JELINEK

"When was the trial? Who was the judge and was there a jury?"

– letter to OTTO JELINEK,
Minister of State for Fitness and Amateur Sport,
from Hanover high school students

When the OHA suspends an entire club for its team's excessive violence, as it did the Brantford Classics in 1986 with Brent Ladds's succinct comment that the Brantford club's "objectives are not consistent with ours," or suspends individual players or team officials because of violence in a particular game, as happens every week, it still does so on the basis of its own investigations, listening to players, coaches, referees, and fans, and then acting, as it has always done, on its own.

As noted, many of the McMurtry recommendations have since been put into effect by the OHA. But still, from time to time, a team that feels unfairly battered and bruised will quit in the course of a game or series. The following case from 1987 is examined here as an example of how today's OHA deals with almost precisely the same type of emergency that brought about the McMurtry inquiry thirteen years earlier, except that in this one there was a rather absurd intervention by a politician.

On March 7, 1987, a junior C group playoff series

between Port Elgin Bears and Hanover Barons began in Hanover. Hanover had finished first and Port Elgin second their five-team league, but there was a major difference in size and age between the teams.

Hanover's coach, Jim Nixon, had been building his team for some years and his players had an edge in size, age, and experience. The much younger and smaller Port Elgin players had been picked specifically by first-year coach Doug Mitchell to his own criteria: speed, attitudes on and off the ice, and scholastic ability, as well as hockey skill. His roster included sixteen rookies, some sixteen-year-olds. In assembling his team, he had considered and rejected several older and more experienced players. He was an elementary school teacher, kinesiology graduate from the University of Waterloo, level-two referee, and a player at Waterloo and elsewhere.

During league play Hanover had lost only two games out of twenty-six, both to Port Elgin, in games where Port Elgin had been badly outshot but won due to excellent goalkeeping. Every time they met, some onlooker was sure to say that it was like boys playing against men. Partly due to Mitchell's coaching style and the qualities he had sought in his players, Port Elgin had been the least-penalized team in the group with 640 penalty minutes. However, next best was Hanover with 797 minutes, followed by Wingham (811), Goderich (1035), and Walkerton (1163).

So Port Elgin and Hanover weren't all that far apart in the matter of playing by the rules, but their intense rivalry had caused some pretty well-known incidents – such as a Port Elgin goalie breaking his stick over a Hanover player's back. The broken goal stick had been saved by a Port Elgin fan or fans and was said by Hanover to have been displayed publicly in the Port Elgin arena. If this indeed happened, along with the broken stick being inscribed with the name of the player over whose back it was broken, it seems to have been more a nut case than anything, but in any event the story itself did indicate the depth of feeling.

Hanover won the March 7 playoff opener 4–0, with penalties equal at thirteen minors, twenty-six minutes for each team. The second game, played the next night and also in Hanover, ended Hanover 9, Port Elgin 0. The penalties this time totalled forty-five minutes for Hanover and forty for Port Elgin. There had been a couple of fights and both teams had suffered injuries, but apart from two they were fairly normal.

The worst injury was to Port Elgin player Mike Chenette. He was cross-checked into the boards, suffered a neck injury, was removed from the ice on the type of stretcher called a fracture board, and spent a night under observation in hospital before he was released. The Hanover player who'd thrown that check was penalized five minutes, the referee ruling that it had not been a deliberate attempt to injure, which under OHA rules would have called for a match penalty and suspension for a minimum of four games.

Another Port Elgin player was cut for fifteen stitches and momentarily stunned when checked heavily but cleanly at the Hanover defence. No penalty was called, but when play went on without a whistle a Hanover player cleared the puck from the net area along the boards near the injured player. Coach Mitchell of Port Elgin subsequently claimed the puck had been intentionally shot at the injured player, hit him, and that this had caused the facial cuts. This was denied vehemently, the counter-argument being that he had been cut by his face mask when he fell.

However, returning to Port Elgin by bus later that night some team members, especially the younger ones, were dispirited and Coach Mitchell even more so. There was talk on the bus about whether there was really any point in continuing the series. Mitchell was particularly distressed by what he later charged were as many as eleven unspecified "deliberate attempts to injure" against his players. After what he said was a sleepless night, it seems that frustration, plus the fear of further injuries, was the ruling factor in his decisions the next day.

In the morning he phoned his school principal to arrange a substitute for his classes and organized a meeting of club executives, players, and parents for that night. He also informed the local weekly newspaper, which sent a reporter. At that meeting, he explained that the issue was whether to continue the series and perhaps risk further injuries, or default. This, among other things, would wipe out the next two home games in Port Elgin and thus cause a substantial financial loss to the home club.

Still, parents and club executives present were mainly inclined to accept the coach's view that for the safety of the players it would be unwise to go on. No doubt some input into that position was the fact that Port Elgin obviously was outclassed anyway. However, it was agreed that the final decision should be left to the players, who then left to meet by themselves in their dressing room at the Port Elgin arena. There, the players first took a vote on how many wanted to quit. Some did not. However, all knew what the coach's position was – and also knew that whatever happened, he wouldn't be coaching in the third or fourth game, if they were played. This was because late in the third period of the second game he had deliberately delayed the game by making line changes one player at a time, slowly, sometimes sending out a player and then recalling him to the bench immediately. After he had been warned, but persisted, he had been ejected by the referee. By OHA rules, such ejection carries with it a two-game suspension.

The players' meeting lasted about a half hour, after which those who had expressed the wish to keep on playing decided to join the majority, which was for withdrawing. Asked directly in later OHA hearings whether the players abandoned the series because of what happened in the first two games, or simply to support what all knew to be the coach's wishes, team captain Geoff Tanner said that it was a little bit of both.

What followed was bizarre. The decision to withdraw having been reached, Mitchell could have got his head-lines by informing the OHA of Port Elgin's intention to withdraw and going public with charges of excessive vio-lence, bad refereeing, whatever. The media thrives on hockey violence stories. When a team has played a full season and won one round of the playoffs (as Port Elgin had against Wingham), then quits with the charge that to continue would endanger life and limb, the issue is never ignored.

In this case, some in the sports media might have felt that if Port Elgin had won the first two games, with just as much violence on both sides, the moral issue would have been a lot more dramatic than a team quitting after it had been beaten badly. But that reaction, however understandable, still would have ranked second to the charges of violence.

Instead, Mitchell proposed that the club would not inform *anyone* of its imminent default. It would spread the word in the local newspaper that the third game, scheduled for Port Elgin on Wednesday night, March 11, would be violence-free. Port Elgin fans would be urged to turn out in force for the event. This was done. The coach's plan – at first agreed to by manager Larry DeMoor, the players, and others – was that on Wednesday night the two teams would finish their warmup and retire to their dressing rooms during ice-cleaning. When the teams were recalled to the ice the Port Elgin players would appear wearing black armbands. They would stand for the national anthem and then skate off the ice, leaving the Hanover players to the no-doubt thunderous boos, or worse, of the crowd.

Mitchell's decision not to let the OHA, or Hanover, know his plans put an unusual complexion on the affair. Often enough in the past the OHA, being informed that a series is getting out of hand, has read the riot act to both clubs, sent a coterie of observers to back up suspension threats, and in so doing saved a playoff. Instead, not only was Port Elgin's commitment as an OHA member being abrogated by not reporting the decision to OHA headquarters, but Hanover was being set up to arrive Wednesday for a third game that wouldn't happen – a fact they would learn under circumstances that Mitchell said in one hearing was part of his feeling at the time that he wanted to make "real assholes" out of the Hanover team. (This phrase was laundered to read "to make a spectacle," in the OHA's final report of its findings.)

In the end, the original plan failed. One reason was that Mitchell phoned several western Ontario media contacts to alert them to the dramatic scenario planned for Wednesday. Brent Ladds has his contacts, too. Two telephone calls on March 10, the morning after the Port Elgin meeting, tipped him off. Later that day, after difficulty in finding Mitchell and DeMoor by telephone, he did talk to both of them, but received no unequivocal answer on whether the game would go on.

The next morning, March 11, manager Larry DeMoor called and told Ladds that Port Elgin was forfeiting the series. Then Ladds called Hanover club officials and told them that they needn't make the trip to Port Elgin; they'd won by default. The Hanover reaction was surprise, disbelief, shock. No one will ever know whether, without the anonymous phone calls to Ladds and his subsequent actions, a very ugly incident might have occurred in Port Elgin that night, with an aroused crowd in the stands and only the team that Mitchell had seen as the mortal enemy left on the ice.

As it was, the original intensely confrontational plan was modified, but only in its most threatening aspect. A thousand people showed up in the arena. What they got was the Port Elgin players skating through their pre-game warmup, going briefly to their dressing room, then returning to line up across the ice for the national anthem. In that lineup, one player had an arm in a sling but Mike Chenette, who had suffered the neck injury, appeared without his temporary neck brace because, he said later, he did not want to draw attention to that injury. Still, it was a moment of some emotion. Coach Mitchell wasn't through yet. Although these events were reported at some length in most major newspapers throughout Ontario, one of the few media eyewitnesses was from the weekly *Port Elgin Beacon-Times*.

After the anthem was played, that newspaper reported, "Coach Mitchell then took over the microphone and, in a sometimes emotionally choked voice, explained" that the Bears had officially ended their season. "Some might consider this sour grapes after losing 4–0 and 9–0 . . . However, we felt that if we continued playing, the series would deteriorate toward a violent conclusion." He also said that, "Hanover has an excellent team who deserved to win and dominated most aspects of both games."

End of phase one, with province-wide media attention.

Phase two took a little longer, and requires a shift of scene to Ottawa and then Minister of State for Fitness and Amateur Sport, Otto Jelinek, former Canadian and world figure-skating champion and an indefatigable fighter against sports violence, his favourite target being hockey. About nine months earlier, in 1986, he had set up a new program called "Fair Play In Sport – Campaign Against Violence." This included an advisory committee, a veritable honour roll of fourteen distinguished sports personalities, including Jean Beliveau, Wayne Gretzky, Abby Hoffman, CAHA president Murray Costello, and others.

Part of the function of those involved was to make

an annual Fair Play Award. The 1987 inaugural award winner was to be chosen by March 15 and flown to Vancouver a few weeks later for the presentation. On March 12, when Doug Mitchell's name burst onto the sports pages, a winner had not been chosen, or at least not announced.

At that point few, if any, of the selection committee had ever heard of Doug Mitchell, let alone tried to match him up with the award's criteria, two of which are: respect for one's opponents (in this case, his opponents were the Hanover team he hoped to make look like "real assholes"); and "consistent demonstration of a respect for officials, an acceptance of their decisions and a steadfast spirit of collaboration with them" (as in the way he broke as many OHA rules as might have stood in the way of his petulance).

There is no intention here to blame Mitchell for what happened; memory of the original event would have died quickly and naturally had it not been for the artificial respiration provided by Otto Jelinek and his Fair Play Award.

It is astonishing to think of a government program moving this rapidly, but exactly sixteen days after the emotional Wednesday night show at the Port Elgin arena, just as the OHA was holding its preliminary hearings into the situation with suspensions sure to follow and Mitchell almost inevitably to be one of them, the sports pages announced the latest development.

The first winner of the Fair Play Award was . . . Doug Mitchell!

Actually, the first news of this decision was not the *official* announcement. One noon Mitchell was speaking by telephone to Lois Kalchman, the freelancer who writes about amateur sports for the *Toronto Star*. In mid-conversation Mitchell asked if he could put her on hold and take another call. She said sure. When he returned, he was

very excited. The other call had been to inform him officially that he had been chosen to receive the first Fair Play
Award.

This was somewhat of a surprise to Lois Kalchman.
She was a member of the Fair Play Advisory Committee
that was supposed to help choose the winner. She hadn't
heard a thing about it. But she knew a front-page story
when she saw one, and that's where this one wound up
in the *Star* the next day. As it turned out, most other
members of the advisory committee also learned the
name of the Fair Play Award's first recipient not by picking
him, or by assenting to someone else's choice, but when
they read about it in the newspapers.

While there was an obvious political tinge, and some
members of the advisory committee later withdrew for
conveniently unconfrontational reasons, Jelinek is said
to have had no part in actually choosing Mitchell. The
word was: "It was run past him for his knowledge and
approval, but that's all." However, with a staff that trigger-
happy, obviously he didn't have to be personally involved
to get the political effect. It was also the general impression that the selection committee all along had been
looking for someone in hockey who would both fill the
Fair Play bill and give a black eye to hockey, which Jelinek's administration had been busy doing in other
instances, as well. However, one must admit that the Fair
Play selection committee was at least prescient enough
(in light of subsequent events in Seoul and elsewhere) not
to make the award to someone in another much more
favoured sport in Jelinek's domain, track and field.

The same day that Lois Kalchman's story in the *Star*
scooped the country, not to mention many or all of her
fellow members of the Fair Play Advisory Committee,
Ladds wrote to Jelinek expressing "our most profound
and deep disappointment" at the "irresponsibility" of the
Fair Play selectors to take this stand without checking

current status of the intense inquiry the OHA was then conducting.

Jelinek replied by supporting the award – he could do little else. To some fairly pointed media questions about the legitimacy of giving an award to a man whose method of dealing with a problem was not widely considered to be what fair play was all about, Jelinek said that the Fair Play nominators had investigated Mitchell *as a man*. In the same story Ladds was quoted as saying *the man* was not the OHA's concern, but the event was. Jelinek also wrote to Ladds telling him that the OHA should not suspend Mitchell.

Queried by the news agency Canadian Press on whether Jelinek's statement would have any impact on the OHA's investigation and decision, Ladds kept cool. "We have to look at this objectively and view the facts, determine whether there was provocation and whether they had good reason for doing what they did," which is more than the so-called Fair Play selectors had done.

If Jelinek had second thoughts about the award, they were privately expressed. The mail reaction he got on the subject tended to be from people who deplored violence in hockey but even more deplored what seemed to them to be a politician reacting to a headline, the Port Elgin default, and making political hay of it before the facts had been determined. From Hanover, 125 students at John Diefenbaker High School signed a letter asking, "We would like to know when was the trial? Who was the judge and was there a jury?" A petition in the same vein was signed by more than 300 parents, hockey fans, and Hanover and district citizens.

Meanwhile, the OHA was conducting its investigation. Meetings with officials and several players of both teams were held on April 6, 21, and 27, May 11, and June 9 and 17. Each meeting consisted largely of questions and answers on individual and group attitudes as well as about what actually happened on the ice and off it. Along the way, as the OHA stick-handled through the charges and counter-charges, some statements didn't jibe with the way the series had ended. One Port Elgin player said, in response to a direct question, that he had not been afraid or intimidated during the series at any time. Another said that he had taken a number of slashes, but nothing out of the ordinary. Others said, sure, they would play against Hanover again.

Mike Chenette, the player injured when checked into the boards, said, "I've been in rougher games, it was just a regular hockey game," but "the check that injured me was a cheap shot." Many players on both teams echoed one of Chenette's phrases, that the games had been "typical hockey."

Hanover's Tom Newbigging, the biggest player on either team, said that he liked to hit, but didn't do so when it would cause injury; that he never started a fight but would not back down when challenged. He pointed out with some pride that he had never received a penalty for instigating a fight. Newbigging felt the two games played were neither hard-hitting nor violent and that Hanover figured it could take Port Elgin four straight anyway and was really thinking of the next round in the junior C OHA playoffs against Norwich. He threw in that he had played against some of the Port Elgin players many times in minor hockey and in particular did not consider Mike Chenette and Geoff Tanner to be quitters, so it must have been the coach who made the decision.

The original situation and something like 25,000 words of testimony were reviewed and summarized by the OHA before Ladds issued his report in late June. Mitchell and DeMoor were suspended for the next hockey season, but the club was not suspended, "and no doubt would continue to provide a lot of entertaining hockey in the Port Elgin area."

This report was the subject of two letters to the OHA

from Murray Costello, president of the CAHA and a member of the Fair Play Advisory Committee, congratulating Ladds and others for such a thorough investigation and noting that "all the facts were revealed and well documented."

Mitchell and DeMoor (counselled by Toronto lawyer Edward C. Hannah) then appealed the sentence to an OHA tribunal that, by the appellants' request, was delayed until October. On the day before the appeal was to be heard Mr. Hannah, by taxi, courier, and other means, sought media support, sending letters to many sportswriters and columnists laying out the Mitchell-DeMoor case. With these letters he enclosed copies of a four-page outline of his grounds for appeal, plus a submission to the OHA by Mitchell and DeMoor on how hockey could be improved and violence lessened. This material went to sports editors and hockey writers at the *Globe and Mail, Toronto Sun, Hamilton Spectator, Toronto Star, Owen Sound Sun-Times, Port Elgin Beacon-Times*. Most of these newspapers used the information with little reference to Hanover's position, or anything else negative to the appeal. It didn't matter much. The OHA tribunal upheld the suspensions. Hannah later petitioned the CAHA to hear an appeal to overturn the OHA decision. Murray Costello replied that the CAHA would only hear an appeal if there had been faulty procedure in the earlier appeal to the OHA, which he judged had not been the case. So the matter was closed, except in the OHA's colourful memory bank.

Chapter Twenty

ALL IN A DAY'S WORK

"I can't see the reason why we would try to 'goon' them when we're up 3-1."

— STAN MCKINNON, manager, Mooretown Comets, on a game called off with 4:41 left in the first period

Violence on the ice is the game's most pervasive public complaint, usually accompanied by the accusatory wail, "Why don't you *do* something?" The story is repeated here and there about the mother at a hockey camp going to the instructor to complain about all the bumping and grinding, and being told, "Maybe you should have put your kid in a tennis camp." A veteran hockey man recently observed, "The rules change, but the *people* don't." Certainly there is no lack of public exhortation of hockey authorities to clean up their act. If there has been a single unifying thread running across this country from sea to stormy sea, it is denunciation of hockey violence. The mere mention of the phrase has a blinding effect, especially on editorial writers. The wise ones know, when getting the assignment at the daily editorial board meeting, that it isn't really necessary to write a new one; just get a printout on last year's and change the names. It has never yet occurred to one of them to write, "There were 5,987 hockey games played in Metropolitan Toronto this winter, and only one of them ended in a riot." In short, hockey is not only our national preoccupation but also our national whipping boy.

The fact is that the OHA version of the game has fostered great non-violent players (Wayne Gretzky, Red Kelly, Dave Keon, Bob Gainey, many more) as well as fine players (their name is legion, but try Bobby Orr and Gordie Howe) part of whose art could be violent to some degree, if the situation demanded. The rules are pretty well standardized with those of the CAHA and the NHL, but in the punishment line the OHA is tougher than most. In each dressing room used by an OHA team during the 1988-89 season there appeared on one wall a large OHA-produced poster, coloured green, setting out *"minimum* suspensions which shall be imposed for infractions which occur in all OHA exhibition, league and playoff games." The warning read that "these suspensions are over and above" any imposed by the CAHA or any other organization whose authority is recognized by the OHA. Further, the line in the poster that reads "Please post this notice in your team's dressing room" is enforced, to ensure that when the heavy arm of OHA law falls on a player or his coach or manager, at least nobody can legitimately act surprised.

So how does it work? In an average playing period from October to April, about 6,000 OHA games are played. In many there isn't much to report except the score. But when game misconducts are handed out, or bench-clearing brawls occur – in short, anything serious – the system for enforcing what the OHA calls "progressive discipline" runs in a straight line from the referee to OHA headquarters. Immediately after the game the referee phones a number at OHA headquarters in Cambridge and dictates into a tape machine details of any substantial trouble he's had. Almost invariably, the most colourful parts of his report are infractions dealt with by the green poster mentioned above. The anti-violence rules set out include the following (a random sampling).

An aggressor/instigator in a fight gets at the very least

a minor and match penalty, usually a fighting major as well, and always an additional one-game suspension. On a second match penalty under this rule, he's suspended for two more games; four on third offence, at which time he also has to appear before an OHA tribunal to explain himself. All these are minimums and may be increased, depending on the player's record and, perhaps, attitude.

When a player leaves the players' bench or penalty bench to get into a fight, or to start a fight, he is ejected from that game and suspended for the next two, *minimum*. At the same time, his coach – who is supposed to have bench control – is also punished: a $300 team fine and his suspension for one game. If it is found on inquiry that the coach ordered one or more players over the side, he is suspended for at least one more game and fined another $150.

If a coach is ejected from a game for any reason, his minimum sentence is suspension for two additional games, as in Doug Mitchell's suspension following his Bad Night in Hanover.

Perhaps the most arresting section on the green poster's crime sheet is that covering match penalties for the likes of hair-pulling, spitting, and other offences against the general social thrust of Making Friends and Influencing People. These infractions not only cause the man's team to play short-handed for the length of time determined by the severity of the original infraction (two minutes, five, or – rarely called, but the rule is there – ten), but also to lose his comforting presence for the rest of that game and any number up to seven additional games. Under these match penalty rules the *minimum* game suspensions are: two for hair-pulling or spitting; three for grabbing a face mask or head-butting; four for spearing, butt-ending, kicking, stick-swinging, or deliberate attempts to injure; and seven for molesting an official. Again, to emphasize, these are minimum.

The public reaction to this list may be, "Ah, hell, but

they don't call all those things." That may be true in some games, but only on the fallibility of an official's eyesight, peripheral vision, or on-the-spot split-second judgement. The times when they do make the calls add up impressively. In the 1988-89 season the number of players called for infractions leading to suspensions, and the number of games they were suspended, were:

Attempt to injure: 47 players, 188 game suspensions, one indefinite suspension, and two suspensions for the entire season.

Butt-ending: 51 players, 204 game suspensions.

Grabbing face mask: 99 players, 297 game suspensions.

Hair-pulling: 9, with 18 game suspensions.

Head-butting (this once-popular pastime is losing its place on the hit parade due to the protection afforded by helmets and face masks):12, with 36 game suspensions.

Kicking: 2, with 8 game suspensions (one player was suspended for 10 games).

Molesting an official: 33, with 231 game suspensions.

Spearing: 92, one indefinite suspension, 368 game suspensions.

Spitting: 8, with 17 game suspensions.

Stick-swinging: which seems to the spectator fairly common in some games but often is linked with another infraction: one four-game suspension.

When you add that up, 354 players were barred from 1,371 OHA games in that one season alone. In almost any other human pursuit, that would discourage the constituents almost to the point of peaceability. The fact that this has not happened is at least partly because the game is the game. Suspensions apart, some players tend to play the game the way they always have – but now find themselves sitting out a lot more than ever before.

The overnight tape, a relatively recent addition to headquarters routine, replaced what used to be, some mornings, two or three hours of taking calls from game officials, and allows immediate action in the most pressing cases.

First duty each morning for the OHA's office staff is to clear the hotline tape and enter details on the individual record card of each player who may have incurred the ref's extreme displeasure.

These cards provide an instant reading on the player concerned. If he has committed a major infraction but has a clean past record, his name in the typed report is followed by the letters NR (for No Record). If his card shows that he has been somewhat less than hockey's version of a perfect gentleman, the card is attached to the morning report. Copies of messages on the tape are waiting each morning on the desks of OHA president Brent Ladds and referee-in-chief Willard Norris. In serious cases the offenders are ordered, with date and time, to attend a disciplinary board hearing at OHA headquarters. This board routinely meets every second Saturday during the hockey season, except when business is so brisk that it is called for every Saturday.

That kind of order in a way represents a further punishment that isn't really a factor until the first time it happens: that is, if the OHA orders attendance at such a hearing, it means that those summoned, usually a player or players and a club official or officials, are obliged to give up a Saturday off in favour of driving, sometimes for several hours, to OHA headquarters to appear at a specific time. Someone from a distance may be summoned for a show-up time later than that for someone closer.

Ladds and Norris estimate how complicated or how simple a hearing will be and write the disciplinary board's agenda accordingly, allowing anything from fifteen minutes to a couple of hours per hearing. The disciplinary committee's make-up rotates among OHA directors on a predetermined schedule, each knowing well in advance which three or four Saturdays a season he'll be required to fulfil this part of the duty of being an OHA volunteer. Usually four or five are on each panel, so sometimes two hearings can go on at the same time.

On the grounds that actuality sometimes tells a story better than dispassionate exposition, one may examine as an example one Saturday in January, 1989, when nine cases were heard. That day's disciplinary committee members were fairly representative of the heart and soul of hockey in Ontario, volunteers who receive no pay and yet year after year help get the job done – playing, managing, coaching, refereeing, or acting as league convenors in their communities across the province. This day they included Larry Clark of Scarborough, whose day job is with the Ontario Ministry of Revenue in Oshawa and who had been OHA chairman from 1986-88; Murray Parliament of Port Perry, a transport company executive who a day later was due to begin intense contract negotiations with the Teamsters' Union; Gord Gottscheu, an Ontario Hydro executive living in Port Elgin; Bill Stobbs of Blenheim, who is Administrator, Manpower Planning, with Union Gas in Chatham; and Don Yeck, a burly product of his home town, Belmont, where he has been arena manager for the last twenty years.

Disciplinary hearings, in most cases, involve players who have been in trouble in the past and who, by whatever they have done recently, might be in line for what the OHA calls "progressive discipline" – increasing the suspensions for each successive infraction. (If you've already had the mandatory minimum four-game suspension for spearing and do it again, you get more than the minimum and so on for all repeat offences.) To emphasize: all suspensions mentioned are the minimum; depending on the hearing, the ante may be raised. After each hearing, the board members discuss the case briefly, reach a decision, and one does a written report that will be passed on to the club within forty-eight hours or less.

The hearings themselves are rather low-key and non-condemnatory, the board chairman opening each hearing with the observation that this isn't a court of law but that hockey's code must be enforced and the meeting's purpose is to give the player and club officials a chance to tell their side of the story.

That day's agenda opened at ten in the morning with the appearance of a Caledon junior C league player who was said to have molested an official and for that had received an indefinite suspension. The board really set its style for the day in this hearing: polite, even friendly, but firm. The referee in question, André Fauteux, described the incident (the player was said to have shoved a linesman while arguing against a penalty for high-sticking). This was followed by the player more-or-less confirming the details except that he'd been fouled by a player the ref didn't notice and had only retaliated. Next came Caledon club officials, who spoke well of the player's general attitude and record (one fight and thirty-six minutes in penalties in thirty games). Molesting an official, throughout all of hockey, is the game's most serious no-no. The player's indefinite suspension was continued for the rest of the regular season, the idea being that next time he's tempted to lay a glove on anybody in a striped shirt he'll think twice.

Five other players (three junior Cs from Dresden, Wellington, and Petrolia; one junior D from Alvinston; and a junior B from Oakville) appeared who were already under four-game suspensions for third offences as instigator/aggressors.

This rule is simple enough. If two players are in an altercation and one suddenly starts throwing punches, he's tagged as the instigator. If two players are fighting and one stops and simply covers up (in hockey this is known as "turtling") while the other keeps hammering away, the latter is tagged as the aggressor. The two transgressions are lumped together for disciplinary purposes. A total of three calls under either or both of those rules adds up to a four-game suspension, with the possibility of more being added. In these cases this day, no further suspensions were added, but the players had pointed out to them, fairly gently, that the next infraction would automatically cost eight games, "and do you really want that?"

Then there was a senior from Lambeth, under indefinite suspension for attempt to injure. He explained that an opposing player had taken a run at the Lambeth goalie, knocking him down. Under hockey's unwritten law that one must defend and protect one's goalie, this player—with a previous record of very few penalties, all of a minor nature—had ("in the heat of the moment, I was sorry right away that I had done it") cross-checked his opponent *not* from behind on the back of the neck, as charged, but with a blow from one side that slid off the shoulder and then on to the side of the neck. After he had left, the board members decided that on this player's generally clean record and his remorseful account of the incident, the six games he'd already missed was enough punishment.

When he left, one board member remarked to another whimsically, "I get the feeling that everybody is telling the truth this morning." Smiles all around. The day's work was moving right along.

The next case was of tampering (trying to get a player to leave one club and join another). A player with the last-place Tillsonburg junior B club had quit his team but wanted to play elsewhere, which is impossible without a release. The Tillsonburg club had refused to release him.

The Tillsonburg coach said he regretted that the player now was out of hockey, but that obviously it was the player's own decision; he was welcome to come back anytime. This coach also mentioned that being a last-place team and naturally not seen as a hockey heaven by its foot soldiers, "we're always getting this kind of thing." The tampering charge was against a well-liked veterinarian, Dr. Wayne Bertrand, a Woodstock club executive. He said that he had only "tried to help the kid," mainly with advice. The boy had contacted him, not the other way around. The tampering charge was dismissed.

The final case, involving the Mooretown Comets and

the Dunnville Mudcats, was the big one of the day. These were two formidable teams, both staffed with experienced players mainly in their twenties. Mooretown Comets had won the OHA senior B championship in 1987 and 1988. Dunnville Mudcats had an even more successful record, in the previous five years winning the Ontario senior A championship four times and the other year losing only in the final. Those players and officials called to the hearing, one Dunnville player wearing dark glasses to cover an injured right eye, had waited several minutes in a rather glowering silence in the OHA's foyer. Their hearing had been scheduled for 2 p.m., because while Dunnville was relatively close, the Mooretowners had a long drive from their home town on Lake Huron south of Sarnia.

Three nights earlier, on January 18, 1989, the two teams had met in Mooretown. This had been scheduled as the second game of a best-of-three series in the early rounds of a national competition for the Hardy Cup, named after George Dudley's co-emancipator of the game in the 1930s. The previous weekend in Dunnville, Mooretown had won the first game of the series 7–1. That game had been rough enough to make the second game's referee, the veteran Lee Richards, aware that he'd better crack down early or things might get out of hand.

Crack down early he did, but it didn't do much good. At the game's extremely early end, he phoned the OHA hotline number to report that he'd stopped the game with 4:41 left in the first period. This had been preceded by a bench-clearing brawl after just over fifteen minutes of play. At the time Mooretown was leading 3–1 and there had been thirty penalties, including seven five-minute majors and fourteen game misconducts.

The next morning when Brent Ladds and Willard Norris got in and digested the bad news a notice was telephoned to both Mooretown and Dunnville clubs requesting their appearance before the disciplinary hearing on January 21, three days after the game.

The notes off the hotline tape had covered the bare bones, as above, as well as referee Lee Richards's comments, which had been typed as follows:

Events leading up to bench-clearing:

#4 K. Pitel (Mooretown) was called for charging on a delayed whistle. After whistle was blown a fight between (Mooretown) #2 Panik and (Dunnville) #22 Mazi started in behind the play. Almost immediately another fight between (Mooretown) #5 Fulcher and (Dunnville) #16 Kielbowich broke out. I took all the numbers down on my pad of the players that were involved in the fighting and by this time two players were in front of the net with their sticks up. These were (Mooretown) #17 Antoine and (Dunnville) #4 McSorley. At this time (Dunnville) #31 Horton was seen leaving Dunnville's player bench and the rest of the players on both benches followed.

After both fights were separated and both teams were told to leave the playing surface #4 McSorley went over to the Mooretown bench and high-sticked another player in the head area.

At this time I instructed the Arena staff to bring out the Zamboni and clean the ice. I then went over to the timekeeper's bench where I was greeted by the Dunnville coach who was on the ice. Finally both teams went to their dressing rooms and we officials went to ours.

The manager of the Dunnville team came to our room and informed me that they were not returning to play. At that time I informed him of his options, being that he was to have a two-minute warning when I returned to the ice and if he did not return his team to the ice the game would be suspended. . . .

The officials and the Mooretown team returned to the playing surface and I announced over the P.A. that a two-minute warning was being given to Dunnville to return. They did not do so and I suspended further play. All the above occurred with 4:41 remaining in the first period.

For the four hours preceding the hearing on this case, referee-in-chief Norris and about twenty of his referees had been meeting in the main OHA boardroom. When they cleared out a little before two, the Mooretown and Dunnville delegations filed in. The disciplinary board of Larry Clark, chairman, Murray Parliament, and Don Yeck sat at one end facing a long table at which four Dunnville players and their coach and manager were along one side, the Mooretown coach, manager, and another non-playing club representative on the other. At the far end were referee Lee Richards, Chuck Nesbitt, a refereeing supervisor (these are former refs who assess the performances of game officials), Brent Ladds, and two other OHA directors.

Larry Clark as chairman handled almost all the questioning, with occasional low-voiced prompting or consultation on some matters by Don Yeck and Murray Parliament, who listened intently and made notes. First he asked referee Lee Richards to report, which Richards did – in a low and rather subdued voice, as if this whole thing was worrying him, as no doubt it was.

He mentioned that the game was supposed to start at nine. Dunnville had not arrived until that time, but dressed and after a brief warmup the game started. Mooretown's first goal came twenty-eight seconds later. The first penalty was called in the third minute of play. The ten penalties called in the first fifteen minutes were unexceptional – boarding, interference, hooking, holding, and a couple of high-sticking penalties to each team. The ref's signed game report detailing these matters was in front of each of the three board members. As he already had made both taped and written reports, he didn't have much more to say. This inquiry was mainly to hear from the teams. Clark asked Tom Wallis, the Dunnville manager, to speak first.

Wallis immediately turned the floor over to centre Jeff Mazi, Dunnville's number 22, the man with the injured right eye behind the dark glasses. Mazi said that just after a McSorley penalty, a Mooretown player had charged the

Dunnville goalie, Larry Wolfe. A few plays later at the Mooretown end, according to later Mooretown testimony, Mazi had hit the Mooretown goalie (which Mazi denied) and had gone on into the corner, which is where the fight began.

Mazi: "We kind of got in the corner a bit and number two (Mooretown's Joe Panik) come in with his stick and elbows up like that (he demonstrated), knocked my helmet off, so then he was my main concern, and I was down on the ice tryin' to hold him off when his hand came up like this (he made an upward clutching gesture with his hand). He was goin' at my eye. So I pleaded to the ref, I said, 'he's got his finger in my eye!' That went on for a little bit, nothin' happened, so we loosened up and the linesmen came in and next thing I remember, I was on the ice, like this (he made a covering-up motion, the turtling effect) and I got a number of blows to the head by number two and number five."

Hearing chairman Clark stopped him there. "A couple of questions. The milling around – that took place directly in front of the net, or off to the side?"

Mazi: "Behind the net, in the corner."

"You made the statement, 'hand in eye,' which at that point in time you thought the finger was . . ."

Mazi: "Yeah, I thought my eye was . . ." He flipped up his dark glasses briefly to show a badly discoloured bloodshot eye with the nearby area a livid bruise.

"Again, some reaction there?"

Mazi: "I was yelling at the ref."

"Again, the blows to the head. What position were you in at that time?"

Mazi (demonstrating): "Down on my knees like this, toward the ice, my head facing toward the ice. I was tryin' to get up. I looked this way (turning his head) I got a shot here. I looked the other way (turning his head the other way) I got a shot there. And I got a bunch of punches on the back of the head."

"You were in a turtle or quasi-turtle position?"

Mazi: "Yeah. I couldn't move. I was being held down."

"You had not entered into any retaliatory action at that time, just the milling around?"

Mazi: "When I was down, the only thing I was trying to do was protect my head."

"And after that?"

Mazi: "After that, our team must've come on . . ."

"Must have . . . Is there anyone who knows exactly what happened?"

Manager Tom Wallis: "I think Jeff can only tell his part . . ."

Mazi: "When after receiving all the blows to the head, I got up and our team was standing around and I just went off the ice."

"Why?"

Mazi: "Because I thought my eye was destroyed and I was covered in blood and I had a lot of pain in my eye."

Tom Wallis then read a handwritten statement from another player, Andy Williams, who was on the ice at the time. Williams wrote that he'd gone into the corner in the Mooretown end when he was boarded by first one and then another of Mooretown's players. "My teammates Jeff Mazi and Charlie Kielbowich skated over to see if I was hurt. Two Mooretown players immediately squared off with Jeff and Charlie and began punching on them. I was paired off with number four of Mooretown (that's K. Pitel) for most of the incident but I was not involved in any of the fighting itself.

"What I recall most vividly is Jeff Mazi on his knees while both number two (Joe Panik) and number five (T. Fulcher) of Mooretown continued to both hold and beat Jeff in a malicious manner. This two-on-one beating occurred about thirty seconds after the initial fight started. It seemed strange to me that neither the linesmen nor the referee were willing to break the fight up. It was actually the only fight occurring on the ice at the time. I recall seeing both linesmen in the corner holding back two Dunnville players while Jeff screamed and pleaded for the referee – who stood beside him, watching – to rescue him from the beating he was taking. It wasn't until both benches finally cleared that the fighting stopped."

He called the attack "blatant," and "the fact that five of Mooretown's biggest players and five of Dunnville's smallest players were on the ice at the time leads me to believe that the attack was wholly intentional. I've played in this league for the last three years and have never witnessed deliberate goon tactics of this calibre. When two players are allowed to beat on one player unmolested I believe that the integrity and reputation of both the league players and officials suffer greatly. It's my hope that this incident will be dealt with firmly by the OHA review committee so that future games are free of this type of brutality on the ice. This letter comes to you from a concerned player who wishes to continue playing and enjoying OHA hockey at the senior level. Sincerely, Andy Williams."

Manager Wallis then said, "Charlie Kielbowich is next. He's the third member of that line that was on the ice at the time (with Williams and Mazi)."

Charlie Kielbowich: "I was comin' in from the left side into the Mooretown zone and what happened is I seen Jeff behind the net with number seventeen (Bill Antoine) and a little pushin' match started and I seen number two (Joe Panik) come in at Jeff with his stick in the air . . . Poor Jeff didn't even have the chance to block the guy already, I seen three punches thrown at Jeff's face and he's still standing there on his feet. That's when one of their players grabbed me and the linesman grabbed me and there's at least one guy that I know givin' me shots on the back of the head when the linesman is layin' on top of me. I got out of that and I look over and I see the guy down on his knees and drillin' at Jeff's head. I try to grab the guy's sweater and then another guy came in and took me out of the play again and then (someone) starts hittin' me on the back of the head again. So I was covered up by the linesman most of the time. So that's actually what I saw."

At this point the chairman said, "After Charlie, then?"

Dunnville manger Tom Wallis leaned forward and spoke along the table to his coach, Terry McArthur, at the other end.

"Terry, could you? . . ."

Terry McArthur had seemed throughout this first part of the proceedings to be taking the matter harder than anyone: listening intently, jiggling one leg nervously. He's a big man with thick dark hair, a former player, and somehow gave the impression that he would say what he felt he had to say, whatever the consequences, but really wanted to be walking out of the front door with all this behind him. He said he didn't know how to start, but then did, admitting immediately that in the last few years his Dunnville team had been the one that went out and did it to everybody else.

"We went through a lot of press and humiliation and being called (names) last year," he said. "We learned a big lesson from it. We respected the OHA on meetings (like this) we had last year and I don't want to get into, you know, a fightin' match between Mooretown and Dunnville across the table, or whatever, I really am not up to that today. But what I saw on the ice at the time . . . I was more concerned with married men with families, that have to go back to work the next day, when this whole incident started. And what happened to Jeff . . . it all stemmed back to last year, it just kept on going through my mind, I didn't want any more suits laid against us, I don't want anything else to happen to our hockey club, regarding . . . we'd already gained the reputation . . .

"There was an article in one of the papers that was cut out by somebody and they gave it to me before the game and it just set the whole limelight (he meant the violent tone) for the game, the way it was going to be played. So all I said to my players was when we get out there, just play hard and do the best we can, let's get out of here and get home, hopefully with two points. And it just seemed like it wasn't going to start that way, from the opening face-off. Like the sticks were up high . . . I had players suspended last year fifteen games, ten games, I don't know how many more. Like Ricky Mowat got fifteen games for swinging his stick once at a goaltender.

"And in this game (meaning the one being debated) Kelly Marr, when the fight broke out, he was smacked over the shoulder across the head with a stick and it was just in the heat of the game, I'm not saying whose fault it is, it just got out of hand. And when everything took place in the corner down there I saw Jeff Mazi taking a beating, two guys on him, I saw blood coming down, he was helpless, I was on the bench, nobody else could get into it, and I sent my boys over the bench.

"They went over the bench and all's I can say in the whole thing, (that being the time) when the referee said that all hell broke out, there was no more fights. There was nothin'! My team went out on the ice and everything stopped. My players went out with the intention of not punchin' anybody. Five years ago they woulda. Last year they woulda. The year before that they woulda. They would've fought. A fight's a fight, that's okay. Like I had guys on my bench, I got two-hundred pounders on my bench, and they went in there and all they said was, get Jeff outta there. And that's what happened. Once we stepped on the ice and went in the corner we got Jeff, he got up and he started comin' toward the bench and we got him off the ice. Nobody else got punched except my goaltender (got into) an altercation at the bench, nothin' broke out after it.

"The whole thing that was dumped on, and you may call the kettle black, what goes around comes around, okay, everybody knows the reputation that the Mudcats had last year, or the year before, unjustifiably or not, that's the reputation we picked up. We had all intentions of goin' (to Mooretown) and playin' a hard game of hockey and fist fights are involved in hockey. A one-on-one is great in hockey. Okay, you know. A fist fight happens. But when a guy is in the corner and takin' a beatin' like Jeff took, I've never seen it like that. I just couldn't justify that happening to a guy that's gotta go to work the next day. The justification to send my players off the bench was to get Jeff outta there and save part of his face. In all sincerity that's what happened in my eyes as a coach stayin' on the bench. I never directed any of my players to punch anybody. We got enough shit last year. I was here four or five times and I didn't want to come up again. . . . What I seen in there I've never seen it happen before and I think it should be dealt with. We were dealt with last year. . . ."

He then looked along the table and gestured to Tom Wallis, the Dunnville manager. "Tommy's gotta say he takes full responsibility for pulling the team out of the game. I can't say that Tom can take that. I can't say that I can take it. You got grown men in that room. With kids it's a different story, a coach is in control. These guys, Ricky Mowat's thirty-five years old. Dougie Siddall . . . these guys were the cattlestones (meaning either catalysts or cornerstones or a combination of the two) of the senior A down there (meaning Dunnville). They're good hockey players, Dougie Siddall, Dave Robertson, Rick Stayzer, them guys carried this league."

Larry Clark interrupted there, noting that because of his position as OHA chairman the previous year he'd been aware of the Mudcats' reputation, "but that was last year."

Next Dunnville speaker was Gerry McSorley, making the point that although he'd been cited by the referee as high-sticking in front of the Mooretown goal when the fight started, he was not on the ice at the time but in the penalty box. McSorley contended civilly that he and Mooretown's John Bernier had been penalized for high sticking fourteen seconds before the main battle commenced, and he had stayed in the penalty box because one of the Dunnville club's officials "who knows that I get excited faster than other people" had gone to the penalty box to keep him company and had told him "not to bother going when things got started. So I was still in the penalty box when the fight started. When it was over the ref came over to the penalty box and was standing there with me and the Mooretown player, so there was no way I was in front of the net."

The chairman checked this with the referee, who for the moment insisted on his original version. However, McSorley's contention was supported by the refereeing supervisor at the game, Chuck Nesbitt, who said, "I just happened to notice those two guys high-sticking in front of the net and the Dunnville one was a big guy with a beard."

As McSorley is a sturdily-built man of medium height, and his teammate Kelly Marr, a defenceman, is big and wears a beard, and the game report's penalty list did support McSorley's contention that he had been penalized fourteen seconds before the balloon went up, the referee's report was revised to subtract one high-sticking infraction from McSorley and leave him with a mere three in that category.

Then it was Mooretown's turn. Stan McKinnon, the Mooretown manager, had come into the meeting jauntily, a contrast to the gloomy mien of the Dunnville delegation – both attitudes no doubt stemming from the same fact, that Dunnville in effect had burned its bridges, given Mooretown its biggest advantage, when it refused to finish the game. Bouncing up the steps on his arrival at the OHA office, McKinnon, encountering a man whose arms were immobilized with a full load of parcels, had kidded, "Got a match?" From that jovial beginning, his manner was that of a man who'd been handed something on a platter and didn't have a worry in the world. He was accompanied by his coach, Peter McNamee, a big former tough guy in the old World Hockey Association, and another off-ice assistant, but no players.

When McKinnon's time came to talk his main strategic line was to agree wholeheartedly with the referee's report. This was not exactly an upset, considering that the referee had reported nothing whatever critical of Mooretown. As a guess, it might also have been strategy that while Dunnville brought along a slate of four witnesses who had been on the ice at the time of the main event, Mooretown brought none – so there were no Mooretown players available who might have been questioned and might have said something that detracted from the simple Mooretown tactic of resting (a) on Dunnville quitting the game and (b) declaring from time to time that as far as Mooretown went, there's nobody here but us candidates for sainthood.

McKinnon's only disagreement with the referee seemed equally shrewd (this is not imputing motive, merely extrapolating from known facts). Because of his penalty record in that and other seasons, Gerry McSorley was the Dunnville player most vulnerable to almost any accusation. He is one of those guys in hockey who, if something happens, is what one might call the world's champion usual suspect. Anyway, McKinnon threw in that sometime around the eight-minute mark he had seen, and said several hometown fans in the Mooretown crowd had verified, a play that the referee had not seen.

"Our player Chris Tomlin was coming along the left boards when McSorley, unseen by the referee, butt-ended him, cutting his right cheek and breaking his jaw. That same player, and this probably does enter into it a bit, in the first game Mr. McSorley was assessed a five-minute and a two-minute for a high stick that broke the same chap's nose."

McSorley, who like many of hockey's tough guys is particularly calm and articulate in his speech, sat impassively as these events were being reported, and even as they were being amplified a little. (McKinnon noted that on the broken-nose play, Tomlin didn't retaliate, just went peacefully to the dressing room to "receive medical attention from a doctor.") But McSorley's coach, Terry McArthur, did not take this testimony impassively. Far from it. The chairman had stopped him once earlier when he had strayed from the game in question. Now McKinnon was straying, free as a bird. McArthur listened, fidgeting, until McKinnon paused. Then McArthur turned to the chairman, Larry Clark, a few feet away.

"Can I get in?" he asked.

Clark: "No. I'm going to listen to him."

McArthur subsided that time and McKinnon went on to speak of other matters, mainly McSorley. The Dunnville goalie had gone to the Mooretown end during the fight, McKinnon said, and on his way back had swung his stick at the Mooretown bench.

"Mr. McSorley also swang his stick (at the bench), and to back up what the referee says, he did leave the penalty box because he came over and hit Mr. Tim Maricle on the helmet with his stick when he got at our bench. So he was out of the box at the time of the altercation, which backs up what the referee said."

McSorley's demeanour during this part of the debate caused one to feel that if he played hockey as calmly as he talked and listened, he'd be a model of deportment. He didn't interrupt, but kept his side of the event until later.

From time to time through his statement, McKinnon — a fast and forceful speaker — passed around news photos of the fight that the Mooretown club had acquired from Sarnia photographers. One point that evidently bothered him was the Dunnville contention that at the time the fight broke out, Mooretown's biggest players were on the ice against Dunnville's smallest. He thought some photos "showed the size of that *b-i-i-i-g* (this word pronounced sarcastically) team we had on the ice." He thought the size was in Dunnville's favour. Nobody asked for a weigh-in, however.

"And I can also say that I can't see the reason why we would try to 'goon' them when we're up 3–1 after beating them in their own building 7–1. I also will say that Mr. McSorley's record in the two previous games in Wallace-burg and Chatham . . ."

"That's not pertinent!" interjected Dunnville coach McArthur, earlier shut down by the chair when he'd got off the beaten track, and still stinging. His words were followed by a jumble of Mooretown's Stan McKinnon saying, "I'm sorry, sir," to person or persons unknown; chairman Clark trying to regain control; Dunnville's Terry McArthur insisting on equal rights to digress; before Clark's voice prevailed with a stentorian, "Terry, if you're not going to follow it, *bug off!* Okay?"

McArthur: "Well, let's make the rules here."

Clark (testily): "I've made the rules. You've got a chance to cross-examine any discrepancy!"

McArthur (forcefully): "Well, when I said something previous about my team . . . (Clark interrupting, but McArthur goes on) . . . you told me I couldn't say that!"

Jumble of voices, finally overridden by Clark speaking directly to McArthur: "I'll determine the rules! If you don't like it, get lost! We're dealing with Mooretown at this point in time, sir."

Stan McKinnon fumbled a bit after all that excitement but then got into the swing of it again with references to McSorley's penalty record (including some misconducts) over the two games he'd mentioned, plus that he had left the penalty bench, hit Tim Maricle, and so forth; plus driving home by what some poets call incremental repeti-tion the heinous nature of several other Dunnville infrac-tions, such as "witnessing the Dunnville coach crossing the ice and giving verbal abuse" to the referee, an event that the game sheet showed had been covered by a game misconduct at the time.

At this point Chuck Nesbitt, the referee supervisor who'd chosen to drop in on the Mooretown-Dunnville game, was called on for his comments. (Such supervisory visits are not known in advance to the referee). Nesbitt opened with words rarely heard in the entire world of hockey: *"In Mr. McSorley's defence . . ."* he began, then repeated that the player the referee had said was stick-swinging with Antoine in front of the net at the time the fight broke out, identified as McSorley, was not. Identification was sure-fire "because I was looking, and this gentleman swinging the stick with Antoine had a beard and was quite heavy set, number five, Kelly Marr."

McSorley then seemed to be on something of a roll, because pretty soon chairman Clark, in an exchange with Dunnville coach McArthur, mentioned that the relation, if any, between Chris Tomlin's broken jaw and an alleged butt-ending by McSorley did not enter into his judgement on the case at hand.

"I cannot read it in the referee's report. I cannot referee the game here, okay? It wasn't penalized, so it's not an issue at this point in time. That's not to say that his record won't be reviewed in conjunction with all players, but in this incident, whether he did or did not butt-end, this committee cannot substitute its judgement for the referee's. So as much as I'm not going to listen to Dunnville's criticism of the referee (this was a reference to Dunnville manager Tom Wallis saying a little earlier, "I can't believe Mr. Richards would even be assigned to that game; if he hasn't got a grudge against us I'll eat *this* table," thumping the table), I'm not going to listen to Mooretown tell us something that Mr. Richards never reported."

After a pause he added thoughtfully, "I can't suck and blow at the same time."

This was followed by McSorley getting yet another break, or semi-break. Referee supervisor Chuck Nesbitt said that he'd witnessed the play where Chris Tomlin got hurt and while his sightline had been slightly cluttered, "to me in the stands it looked like a good check, but it could very well have been a butt-end, okay?" Again McSorley listened impassively.

The Mooretown image to that point had been heavily based in steadily self-righteous viewing with alarm by Stan McKinnon who, however, had naturally not referred to the fact that his team was averaging a fairly high forty-five minutes a game in penalties so far in that season. Now when the chairman turned back to him, McKinnon said that having listened to so many others, his coach should speak.

Until then Peter McNamee, the Mooretown coach, had been sitting in attentive silence, occasionally shaking his head with a disbelieving smile at some contention from the Dunnville side. McNamee, a veteran of many a hockey battle in his eight years as a pro and elsewhere along the way, gives the impression – and admits freely – that he had been a tough one.

He opened by referring to the "good check" reference by Chuck Nesbitt. "Just on that little point about a 'good check,' it's not obvious to me that if it's a good check, how did he break Chris Tomlin's jaw? That's just an aside. Whatever relevance it has to this game, it had a great deal to the first. Fine! Dunnville has the reputation for this, that and whatever, and I didn't really give a shit, because that's not what our team is . . . We're going down there, we've got a good hockey club, beat them on the merits of the game. Fine! I don't give a shit that they're the worst team in the world with their sticks, their jabbing, and everything else. Unfortunately, when one of our better players, okay, gets a broken nose in the first game from a high stick . . . you're setting the tempo (for the series), okay, that this is how we play the game.

"The last minute of the first game when we're winning 7–1 they got two penalties for slashing. Fine. We go home. We'd won the game and set what you might call the pace for the next game. To our players I say, 'Guys, we're winning, (we're in) our building. Play the game, use your head, yes, it's probably going to be a little rougher and things like that but sticks have no part in the game.' Eight minutes into the game, whatever, the same player gets a broken jaw, a butt-end that you sit and see. Fine! Because the referee doesn't see it, doesn't mean it didn't happen. I'm not blaming him for that, but the point is, it occurred.

"Now we've got continuation of the same type of play from the last game, except we're winning three to one. So this gentleman here (he points across the table to Jeff Mazi), our goaltender has the puck and this gentleman here goes down and bumps into him, right?"

Voice from the Dunnville side, "You got pictures of that, too?"

Jumble of rejoinders, brought to order by the chair.

McNamee apologizes and continues. "So anyway, he bumps into our goaltender. Our goaltender has allowed two goals in basically four periods and is playing well. What ensued after that is our guys hitting this gentleman (nodding at Mazi), I use that term loosely, the gentleman from Dunnville, right after hitting our goaltender, because if our goaltender's out, he's playing a key role, we have to put our substitute in, who, last time we played, they had five goals on him. So it only stands to reason that you protect your goaltender. And then the fight ensued. Now, an individual to be on the ice in a turtle position and look up and say, 'oh, six hit me,' and then (turns his head to mimic Mazi) 'now it's two hitting me.' I can't understand how an individual taking a terrible thrashing has the opportunity at the time to look around and check out numbers."

Mazi, from across the table: "I can remember two's face! I can remember the other guy!"

In the quick jumble of voices that followed it was difficult to sort out who was saying what except that there
were a lot of voices, mostly loud. Stan McKinnon, at
McNamee's left, could have been one, aghast at hearing
Mooretown's holier-than-thou stance being undercut by
his coach scoffing at a guy who, whatever his initial role,
had taken eye damage that might turn out to be worse
than any broken jaw. Then McNamee suddenly was saying, "I'm sorry, I'm sorry, it's my fault, but . . ." and
Larry Clark storming at him, "If you're going to play the
sarcastic! . . . they can play the mind game, too!"

McNamee went on to say that it was very difficult,
because *why* that (the attack on Mazi) occurred is that
"now we've got one of our key players, Chris Tomlin,
with a broken jaw – he's the second leading scorer on our
team, okay? Now we've got a gentleman who goes down
and hits our goaltender, okay? Well, obviously, to me . . .
that's what precipitated the fight in the sense that, you
know . . . we wanta play a game of hockey, we're winning,
we don't need to go out and get penalties and everything
because we're ahead. So what happens after that, fine. Joe
(Panik, #2, the Mooretown captain) is winning the fight
or whatever the case may be, then their player goes over.
What I'm saying is that why the first game is relevant is
the penalties that were taken against Tomlin in the first
game and it continues into the second game and on top
of that they hit our goaltender! Now once . . . hold on a
sec, Stan . . . (this last in a low voice to the anxious Stan
McKinnon beside him, who seemed trying to slow him
down) . . . now once the brawl started, I'll call it, quote
unquote, the *altercation* started, their players went over
(the boards) first. . . ."

"I try to keep my players for as long as I could, fine,
they went out and it's absolutely right, nothing happened
after that, okay, *except* number whatever his name, four,
there, four for them (he meant Gerry McSorley), comes
over to our bench, swings his stick at us, right? At Tim

Maricle, and hits him! Then the goaltender comes up the ice and comes over and swings his stick at us!"

Here Mooretown coach McNamee spoke directly across the table to Dunnville coach McArthur. "As you pointed out and I agree with you a hundred per cent, these people with families, jobs, they're playing a good competitive brand of hockey, the last thing anybody wants to do is lose an eye, get a jaw broken, get a spear. They gotta go to work, they got bills to pay. That's the kind of thing I like to see stopped."

Chairman Clark then summarized what McNamee had said: "That basically, the tempo of the game was not developed solely by Mooretown, but also by Dunnville, by virtue of either deliberate actions or actions that resulted in injury or potential injury to your player in the form of broken jaw, broken nose, and a goalkeeper that was run into."

A few peripheral arguments followed. Tom Wallis for Dunnville argued that the bump on the goaltender had not been serious, and asked the ref for his opinion, which was that "I did not witness any play of running the goal-tender." Stan McKinnon said that a Sarnia reporter saw it and reported it. "I saw it, fans saw it, and the goalie felt it." To this Dunnville's Tom Wallis noted dryly that previously McKinnon had said he agreed with everything the referee did, said, and reported, and now was obviously not agreeing.

Next up was Gerry McSorley, who had been listening intently to the backing and forthing, and had what he thought was some needed clarification regarding his role, especially the stick-swinging at the Mooretown bench, in which he admitted some part but, he wished to state, with extenuating circumstances.

When the ruckus seemed to be over, he said, "I had gone from the penalty bench right to the dressing room. Because one of our veteran players, Rick Mowat, had come over and, like, because I'll get excited before most people, he had come right over to me and took me to the dressing room. That's where I went, right there. Then I did come back to ice."

The reason, he said, was that from the dressing room he could see the Mooretown bench and what he saw was that his team's goalie, Larry Wolfe, returning down the ice after the fight, had stopped and was "standing in front of the Mooretown bench and he had hit one guy, who was coming towards him . . . and then another guy had come at him.

"He (Larry Wolfe) hit him with his blocker (the big goalie mitt) and then I saw the big guy, because . . . no prejudice or nothin' like that, but the big Indian, that's the way I remember him, Tim Maricle . . . him and Larry going with the sticks, no contact or nothin' like that, other than the sticks, but when I saw that I had come from the dressing room and had went over to Tim Maricle. As far as a crashing down or slash over the head or the side of the shoulder, no . . ."

Chairman: "Did you wave your stick in his direction?"

McSorley: "I certainly did."

Chairman: "Make contact?"

"I made contact with his stick, because he'd put his up. But I mean, like my main (reason) was . . . like Mooretown says, you've got a goalie, he is yours, and I'm going to go over there and protect him. Like, if we lose Larry we've lost an integral part of our team, so I went over and took on Tim Maricle. I don't believe there was any body contact made, there was contact made with each of our sticks."

Question from the chair: "Was Mr. Maricle on the ice or on the bench?"

McSorley: "On the bench. He was leaning over. A trainer, or whatever, was holding on to Mr. Maricle."

From there the chairman read the last part of the referee's original written report, about warning the Dunnville manager that if he did not return his team to the ice, the game would be suspended. Which it was, with 4:41 remaining in the first period. The chairman then once again summarized the opposing points of view, including that Mooretown did not feel any of it justified refusing to continue, and asked Tom Wallis for his reason in that refusal.

"Because I felt that the officiating was to the point where the control of the game (indicated) that it was beyond control," Wallis said. He made other criticisms of the referee and then said, "the safety of the players is why I pulled them off the ice."

Referee supervisor Chuck Nesbitt, asked for a final comment on the refereeing, said he and Tom Wallis had "gone off to a corner of the arena and I said to him that he might be in a pile of shit for pulling his team and everything, but there was nothing mentioned there about the officiating."

"I wasn't about to get into that there," Wallis said.

Wallis then asked if his coach, Terry McArthur, could say something. Permission was given.

"Okay, now," McArthur said, "we've heard what went on and it's just like a husband fighting with his wife. We've eventually said our things about everything that went on." The decision not to go on with the game was made by everybody. "We knew what had happened to us last year and we thought, piss on it. We knew what was going to happen if we went back on the ice and I think the smartest move that we could've made was not to go back on the ice, in the heat of the whole thing. I knew that if we'd have gone back on the ice, all hell would have broken loose again." Didn't the Mooretown coach's remarks about things that had happened being the reason why Jeff Mazi was hammered add up to one thing? "Is he not saying that because of the things that happened, they're going to get even? My players didn't want to get suspended, hurt. They made the decision (to quit) and I just went right along with it and so did Tom."

Chairman: "A corporate decision."

A Dunnville player: "I can vouch for that."

Tom Wallis: "Nevertheless, I take responsibility because of the position I had with the hockey team."

There were a few wind-up remarks, including Mooretown coach Peter McNamee saying, "I apologize for being sarcastic."

Others spoke briefly, including a difference of opinion between the managers as to an Ontario Provincial Police investigation instigated by the Dunnville club into the injury to Jeff Mazi's eye, with the possibility of charges being laid. Mooretown manager Stan McKinnon said bringing in the police would be bad for senior hockey and that his club felt it had justification, as well, to seek to have charges laid, but did not wish to.

Wallis: "If you feel that, you should do it."

In the disciplinary committee's three-page report prepared a few days later, the conclusions were that:

There was no justification for Dunnville refusing to continue the game, therefore the game and series were awarded to Mooretown;

Tom Wallis, Mooretown manager, was suspended for one year;

Another game between Mooretown and Dunnville, originally scheduled for four days after the abandoned game, was suspended pending further review;

And that if the two teams did meet again this season, both should appear before an OHA committee to ensure proper conduct of play throughout.

All of which seemed reasonable.

A footnote is that subsequently Gerry McSorley had to appear before another disciplinary committee because in another game he had been penalized for attempt to injure. One of his lines during that hearing was, calmly, "If I'd been attempting to injure him, he wouldn't be here today."

Chapter Twenty-One

A NEW CENTURY

"What we're proposing is that the OHA should consist of five zones into which the MTHL would disappear, the OMHA would disappear, the NOHA would disappear – and so would the OHA, because I don't see any reason why they should throw their stuff in the pot and not us. Now we might all choose to call it the OHA when it's finished, but tentatively we're going to call it the Ice Hockey Federation of Ontario."

– COLIN MACKENZIE, OHA chairman,
stating the views of the executive
on what must be done to send the OHA
into its second century in good health

"A few years back we sat down and asked the question – if you looked at the present structure of the OHA and you were running a business and it was your money on the line, would you run your business the way the OHA is being run now? Unanimously around the table we said no."

– BRENT LADDS, president, OHA, in a 1989 interview

Entering its second century, OHA annual budgets continue to rise. The projected budget for the 1989-90 season was more than $1 million, not a huge amount when

337

one notes that the five-person staff trains, assigns, and supervises nearly 400 referees and linesmen every week, organizes playoffs, participates in injury research, operates (mainly on a user-pay basis) schools for coaches, referees, and trainers, enforces its playing rules through dozens of disciplinary hearings and subsequent tough suspensions each year, and pays whatever it costs to protect itself in courtroom challenges.

Apart from the steep increases in club registration fees for the 1983-84 season, which met immediate but not long-term needs, there have been few alleviating sources of funds – a sponsorship arrangement with a succession of breweries, for one. Government funds, trumpeted politically in large numbers (one cabinet minister mentioned the sum of $17 million for little more than a year's help for hockey) as being good for the game from a safety standpoint, are difficult to trace in specifics. What little has gone to the OHA was never for the support of the organization as a whole but for specific projects, and sometimes for only a portion of those. In the main the problem of making ends meet remains and increasingly indicates the need for major changes, those being the purview of the chairman and his executive, under whose policy directions the OHA president operates.

Colin MacKenzie, a bespectacled widower and father of seven, was elected chairman of the OHA at the 1988 annual meeting after six years as finance chairman, so he knows the problems firsthand. He is also chairman and chief executive officer of Electro Sonic Incorporated, a successful electronics company in Toronto, and habitually is at his desk early every morning answering his own phone to keep both organizations humming. Like every OHA top man before him, with the possible exception of John Ross Robertson, he served his hockey apprenticeship in the trenches. In the 1970s he managed the Seneca Nationals junior B team, OHA champions in 1979. A few years earlier one of his players was Wayne Gretzky. That happened when Gretzky, then fourteen or so, tried to switch from an OMHA team in Brantford to a more challenging Toronto team in the MTHL. Brantford refused to release him. The Gretzkys appealed to the Ontario Supreme Court and lost. Enter Colin MacKenzie. His junior B Seneca Nationals were OHA, not OMHA, so the previous transfer refusal did not apply (he thought).

So he signed Gretzky to a junior B card and moved him in with the Seneca Nationals. Brantford protested. Dave Branch was OHA secretary-manager at the time. MacKenzie phoned Branch and stated his case in such loud and emphatic terms that Branch had to ask him to lower his voice, the office secretary was blushing. But Gretzky stayed with MacKenzie's team

Later MacKenzie succeeded Larry Clark as convenor of the Metro Junior B league, landed on the OHA board to help with essential financial restructuring in the early 1980s, and became a vice-chairman in 1986 and chairman in 1988. And now, if plans formed by MacKenzie and his executive to sail the OHA into its second century financially and artistically healthy are put into effect, they will constitute the most profound change the organization has ever undergone.

The beginning of this era of change was signalled dramatically early in 1989 when the executive authorized MacKenzie to communicate with the Northern Ontario Hockey Association, Metropolitan Toronto Hockey Association, and Ontario Minor Hockey Association – terminating their affiliation agreements with the OHA on June 1, 1989.

Explaining this drastic majority decision, MacKenzie said this would provide room for development of the OHA's successor, by whatever name, into a single unified organization divided into five large zones, each with its own leagues, groupings, categories, and autonomy under a revised constitution. All the current advantages would survive, plus several new ones – especially in the sense that players in any area would not be forbidden by narrow territorial boundaries to seek their own level of play. For instance, if a Huntsville or Sarnia or Aurora or Markham player, or a player anywhere in Ontario, didn't have a league available to him that was up to his proficiency, there wouldn't have to be a jurisdictional battle involving the OMHA, MTHL, NOHA, or whoever; he would be free to move to another club in the same zone, or an adjoining zone, that did meet his development needs. (This is already the case in women's hockey.)

Current residential restrictions, especially the stringent ones affecting the MTHL and the OMHA, would disappear into the zone system. As an example, the Toronto area zone, which would encompass present MTHL boundaries and some OMHA territory, would offer all players and clubs more flexibility. This would include guaranteeing each player with the appropriate skills the right to belong to a team eligible for national and provincial playdowns, which is now not always the case.

These proposals, as outlined in the spring of 1989, suggested a series of meetings in which the organizations involved would hammer out a new constitution acceptable to all. Maintenance of all rights and privileges in the present system was promised. All levels of hockey would be represented on the new organization's board of directors, but for the common good none would be allowed to dominate. To most outside observers, these revolutionary proposals seemed drastic, but sound. There were two main hitches, one major, another relatively minor.

The minor hitch was of long standing: the new plan would still not meet the provincial government's stated ideal: a governing body of all hockey in Ontario, nothing less. Until now there has been no such animal. The OHA, NOHA, OWHA, OMHA, and MTHL represent 88 per cent of registered hockey players in Ontario (Thunder Bay and Ottawa District the rest), but 88 per cent isn't 100 per cent; close doesn't count.

The Ontario Hockey Council as recommended in the McMurtry report of 1974 was a move to achieve the required unanimity, but this didn't work well because the divergent elements – including not only hockey people but McMurtry's mix-in of academics – couldn't agree on how it *should* work. When the OHA claimed primacy on the grounds of sheer size, plus its eighty-four-year record, the government said forget it.

Tinkering with terms of reference and changing the Council's name didn't seem to help: Sports Ontario and Hockey Ontario foundered on the same rock. The current manifestation is called the Hockey Development Centre for Ontario. It includes virtually every Ontario organization in the game, among them the Ontario Hockey League, but it has no governing function, being mainly concerned with funnelling money into various specific projects.

These include injury research, public attitude surveys, and other hockey-related programs such as those for referees, coaches, and trainers. It is worth noting that in the early 1980s, when the OHA had backed out of Hockey Ontario over disagreements with the standards governing allocation of funds and decided to go it alone again, for several years the OHA ran its own referee-supervision program without financial help.

"That was a case," said Brent Ladds, whose job is to carry out executive policy, "where we felt we had to do it whether we had the money or not. We've always placed a great deal of emphasis on referee supervision. Even in 1988 when we were back in the Hockey Development Centre, we spent $28,000 on referee supervision against a $12,000 grant from the ministry. The other $16,000 we put up ourselves."

Colin MacKenzie, as designated main spokesman for the proposal that the whole system be rocketed into the future, adds an assurance that whatever happens to the big-change idea, "we'll do our job whether we get outside money or not, and we'd rather *not* have to use outside money, but that's not always possible."

All concerned agree that the Hockey Development Centre works quite well within its limits. But hockey still faces the central problem – fragmentation of effort among the province's several hockey and hockey-oriented organizations instead of the government's not unreasonable ideal: one, answering for all. That is what Colin MacKenzie's administration wanted to rectify with the idea for a single unified organization. It could take in everybody, including (in time) Ottawa and Thunder Bay when and if they so wished. But because of the size of the OHA and its affiliates, the effect there would be the greatest – more to change, more leagues, more players, more long-established customs and rules, and perhaps more entrenched opinion that in the end the old way was the best way.

However, to MacKenzie's way of thinking the OHA and everyone else in the game had to face this crunch. The precise nature of the changes would not be known until his plan could be threshed out, changed if necessary, voted upon and, he hoped, put into practice – the sooner the better.

Which brings us to what showed up immediately as the major hitch. The instant reaction of the OMHA and MTHL, representing huge minor hockey empires, was that they wanted no part of giving up the large degree of autonomy granted them over the years by the OHA.

They got together and quickly agreed on plans to form a new organization of their own and seek recognition from the CAHA as an entity separate from and not beholden to the OHA. The CAHA's refusal came along with the fervently expressed hope from its president, Murray Costello, that all parties could get together, keep negotiation lines open with the hope of hammering out a workable compromise.

As the OHA-NOHA-OWHA on one side and MTHL-OMHA on the other met, planned, and wrangled more or less immovably through July and into August, rarely was heard an encouraging word. The clost-knit MTHL had been led for many years by John Gardner, who seemed implacably opposed to giving up any of his leadership position. The OMHA situation was no more promising. Its annual meeting in June had been featured by the organization's lawyer, Wally Scott, being cheered and applauded in a rambling "we'll fight 'em on the beaches" speech, long on emotion and short on facts, which more or less charged that the OHA was trying to improve its own financial situation with a blatant takeover. Around the province, local OMHA groups were much less militant. "OMHA split with OHA restricts local minor hockey players," read a Peterborough banner headline. This reflected fears in other communities. The carefully and even lovingly constructed local minor hockey associations were openly concerned that if the battle continued they'd be shut out of those regional, provincial, and national championships and tournaments for which OHA and CAHA affiliation is a requirement.

On the other hand the OHA was prepared to carry on its own business whatever else happened, so was keeping cool, not burning any bridges, hoping that some method could be found to persuade the MTHL and OMHA that their world need not necessarily come to an end.

The crisis was settled with remarkable suddenness. In the first week of August the dissident minor hockey organizations were still breathing defiance, meeting in Barrie, and then announcing the formation of something called the Central Canadian Hockey Association. However, a few days later Murray Costello of the CAHA persuaded the combatants to make one last-ditch attempt – a meeting on the night of August 14, 1989, in a Toronto airport hotel.

Exactly what happened at that meeting was not put on public record, but the next day Costello simply announced that peace had broken out. An interim flagship organization for Ontario hockey had been agreed upon, to be called the Ontario Hockey Federation (not far from Colin MacKenzie's original suggestion as a name). All main hockey groups had agreed to become equal members, to administer hockey in their respective jurisdictions as before, and over the next three years to work out a permanent structure for the betterment of the game. Costello himself would be interim chairman. Brent Ladds, while continuing as OHA president, also would be executive director of the new organization.

Much more importantly to the hundreds of thousands of players and volunteers far removed from the game's committee rooms, very little change would be visible at ice level. There would still be the thousands of hockey games every week, as before, from the tiny tots and novices to the more robust realms of the peewees, bantams, midgets and juniors to the leagues, no matter how tough, where grown men worked by day to support their families and two or three times a week would practise and play for keeps in the game they love.

The changes had not come easily, but one way or another the OHA, however altered its mandate, was skating into its second century.

ACKNOWLEDGEMENTS

I've been helped a great deal in researching this book. Newspaper microfilm facilities at University of Waterloo, Queen's University, and Trent University were my fall-back position when I couldn't find anywhere else the kind of close-in observation that only journalists of long ago could give. Most persons interviewed on specific events both on and off the ice are credited by name in the book, but I also had library research help from the late Joan Taylor in Toronto, Paul Kirby in Belleville and Toronto, and especially I thank Toronto's Lois Kalchman, whose encyclopedic knowledge of the hockey scene's quirks and quarrels is equalled only by the enthusiasm with which she digs for facts. I thank again Frank Buckland of Peterborough for his painstaking research back to the OHA's beginnings. Thanks also to the Ontario Hockey Association itself for research assistance and for unstintingly opening its books and records to me, while leaving me totally free to tell the story as I saw fit.

Scott Young
Cavan, Ontario

Appendix:

OHA Chief Executive Officers

(From 1890 to 1980, elected presidents ran the OHA. In 1980, a full-time president was appointed to carry out policies of the elected chairman and his board of directors.)

PRESIDENTS

Year	Name	Residence
1890-92	A.M. Cosby	Toronto
1892-94	H.D. Warren	Toronto
1894-96	C.A.B. Brown	Toronto
1896-97	J.A. MacFadden	Toronto
1897-98	Alexis Martin	Toronto
1898-99	A. Creelman	Toronto
1899-1905	John Ross Robertson	Toronto
1905-07	D.L. Darroch	Collingwood
1907-09	D.J. Turner	Toronto
1909-11	Louis Blake Duff	Welland
1911-13	H.E. Wettlaufer	Berlin
1913-15	Charles Farquharson	Stratford
1915-17	James T. Sutherland	Kingston
1917-18	Sheriff J.F. Paxton	Whitby
1918-20	R.M. Glover	Peterborough
1920-22	A.E. Copeland	Midland
1922-24	W.A. Fry	Dunnville
1924-26	William Easson	Stratford
1926-28	George B. McKay	Toronto
1928-30	Richard Butler	Lindsay

1930-32	Frank Hyde	Woodstock
1932-34	J. Percy Bond	Peterborough
1934-36	George S. Dudley	Midland
1936-38	Alvin H. Schlegel	Preston
1938-40	James Douglas	Brantford
1940-42	Ross E. Clemens	Hamilton
1942-45	F.W. (Dinty) Moore	Welland
1945-48	George Panter	Gravenhurst
1948-50	J.J. McFadyen	Galt
1950-52	J.M. Roxburgh	Simcoe
1952-53	S.E. McTavish	Oshawa
1953-55	M.L. (Tory) Gregg	Wingham
1955-57	Frank Buckland	Peterborough
1957-59	Lorne Cook	Kingston
1959-61	Ken McMillan	Georgetown
1961-63	Lloyd Pollock	Windsor
1963-65	C.G. Patterson	Guelph
1965-67	Matt Leyden	Oshawa
1967-69	Jack Devine	Belleville
1969-72	Clarence Schmaltz	Walkerton
1972-74	Frank Doherty	Thorold
1974-76	Cliffe Phillips	Newmarket
1976-78	Hugh McLean	London
1978-80	Larry Bellisle	Penetanguishene

CHAIRMAN, BOARD OF DIRECTORS

1980-82	William Ruddock	Toronto
1982-84	Pat Doherty	Kitchener
1984-86	Bob MacKinnon	Oakville
1986-88	Larry Clark	Scarborough
1988-	Colin D. MacKenzie	Toronto

INDEX